USING TRAUMA-FOCUSED THERAPY STORIES

Using Trauma-Focused Therapy Stories is a groundbreaking treatment resource for trauma-informed therapists who work with abused and neglected children ages nine years and older, as well as their caregivers. The therapy stories are perfect accompaniments to evidence-based treatment approaches and provide the foundation for psychoeducation and intervention with the older elementary-aged child or early pre-teen. Therapists will also benefit from the inclusion of thorough guides for children and caregivers, which illustrate trauma and developmental concepts in easy-to-understand terms. The psychoeducational material in the guides, written at a third- to fourth-grade reading level, may be used within any trauma-informed therapy model in the therapy office or sent home for follow-up. Each therapy story illustrates trauma concepts, guides trauma narrative and cognitive restructuring work, and illuminates caregiver blind spots; the caregiver stories target issues that often become barriers to family trauma recovery. No therapist who works with young trauma survivors will want to be without this book, and school-based professionals, social workers, psychologists, and others committed to working with traumatized children will find the book chock-full of game-changing ideas for their practice.

Pat Pernicano, PsyD, is currently a psychologist with Personal Counseling Services and served as the director of clinical services at Providence House for Children between 2007 and 2013. She is associate professor on the clinical faculty at Spalding University, where she has taught in the PsyD program since 1996.

USING TRAUMA-FOCUSED THERAPY STORIES

Interventions for Therapists, Children, and Their Caregivers

Pat Pernicano

Routledge
Taylor & Francis Group

NEW YORK AND LONDON

First published 2014
by Routledge
711 Third Avenue, New York, NY 10017

and by Routledge
27 Church Road, Hove, East Sussex BN3 2FA

Routledge is an imprint of the Taylor & Francis Group, an informa business

Library of Congress Cataloging in Publication Data
Pernicano, Pat, 1954-
  Using trauma-focused therapy stories : interventions for therapists, children, and their caregivers / Pat Pernicano.
    pages cm
  Includes bibliographical references and Index.
  1. Psychic trauma in children—Treatment.   2. Child psychotherapy.
  I. Title.
  RJ506.P66P48 2014
  618.92'8914—dc23

                                                    2013029638

ISBN: 978–0–415–72691–7 (hbk)
ISBN: 978–0–415–72692–4 (pbk)
ISBN: 978–1–315–85600–1 (ebk)

Typeset in Stone Serif
by Swales & Willis Ltd, Exeter, UK

CONTENTS

CHAPTER 41   Neurobiology and Trauma   230

CHAPTER 42   Caregiver Stress and Self-Care   240

PREFACE: USING TRAUMA-FOCUSED THERAPY STORIES

This book is intended as a treatment resource for social workers, psychologists, expressive therapists, and counselors who work with abused or neglected children ages nine years and older, as well as their caregivers. It is particularly difficult to communicate trauma concepts to children and their caregivers, yet it is important that they understand how abuse and neglect impact attachment, behavior, cognition, moods, and relationships. Children in older elementary through young teen age-groups have, to this point, been neglected with regard to treatment resources; they are, however, avid readers in their areas of interest (dinosaurs or historical fiction, the Harry Potter collection, or the books within *A Series of Unfortunate Events*), creative organizers (scrapbooks and journals), faithful viewers of Discovery Zone and Animal Planet, and receptive to new ideas. Many abused children in these age-groups are eager to *learn about* the impact of abuse and how to heal that impact.

There are many excellent clinical and academic resources that address interpersonal neurobiology, attachment, post-traumatic stress, and the impact of trauma (Badenach, 2008, 2011; Bremner, 2002, 2003, 2006, 2012; Briere, 2012; Briere & Jordan, 2009; Briere & Langtree, 2008; Briere & Scott, 2006; Cozolino, 2006, 2010; Perry, 2009; Perry & Hambrick, 2008; Perry & Pollard, 1998; Perry & Szalavitz, 2006; Schore, 2001; Siegel, 1999, 2010; and Siegel & Hartzell, 2003). There are also first-rate trauma-informed treatment approaches for working with children and families (Blaustein and Kinniburgh, 2010; Cohen, Mannarino, & Deblinger, 2006, 2012; Crittenden, 2008, 2013; Drewes, 2009; Gil & Briere, 2006; Greenwald, 2005; Lieberman & Van Horn, 2008; Malchiodi, 2008; Pernicano, 2010a and 2010b; Saltzman & Goldin, 2008; and Tinker & Wilson, 1999). The author makes the assumption that the reader already has core knowledge and skills in these areas, as this book is not meant to educate about trauma but rather to translate trauma concepts for clinical use with children and caregivers.

The book also is not intended as a stand-alone treatment model or "cookbook" for trauma intervention. The material is meant to be integrated and used adjunctively with available treatment approaches such as: Child–Parent Psychotherapy (CPP); Trauma-focused Cognitive Behavioral Therapy (TF-CBT) (Cohen et al. 2006, 2012); Attachment, Self-regulation, and Competence (ARC) (Blaustein & Kinniburgh, 2010); Mindfulness-based Stress Reduction (MBSR) for school-age children (Saltzman & Goldin, 2008), and child-focused Eye Movement Desensitization and Reprocessing (EMDR; Tinker & Wilson, 1999) among others.

Part I, *Therapist Guide for Use of Trauma-Related Therapy Stories*, includes a brief overview of the impact of child trauma on development and functioning, as well as information about how to develop and use trauma-related stories with children and caregivers. The author provides case examples to illustrate the development and use of such stories in addition to explaining how to move from stories to intervention. The case study used in the first chapter—in which therapy stories were central to the change process—is included with permission of the mother.

Parts II, III, and IV are sections of therapy stories: Child, Adolescent, and Caregiver. The stories allow easy identification with characters and themes, illustrate trauma concepts, guide trauma narrative and cognitive restructuring work, reduce avoidance or denial, illuminate caregiver blind spots, and lead logically into one or more treatment interventions.

Parts II and III, the Child and Adolescent stories, address issues and symptoms that arise following trauma as well as the coping skills needed to reduce symptoms and build efficacy. A section of stories for caregivers in Part IV targets *adult issues* central in cases where caregiver behavior or the presence of cross-generational trauma (abuse, neglect, or witnessing domestic violence) impedes child or family progress.

The decision was made to include a set of adult stories in the book because caregivers' own prior trauma experiences may interfere with the capacity for attunement, the development of positive attachment and parenting strategies with children, and result in barriers to healthy adult functioning. Many caregivers with early trauma self-medicate through the use of drugs and/or alcohol and select partners who can rekindle childhood experiences of rejection or abandonment. Adult treatment, including attachment work, needs to take place with caregivers in order to ensure safety and successful reunification: this is particularly the case with those who were themselves abused or neglected as children, who witnessed domestic violence, who had substance-abusing parents, or who have been adult victims of intimate partner violence.

The psychoeducational material in Parts V and VI, the Child and Caregiver Guides to Trauma, written at a third- to fourth-grade reading level, reviews trauma concepts and parallels the story themes. The word "caregiver" refers to any caring adult involved in the life of an abused child, so the materials may be used in a variety of settings, including treatment, school, and child welfare. The caregiver section may be used with parents, teachers, caseworkers, foster parents, or kinship placements.

The Child and Caregiver Guides introduce readers to Bruce Perry's Neurosequential Model of Therapeutics (Perry, 2009; Perry & Hambrick, 2008; Perry & Pollard, 1998) and the state-dependent functioning materials used in the Child Trauma Academy Video Training Series (Perry, 2004). The guides and appendices describe the ways in which traumatic stress impacts child development at different ages and stages and how adult responses to child victims can exacerbate symptoms or help children develop better self-control.

The stories are intended to be read with the child and caregiver to allow interaction, and the simple questions following the stories allow the child to apply the material to his or her own life. The Child's Guide to Trauma includes workbook-type activities to help young clients think about and process home life and traumatic experiences in step-by-step ways that will not be overwhelming and which will allow them to be active participants in their treatment. The material in the Caregiver's Guide to Trauma allows a caregiver to better understand the child in the context of the his or her past experiences and educates the caregiver about the ways in which caregiver behavior can exacerbate symptoms or support recovery.

Those working with abused and neglected children realize that many of their young clients do not meet diagnostic criteria for post-traumatic stress, yet these children present with a constellation of attachment-related life problems and traumatic stress-related symptoms that are deeply tied to prior life experiences (Briere, 2012). John Briere pointed out during a 2012 workshop that when working with victims of complex trauma, it is hard to know "which exactly of the 14 prior abuse episodes" most triggers stress and impacts current functioning. Bruce Perry (2009) points out that an abused child's brain continues to exist in a state of fear unless something changes via treatment and interpersonal relationships. It is hard for a child to "behave," have good relationships, and live a normal life while existing in a state of fear. It is important that adults living with such children recognize the signs of complex trauma and intervene to help children recover from past abuse and neglect.

As mentioned earlier, this book is not intended as a "stand-alone" protocol; rather, the stories and psychoeducational material can be easily incorporated into other evidence-based models of treatment. They should, however, be read and worked through with the child and parent and the work continued at home to solidify and expand upon the work of the session.

The best and heartiest stew has many savory ingredients, and the finished product is tastier than any of its individual components. It should be no surprise, then, that the flavor of an already delicious casserole can sometimes be enhanced, made richer and more satisfying by adding a new ingredient. It behooves us to incorporate new ingredients in trauma intervention, especially ones that impact the child's relationships with caregivers; ultimately it is relationships that result in neurobiological integration of emotion and cognition and improve the capacity for self-regulation.

Note: The author acknowledges that perpetrators can be men, women, or older children. For simplicity's sake, the author has chosen to use the word *he* throughout this book as an inclusive term. Readers are encouraged to substitute whatever word suits the nature of their work with children and families.

The stories and psychoeducational guides for use with children or caregivers in treatment are available to download as eResources here: www.routledgementalhealth.com/9780415726924

ACKNOWLEDGEMENTS

This book has been a work in progress, and the concepts and content have emerged and evolved over time. I am especially grateful to Anna Moore, Routledge editor, who understood the importance of publishing practical material for use with traumatized children ages nine to 13 and their caregivers. Thanks to the assistance of Patricia Zline at Jason Aronson, my previously published stories have been included in this publication. Dr. Bruce Perry, whose theory and research contribute widely to trauma-informed practice internationally, was kind and gracious in providing articles and material from the Video Training Series at the Child Trauma Academy and in offering guidance about concept fidelity.

I thank the children and families who over the years taught me about trauma and gave me opportunities to help mend their lives. Their lives and treatment experiences are woven into the therapy stories in this book, and their stories will help other children and families participate more fully in their own care.

There are many graduate students and colleagues who encouraged me to develop a trauma-informed workbook and assisted me in those efforts. Special thanks to Ashley Casto for her valuable editing and feedback on the manuscript. Thanks also to my colleague Dr. Meg Hornsby, who piloted some of the state-dependent learning material. Dr. Allyson Bradow took the time to read the stories with her seven-year old-daughter, who one evening asked, "Instead of watching my program, can we read another story?" The material was clearly child-friendly!

A special thank you to my psychologist husband Kevin, for encouraging my writing and contributing to the final edit. Without his support and co-regulation I would not be capable of doing this work. My son Sam brags that his mom is a "famous author." I am certainly not famous but I am grateful to be an author and to have the privilege of sharing my work with others.

PART I

THERAPIST GUIDE FOR USE OF TRAUMA-RELATED THERAPY STORIES

CHAPTER 1

OVERVIEW: IMPACT OF TRAUMA ON CHILD DEVELOPMENT AND CAREGIVING BEHAVIOR

1.1 Complex Trauma—A Case Example

A twenty-something mother of four had been referred by the local child welfare department to participate in a six-to-12-month family-in-residence program where families receive campus housing, case management, transportation, linkage to community resources, and treatment services. The program offers parent education, parent–child interaction skills training, trauma-informed play therapy, family and individual therapies for trauma recovery, a women's relationship recovery group, and a dual diagnosis group.

The mother moved into the program with her two boys, one a preschooler and the other in elementary school, and child welfare officials wanted her and her children to be self-sufficient within six to nine months. The mother's own sexual abuse had begun at age four at the hands of her older brother and lasted eight years. When she was nine, her first *boyfriend* (client's term), age 16, began molesting her although she did not initially understand that this had been a form of abuse. Her three marriages had been unstable, her partners emotionally and physically abusive to her and her children.

Interestingly, this mother had never had difficulty maintaining employment, but she left her children in the care of unstable friends for days at a time. Early in the program, she had difficulty multitasking and became easily overwhelmed, confused, and depressed. When her sons hit her or yelled at her, staff observed that she became scared and tearful. She reported that it *felt* as if she was being abused *all over again*.

Psychological testing showed cognitive deficits and other psychological problems: poor abstract reasoning, slow processing speed, impaired working memory, features of dependent personality, and symptoms of trauma and depression. The treatment team set therapy goals that took her limitations into account and referred her for a psychiatric evaluation, at which point she began taking antidepressant medication.

As her children began to disclose prior physical and sexual abuse at the hands of her partners, she experienced nightmares and flashbacks about her own abuse. Her own mother had been sexually abused as a child and had not understood how to protect her daughter.

With regard to the children, there were many emotional, interpersonal, and cognitive developmental delays to address. Their mother's parenting skills included yelling, ignoring serious safety risks, and putting the children in their rooms for long periods of time. All four of the children in this family were *hyperactive and emotionally dysregulated*. Expressive language and communication deficits were present. We learned through communication with the school that the children did not own a toothbrush or know how to brush their teeth; the mother believed that teeth develop cavities if brushed too much. One of the older children had been shown pornography by an older family member and had become sexually reactive with his brothers prior to entering the program, so a safety plan had to be implemented around bathing and privacy.

The mother showed visible favoritism for the younger child, since the older boy looked like and reminded her of his abusive father. The younger child had failed to thrive in his first year of life. When he joined his mother to live on campus, he would not sit and eat at the table and instead wanted to be fed. He had delayed speech, would not walk on his own, and hit his mother during angry outbursts that lasted between 20 and

30 minutes. He had nightmares and was terrified of being in the bathtub. His older brother had soiling accidents and poor eye contact. His intense *rage meltdowns* lasted up to 30 minutes, and his play was regressed and compulsive.

Child Services was often more concerned with the cleanliness of this mother's home than with the bonding that was taking place with her children, and they wanted a *quick fix*. One social worker said to the mother, "You need to forget about all this therapy stuff and focus on taking care of your home and your finances," and at one point was going to recommend termination of parental rights rather than give the family three additional months in the program to complete trauma work. The treatment providers and the case judge understood the need to address the family's complex issues, however, and so the mother was granted the extra time to continue her family's slow and gradual healing progress.

It should be mentioned that this well-intentioned mother attended every session, did her psychotherapy homework, and called staff for advice when she did not know what to do. She participated in parenting classes and learned how to make informed choices and use consistent discipline through repeated feedback. She practiced problem-solving skills and rules for dating relationships that helped her override her lack of common sense. In time, she became more nurturing, emotionally regulated, and attuned to her children. She also became very *attached* to the campus therapy staff and used those attachments to *grow up*.

In retrospect, a turning point for this client was a set of therapy stories that touched her emotionally and helped her understand and talk about her childhood trauma experiences. The reader might be curious about how a woman with somewhat low cognitive functioning became interested in reading therapy stories. Early in placement, a story was used in the women's group, and she asked me if I had "any more." She borrowed a book of trauma-related therapy stories, read each one, wrote answers to the story questions in her journal (without prompting), and dropped in weekly to talk about how the characters reminded her of her life. She took time to think about and process what was in the stories. About eight months later, when she was coping much better, she said to me, "You know you always reminded me of my grandmother. She was the one person in my childhood that made me feel safe. Thank you for being there for me." I did not realize until then the ways in which our discussions had contributed to the development of a positive adult attachment.

The therapy stories were well matched to someone with cognitive and emotional deficits. Reading them grounded the client and helped her understand, week by week, how her childhood trauma had inflicted damage and how she might *take charge* of her life and function better as an adult. She became aware of and better able to manage her behavior and emotions in the face of trauma cues; she also developed a strong attachment to her children.

This client *changed from within*, at least in part because of stories that brought back memories, allowed her to process her abuse, allowed her to *feel and behave more like an adult* around her children, and helped her develop a significant attachment with persons who cared about and believed in her. She came to believe that she could give her children a better life.

For her children, it was a story about *Lucky the Junkyard Dog* that gave them words to talk about their past abuse. They identified with Lucky's fear and discussed why he was still scared long after his abuse. The older boy did a *Mad List* (Pernicano, 2009) with his therapist and he began to engage in trauma-focused play therapy. He delighted in a bathroom intervention where he could poop and pee (like a dog) in the toilet and flush the waste down on his perpetrator's head in the sewer.

It took over a year, but her youngest son is now doing well and sets good boundaries for privacy, seeks out his mother when he is distressed, has normal weight and eating habits, is making friends at preschool, has age-appropriate verbal skills, and openly displays affection. His older brother eliminated soiling, plays well with his younger brother, is attached to his mother, and is able to talk about his trauma. At the present time the mother is employed, lives back in the community, and parents her children in a *good enough* fashion. Child welfare is in the process of closing her family's case.

This case illustrates the complex needs encountered in families that experience cross-generational and repeated trauma: interpersonal, emotional, cognitive, and environmental. With these types of families, change is needed at multiple systemic levels and must be matched to the cognitive, emotional, and developmental functioning of the children and their caregivers. Fortunately, treatment providers are now better able to access information and training in evidence-based practice, both online and through comprehensive training programs. Providers are referred to the National Child Traumatic Stress Network (www.nctsn.org/), the SAMHSA evidence based repository (www.nrepp.samhsa.gov), and the Child Trauma Academy (www. childtrauma.org) for resources.

1.2 Diagnostic Clarification

Traumatized children, especially those with complex trauma, present for treatment with any number of symptoms: somatic complaints, disruptive behavior, attention problems, stubborn defiance, odd thinking, mood swings, poor eye contact, rage outbursts, obsessive compulsive habits, attachment difficulties, rule violations, oppositional behavior, delayed language, or poor social reciprocity. Clinicians need to be aware of the ways in which trauma impacts child development, functioning, and behavior and assess carefully in areas often not shared spontaneously by caregivers.

Recently, a ten-year-old boy and his mother sought treatment for his *school and anger problems*. He had been diagnosed with attention deficit hyperactivity disorder (ADHD) by the school based on an ADHD screening measure, and they were recommending medication. He was restless and inattentive in class and, over a two-year period, displayed interpersonal conflict. He had difficulty keeping friends, did not concentrate on his work, and needed a lot of attention and validation from the teacher. His parents were seeking a second opinion.

During assessment that included parent interview and social-emotional personality testing, it became clear that the child's significant anxiety was interfering with his focus and attention. He ruminated about school incidents in detail, used "victim" language, and shared concerns about his friends (and him) getting hurt by bullies. He often felt the need to step in and protect them. During the interview with the boy and his mother, the therapist asked if things were happening at home (like arguments) that might be upsetting him and setting the stage for his anger outbursts. The mother acknowledged that the dad had "a *very* bad temper" and was quite intimidating, to the point of verbal abuse (and prior partner violence). The child said that he worried a lot about his parents' fighting and kept thinking something worse might happen. This boy met all the criteria for ADHD, but his symptoms were better explained by a diagnosis of anxiety triggered by verbal abuse that was occurring in the home.

Diagnoses of disruptive behavior disorder (DBD), ADHD, oppositional defiant disorder (ODD), psychosis, bipolar disorder, obsessive compulsive disorder (OCD), or pervasive developmental disorder not otherwise specified (PDD-NOS) may not be *wrong* given the presenting symptoms (see Appendix D), but evidence-based treatments for these diagnostic conditions alone will not address root family problems of attachment and trauma. The neurobiological dysregulation of abused and neglected children results from the cumulative impact of a lifetime of highly stressful life events.

Traumatized children need to develop and maintain relationships with nurturing, consistently responsive adults within stable, predictable environments, whether in a group home, residential placement, foster, kinship, or biological home. The importance of attachment through the lifespan has never been questioned, but with growing knowledge about interpersonal neurobiology we now better understand what goes on when parent–child relationships break down and how to remediate those difficulties. We also understand the harm that comes when children are forced to endure multiple placements and repeatedly lose attachment figures.

In Patricia Crittenden's *Dynamic Maturation Model of Attachment* (2013), attachment patterns are understood as adaptive, protective strategies used by children to reduce arousal/stress and cope with different types of caregiving. Infants are dependent on the caregiver, and their attachment strategies are meant to ensure survival in response to caregiver expectations and behaviors. By preschool years, relationship co-regulation should be present, whereby the child is able to seek care (when the attachment behavioral system is activated by stress), engage in mastery-related activities, and self-regulate when the parent is absent.

With consistent, congruent, sensitive care that is responsive to the child's individual needs and personality, the child develops true, integrated cognitive and affective information about the self and caregiver. When the caregiver is punitive, non-validating, inconsistent, non-congruent, or demanding, the child "twists" him/herself to match the parent's needs or view of reality and develops a *false self* (Crittendon, 2013). In doing this (to survive, increase consistency, protest the lack of congruence, gain approval, or seek attention), the child's view of self and others becomes distorted.

Caregivers' own mental health symptoms, prior abuse, attachment deficits, mistaken beliefs, lack of developmental understanding, and relationship problems make it difficult for them to develop *secure attachments*. Mental health systems are sadly lacking in appropriate trauma-informed treatment for the neglectful or abusive caregiver. Therapists working with traumatized children should ensure that caregivers have adequate cognitive coping skills, can engage in effective attachment strategies, and manage their own distress.

It is unwise and even risky to work with a traumatized child without active caregiver involvement. Attachment strategies develop within a cultural and family context and are sustained by the pattern of interactions within the family. The child's behavior serves an adaptive purpose to maintain safety and security within a family context; therefore, a change in the child's functioning can stress the parent–child dyad and alter family dynamics. If professionals take away an adaptive yet unhealthy parent–child strategy without offering something in return, they risk negatively disrupting the family system and bringing harm to the child.

For example, an 11-year-old boy had been exposed to multiple episodes of abuse at the hands of his older sister, largely due to his mother's blind spots and non-protective behavior. He was serious-natured, provided compulsive caregiving toward his mother, performed very well in school, and dealt with his own distress through rigid coping strategies. The therapist's first inclination was to move him more into a *child role* and teach his mother to be more protective. Yet early on during sessions, his mother smiled oddly and her eyes had a glazed look either of medication or dissociation. She laughed inappropriately and did not make good eye contact.

The client loved drawing and creating therapy stories (most of which were about someone being ugly or defective) and we ended most sessions with this activity. About six sessions into treatment, at the end of a family session, the client mentioned a test at school where he had missed three questions.

He then pulled out the dry erase board, smiled and said, "Don't forget this!"

He wanted to go first, so he drew his picture and told a story about a boy that entered a science competition.

He had a big birthmark on his face, spiked hair and looked funny. He did not think they would let him enter the science competition because he looked different from everyone else. They let him enter, and he ended up being one of three finalists. In the final round, the boy looked out into the audience. His mother was not there. He started worrying about her and got distracted. He missed three questions because he could not focus, so he did not win. Later he tried to tell his mother what happened but she just smiled.

As he finished the story, he looked at the therapist with a solemn look on his face and said, "That's like me." His mother sat across from him with a smile on her face, tears in her eyes.

With some help, he was able to talk about being abused by his sister and that he wanted his parents to take it *seriously*. The therapist talked with him and his mother about a safety plan he could be in charge of, given the family circumstances and his mother's visible limitations.

After his mother went back to the waiting room, the therapist said, "I really like your story. In a few places it did not turn out the way I expected. Would you like to hear how I thought it would go?" He was curious and agreed.

The boy had spiky green hair and a big birthmark on his face, so he did not think he would be invited to compete in the science competition and he assumed no one would like him. But he was wrong. He entered the contest and they said, "Thank goodness you are not like everyone else. We need someone new and different. All these science contest kids are geeks, nerdy and too serious, and they all look alike. You are *one of a kind*. We need someone who is one of a kind." The boy competed and in the finals, he looked out and saw his mother was not there. Well, his mother was often not all there, and he had come to know and accept that. He took a deep breath, focused on the questions, and managed to win the contest, not that winning or losing was the most important thing. Later he told his mother he had won. She smiled, and he knew she was really proud of him.

Not surprisingly, he smiled at the therapist's story.

It is important to assess caregiver expectations with regard to communication, discipline, and parent–child interaction as well as the ways in which family members manage stress. When a child does not live up to unrealistic, pre-conceived caregiver expectations, problems may arise.

Information about caregiver–child interaction may be gathered throughout treatment and interventions tailored to those interactions and family dynamics. A parent who seems disconnected, sits across the room, texts during session, allows the child to wander untended, or ignores a child's needs may have difficulty tuning in to the needs of a child. Does the parent push, hold, slap, caress, or hug the child? Does the parent readily touch the child to comfort or redirect? Does the parent move abruptly toward the child or demonstrate calm patience? What is the quality and intensity of the parent's mood in response to the child's behavior? It is important to note whether caregivers are *on the same page* regarding values, child discipline, and communication; and subtle cues, such as a mother always looking at her partner before speaking, provide useful information. It can take a while to *put the pieces of the family interaction puzzle together*, and the conceptual *roadmap* may change as new information emerges.

1.3 Evidence-Based Practice

There are a variety of evidence-based trauma informed therapy approaches that facilitate cognitive, emotional and behavioral change.

Regardless of a therapist's theoretical orientation, the PRACTICE *elements* included in Cohen et al.'s Trauma-focused Cognitive Behavior Therapy (TF-CBT) are critical ingredients in trauma recovery: psycho-education and parenting, relaxation (and stress reduction), affective identification and expression, cognitive coping (to lay the groundwork for later restructuring), trauma narrative development, *in vivo* exposure, conjoint child–caregiver sessions, and enhancing future safety, relationships and self development.

Therapists will also find the Attachment, Self-Regulation, and Competency (ARC) model developed by Blaustein and Kinniburgh well suited for work with traumatized children and caregivers with multiple, prolonged traumatic stress. ARC includes relationship development (resilience through attachment), self regulation, and dimensions of cognitive and emotional competency. It also suggests intervention for the management, identification, modulation, and expression of affect. The competency component of the program, in addition to self-efficacy, addresses executive functioning and individuation. It is a *must-read* for every trauma-informed therapist.

Child–Parent Relationship Therapy (Landreth & Bratton, 2006) strengthens the relationship between the caregiver and abused child. Dialectical Behavior Therapy (DBT) helps abused teens learn to regulate moods and combat faulty beliefs. Schema Therapy and Acceptance and Commitment Therapy (ACT) assist older teens in developing new coping abilities.

Parent–Child Interaction Therapy (PCIT) (Zisser & Eyberg, 2010), Filial Therapy (VanFleet, 2005) and Child–Parent Psychotherapy (Lieberman & Van Horn, 2005, 2008) are excellent models of evidence-based parent–child training. PCIT is an empirically supported treatment for behaviorally disordered young children with an emphasis on improving the quality of the parent–child relationship while changing patterns of parent–child interaction. In this model, parents are taught specific skills to establish a nurturing and secure relationship with their child while increasing their child's prosocial behavior and decreasing negative behavior. This treatment focuses on two basic play-based interactions: Child-Directed Interaction (CDI) for strengthening the parent–child relationship; and Parent-Directed Interaction (PDI) for specific behavior management techniques. We have found that the Child-Directed Interaction allows the parent to become more sensitive to the child, build positive attachment, and respond more consistently.

EMDR and Mindfulness-based Stress Reduction training are effective treatments with school-aged children for emotion focused right-brain work and neurobiological integration. EMDR is being used clinically with children for both single and complex trauma (Gomez, 2013; Lovett, 2007; Tinker & Wilson, 1999).

Gomez speaks succinctly of how EMDR impacts neural pathways and cites controlled randomized studies with children. EMDR taps into use of memory function and right-brain experiential contributions to trauma. The interventions activate right-brain areas through sensory stimulation (tapping, tones) and then integrate those neural pathways with left-brain functions through verbal processing. The Child Welfare League of America (CWLA) now includes EMDR as one of their approved evidence-based practices for traumatized children.

Mindfulness-based Stress Reduction training for school-age children and a wide variety of mindfulness practices are also recommended interventions with abused children, since they allow the child to improve self efficacy, increase cognitive focus, achieve relaxation, improve distress tolerance, and seek body/mind integration. Some mindfulness resources are listed in the parent resource list in the appendix and these practices offer opportunities for caregivers and children to practice breathing, meditation, and acceptance together at home.

And finally, play therapy techniques have long been used in trauma intervention within both psychodynamic and cognitive behavioral therapies (CBT; Drewes, 2009; Gil & Briere, 2006; Kaduson & Schaffer, 2003; Malchiodi, 2008; Markell & Markell, 2008; McGee & Holmes, 2008; and Pernicano, 2010a and 2010b). Play therapies may be integrated into almost any trauma-informed work, and they can be tailored to the age and developmental functioning of the child.

1.4 The Four "F" Words: Stages of the Trauma Stress Sequence

Freak out, Freeze, Flight, and Fight (the four "F" words) are terms used by this author in the Child and Caregiver Guides and Appendix B to describe the neurobiological stages of the stress response, in part because they will be easy terms for readers to remember. The stages—and behaviors during each stage—parallel the child's brain functioning under stress and the neurobiological resources being used to deal with threat to the child's well-being (Bremner, 2012; Cozolino, 2006, 2010; Perry, 2004a, 2004b, 2006, 2009; Perry & Hambrick, 2008; Perry & Pollard, 1998; Siegel, 1999). The nature of stress, and its impact on brain development and functioning, have been widely researched in recent years.

When I worked in a residential treatment program for teens and later in a group home/family reunification program with infants, preschoolers, and school-age children, I observed the ways in which staff or caregiver behaviors triggered dysregulation. Child functioning reliably changed in the face of threats, ultimatums, a loud or harsh tone of voice, fast movements toward the child, criticism, lack of consistent attention, and/or visible frustration. Abused and neglected children of all ages were especially sensitive to changes in vocal tone or facial expressions; they also reacted to both verbal and nonverbal signs of stress in the staff.

It was clear that certain staff had a knack for helping children calm down; they softened their voices, ensured proximity, provided nurture, and lessened control. Other staff *unwittingly triggered fear and protective responses* in children—responses that looked a lot like anger or defiance. A fearful, angry, defiant child was usually given a behavioral consequence for his or her perceived actions, yet it was often the caregiver who needed to learn to engage with the child in a less threatening manner.

One staff member, when discussing the defiance of the teens in the group home, said zealously, "We need to show them who is in control/in charge around here!" I replied, "What we need to do is help them gain better control over their own moods and behavior." This person did not realize that traumatized children need to be given as much control as possible in order to reduce their fear and help them feel safe. His power-control strategies often led to physical management with the young people, and he did not understand that his behavior triggered negative caregiver–child interactions.

In searching the web a number of years ago for materials (on trauma-informed treatment) that I might use in teaching and training, I came across the Trauma Academy Web site (www.childtrauma.org). Dr. Bruce Perry and his colleagues have written extensively about what I observed in my clinical practice with traumatized children and their caregivers, i.e. that treatment needs to be "matched to" a child's strengths and limitations, and that the age of onset and duration of abuse (beginning in infancy) have neurobiological ramifications (Perry, 2004, 2006, 2009; Perry & Hambrick, 2008; Perry & Pollard, 1998). The Neurosequential Model of Therapeutics trains professionals to evaluate and "map" a child's neurobiological capacities and identify interventions that utilize skills already mastered by the child (Perry, 2009; Perry & Hambrick, 2008; Perry & Pollard, 1998).

At a play therapy convention several years ago in Louisville, KY, I attended a workshop that incorporated Dr. Perry's training materials on state-dependent functioning (2004a, 2004b). These materials describe how children react neurobiologically (to cope with stress) following trauma, and how caregiver behaviors can either escalate a traumatized child's stress and fear orhelp children calm down and regain control. Perry's materials integrate much of what we have learned over the past 20 years about traumatic stress; a chart in the training materials walks one through the stages of neurobiological coping that occur as a child is increasingly stressed. The Child Trauma Academy training materials are available for purchase at www.childtrauma.org and are strongly recommended for those working with traumatized children and their caregivers. I provide my own example of state-dependent functioning in Appendix B following on from the chart in Perry's training materials and summarize in the Caregiver Guide how caregiver behavior can exacerbate or alleviate fear in a traumatized child.

In my practice, I find it helpful to give copies of Appendix B to caregivers and review the material in session using examples of their recent parent–child interactions, to bring points home. Once a caregiver understands the connection between child functioning and trauma, that person can adapt his or her response to the child. Following is a quick review of the freeze–flight–fight response that can occur in children following trauma.

1.4.1 Freak Out

Since an abused child's brain and nervous system remain in a state of fear even after the mistreatment ends, the child is likely to be vigilant and watchful and less calm than a non-abused child. In essence, children who have undergone this trauma are *on the lookout for the abuse to happen again* and their nervous systems remain at a higher level of arousal (Perry, 1998, 2004a, 2004b, 2006, 2009). These children are easily startled or *triggered* by sensory, interpersonal, or environmental cues that remind them of past abuse. *Vigilant* children also become easily stressed by raised voices, multiple demands, signs of adult criticism or frustration, and perceived failure. As their stress increases, they find it hard to think clearly and are less likely to pay attention or comply with adult directives. When the children are startled, they become highly alert and *freak out* (a state of internal dysregulation).

If a caregiver misunderstands a child's fear-based stress response and becomes more frustrated with him or her, the child is likely to *freeze* or become very emotional. The caregiver can be coached to notice early signs of stress and dysregulation and intervene to prevent the freeze; this can include helping a child *calm down* with mindfulness, relaxation, and guided imagery.

1.4.2 Freeze

Freeze is the second stage of the stress response. Here, the child is in a state of alarm and may be too afraid to move or talk because he or she perceives that something bad is about to happen. During *freeze*, a child might become suddenly very emotional or simply more quiet and watchful, *like a deer in the headlights*. A child in *freeze* may seem inattentive, disobedient, disorganized (doing random things without a clear goal), or paralyzed (still).

The goal is for caregivers of children in *freeze* to help those children relax and regain control. During *freeze*, most children respond to slow movements, light touch, invited contact ("do you want a hug?"), and quiet soothing words. These responses can reduce the child's *fear* and help the child calm down and regulate affect. A loud or threatening voice, a raised hand, or a finger pointing in the child's face will increase fear for a child in freeze (Perry, 2004a, 2004b).

1.4.3 Flight

Flight, the third stage of the stress response, occurs when the child's fear or stress increases to the point that he or she perceives the need to *escape* in body or mind to ensure protection or survival. The midbrain is activated prior to *flight*, and the child's response will be a form of shutting down (during which he or she is not capable of listening or talking) or escape (running or hiding from the perceived danger). A child in *flight* might leave the room or run from the therapist or caregiver due to the increased state of fear. During *flight* the child is unable to think and is emotionally reactive (likely to do or say something without thinking). Dissociation is a serious type of flight that may result from severe or repeated trauma during early childhood, where a child goes somewhere else in his or her mind and tunes out reality.

It is helpful to remain quietly present or offer an attachment object (pet, blanket, stuffed animal, etc.) when a child starts to tune out or appears ready to run. It also helps to reduce noise and distractions and to *disengage* (back off or give the child some space). When the child is in *flight*, a caregiver should not raise his or her voice, lecture, threaten, show increased frustration, show fear, grab the child, or make demands/ultimatums (Perry, 2004a, 2004b). If an adult responds in any of these ways, the child is likely to move into *fight*.

1.4.4 Fight

Fight is the final stage of the stress sequence, and is a state of terror during which the child is concerned only with self-protection and survival. During terror, or *fight*, the child's brain moves to a primitive, lower level functioning (brainstem); he or she cannot think or reason, although a caregiver may interpret this response as willful defiance or intentional aggression. A child's fight may be verbal or physical. Once in a state of *physical fight*, the child may hit, bite, throw things. or kick anyone that comes too close.

Therapists need to teach caregivers the difference between a *meltdown that arises out of fear (self-protection)* and a *tantrum that comes from defiance (oppositional)*. These can look very much the same, but when adults can't tell the difference, children get accused of *acting out on purpose* when in fact they are actually trying to stay safe. Traumatized children do not *behave well* until they feel safe, can self-regulate, and develop the capacity for cause–effect thinking. If a caregiver grabs, shakes, harshly restrains, or screams at a child in *fight*, it will remind the child of prior abuse and intensify the child's fear. The caregiver should give the child space to calm down and focus on safety and protection. Restraint should not be used with an abused child except as a last resort to maintain or restore safety, since restraint itself can trigger fear.

1.5 Working within the Developmental Context

The Neurosequential Model of Therapeutics (Perry, 2009; Perry & Hambrick, 2008) is beyond the scope of this book, but the model stresses the importance of assessing a child's developmental strengths and limitations, understanding at what ages trauma occurred, and matching interventions to a child's neurobiological and developmental limitations and competencies. Due to the neurobiological impact of trauma (which differs by stage of development), a child may subsequently have functional limitations. A child's play capacity, sensory-motor skills and cognitive/language development need to be carefully evaluated early in treatment, since they establish the scope of developmentally appropriate interventions. For example, expressive or receptive communication difficulties may indicate the need for play or expressive therapies even with older children. The treatment provider also needs to help the caregiver respond appropriately to the child's developmental needs.

Many traumatized children, especially those who have undergone complex trauma, have developmental delays. It used to be thought that children would recover better than adults from the experience of traumatic events since their brains are malleable and still developing. However, neurobiological research suggests that the experience of overly high, debilitating stress (during prenatal development, infancy, or childhood) can result in changes to the developing brain and nervous system that impact attachment, health, and coping, and may last into adulthood if left untreated (Bremner, 2012; Briere, 2012; Cozolino, 2006, 2010; McCollum, 2006; Perry, 2006, 2009; Perry & Hambrick, 2008; Perry & Pollard, 1998). It is unclear whether neurobiological differences are present in individuals prior to their experience of trauma or *caused/exacerbated by* high stress/trauma; this seems a moot point given evidence for prenatal transmission of stress.

1.6 Psychoeducational Needs of Children and Caregivers

It is important to educate children and caregivers about the impact of trauma on child development, including cognitive processing, mood regulation, and parent–child attachment. Caregivers such as teachers, foster and adoptive parents, and kinship care providers need to understand the many types of cues that can trigger fear and arousal in abused children, even those abused or exposed to violence preverbally. Caregivers who believe children were *too young to remember their abuse* will be better able to put a child's behavior in context once they understand that trauma memories and triggers can be sensory (right-brain, non-verbal, limbic) and/or cognitive (verbal, left-brain, hippocampus-mediated).

In doing caregiver–child conjoint work, it is important that the therapist evaluate the caregiver's own trauma and attachment experiences, as memories of these may be triggered by, and impact, the child's therapy process. Avoidance of trauma work by the caregiver can be related to his or her unresolved trauma.

Mental health providers become positive advocates for abused children in school and other settings. They can help caregivers understand the sorts of things that trigger a child's fear and learn to respond in ways that reduce the risk of further trauma. It is not surprising that many children with prior trauma end up suspended from school, incarcerated, or hospitalized when adults misread signals and respond in ways that intensify their fear. Ross Greene's *Explosive Child* (2001) and *Treating Explosive Kids: The Collaborative Problem-Solving Approach* (Greene & Ablon, 2006) describe the problems of "inflexible" children and the ways caregivers can negotiate with them and collaborate in order to solve daily problems and prevent aggressive outbursts. These strategies can be very helpful with abused children, since many of them move quickly into power struggles or arguments with caregivers and teachers when they feel threatened. Dr. Greene's model teaches listening, reflection, and empathy skills so that adults and children work together to solve problems (see www.ccps.info and www.livesinthebalance.org).

As noted above, many caregivers mislabel child stress/fear responses as willful defiance or "ignoring," and are unaware of the ways in which their behaviors trigger children's protective responses. For example, a young boy whose diagnosis fell on the autism spectrum recently had a temper tantrum when transitioning from his father's to his mother's for the weekend, saying he didn't want to go. Rather than ask why, his parents put hands on him to try to get him in the car. He completely *lost it*, biting, kicking and screaming. When asked by his therapist why he didn't want to go, the child said that his mother's husband *picked on him* and scared him. This was the same man that had abused him four years prior. He denied current abuse, but referred to harsh discipline, a "look" on his stepfather's face, and comments made that raised his anxiety. I explained to the boy's father that his son seemed to be reacting out of fear, not defiance. Therapy was bringing up (triggering) memories of prior abuse, and the child remained in a state of fear around the mother's husband.

Caregivers sometimes judge that children behave in the ways they do *on purpose*. Therapists need to help caregivers understand that some behaviors of abused children have a *purpose (are goal-directed)* but are not necessarily *on purpose*, i.e. done deliberately. The goal of such behaviors is safety and survival—they help the child cope with stress and avoid future abuse. A sudden change in a child's mood or attitude, even *bossiness, backtalk, sudden oppositional stubbornness, or arguing*, can be a child's attempt to regain control or take charge in the face of a stress trigger.

Conversely, *on purpose* behavior is left-brained, rational, and intentional; the child knows what he or she is doing and why. *On purpose* behaviors require planning, foresight, and self-control; many abused children have not developed these skills. They do not plan well, do not think ahead, and tend to react to (rather than act on) their world.

I have heard caregivers say, "He wants his own way," as if having control is a bad thing. Therapists can help caregivers understand that an abused or neglected child felt helpless and out of control during the abuse and now needs to feel more *in charge* or *in control*. If we are to be very honest, we all find satisfaction in autonomy and doing things our own way. Children, especially abused children, need to feel in control of their lives and decisions.

1.7 Developmental Considerations

1.7.1 Trauma Therapy with Caregivers and Infants or Toddlers

Therapists often become involved in court-ordered assessment and intervention in order to increase caregiver sensitivity to infants or toddlers exposed to abuse, neglect, or domestic violence and to educate caregivers about child development.

A number of caregivers have been referred to our program for family reunification when their infants, some of whom were born addicted to drugs or exposed to significant abuse or neglect, are five–12 months of age. These infants may be much too quiet (few vocalizations), non-responsive (little eye contact), fussy, or irritable. A good number of these infants do not start crawling until eight–ten months of age. If they are mobile, they move out of sight of the caregiver with little regard for safety.

A twenty-something mother who had lost parental rights on four older children moved in with an infant and toddler. The baby, who had been in foster care since birth, was engaging and active, seeking proximity to her mother and fussing when left alone.

"She is bad," said the mother. "She never lets me sleep in the morning and doesn't want to stay in the playpen. Why can't she be more like her big sister?"

She considered the toddler a "good girl." The older child stayed to herself, showed little curiosity, did not fuss or cry, and avoided interpersonal contact. She was not yet talking and averted her eyes when approached. She pretended to not hear requests and hardly ever smiled or laughed. She did not show interest in other toddlers or children.

After a few months in the program with intensive in-home therapy activities, the two-year-old began to smile, approached program staff to be picked up, made better eye contact, increased playful behavior, and signaled distress to her mother. She was no longer happy to be left alone, and her mother was not entirely happy at the changes in her formerly "good" baby. In time she came to accept that the changes in her daughter were healthy ones, and she began to see the ways in which her behavior impacted her children.

The age at which trauma occurred, availability of secondary attachment figures, and the quality of attachment in the home subsequent to the trauma in part determine the neurobiological impact of abuse and neglect. With intensive parent–child treatment, an infant can often reach normal developmental milestones within about six months.

Treatment with infants and toddlers focuses on attunement, improving caregiver–child emotional and cognitive attachment strategies, and increasing understanding of child development. Attunement is a synchronized, *brain-to-brain* neurobiological connection between caregiver and child that develops through interpersonal stimulation. This takes place through mutual face-to-face interaction, during which the caregiver *reads and responds* to the baby's arousal and cues. An attuned connection between the caregiver and infant facilitates healthy neurobiological development in the child. Infant mental health providers train caregivers to use touch, vocal inflection, facial expression, and eye contact to connect with the infant and to respond consistently to a child's verbal and non-verbal cues.

1.7.2 Trauma Therapy with Caregivers and Preschool Children

Abused children may engage in mechanical, rote, repetitive play as preschoolers. When this is the case, their play lacks emotional expression and mastery and they do not use or respond to pretend play. When rote play is observed, therapists and caregivers can use sensory-motor activities (music, rhythm, rhyming, and massage) with the child to enhance bilateral brain development and integration. Sensory-motor play is a precursor of language development, and as the child develops language and strong attachment relationships, his or her play behaviors will mature as well.

Play therapy helps children identify and express feelings, solve problems, and talk about their abuse with their caregivers. Caregivers should be pulled into and involved in the child's play therapy. When abused children start to use make-believe play, they often display themes of power-control, victimization, monsters, good/evil, and safety. They may bury "bad guys," fight alligators, or seek help from superheroes. Caregivers may be caught off guard by the level of the child's anger and emotional intensity in play, but therapists can help them understand the difference between fantasy play (which helps resolve trauma) and real aggression. Caregivers can also be encouraged to allow frequent child directed play to give an abused child a sense of autonomy and control.

1.7.3 Trauma Therapy with Caregivers and School-Age Children

Many abused or neglected children, especially those placed in out-of-home care, begin to display disruptive, disorganized, oppositional, or aggressive behavior during elementary school years. Others present with separation anxiety, obsessive compulsive symptoms, or depression. Therapy is usually a mix of structured, activity-focused, cognitive behavioral treatment and creative expressive or play therapy interventions. Children at this age are able to express feelings, answer questions, and process life experiences. During the elementary school years, children enjoy competition, play games with rules, and engage in advanced pretend play through story creation or dramatic enactment.

On the other hand, some abused children respond poorly to competition and losing in games, since this elicits uncomfortable feelings about power and control (one up/one down); as a result, they become stressed and shift to a self-protective or aggressive stance. If caregivers or therapists notice this tendency, play can be adjusted to a lower developmental level until the child can tolerate this type of interpersonal stress when interacting with peers and playing with others.

Some cognitive-behavioral therapies such as social skills- or self-control training require higher level brain development and are not appropriate for children with delayed language or expressive communication difficulties. Language-driven CBT requires that a child have adequate executive functioning (be able to think and plan ahead, use self-direction and self-control); be able to use cause–– thinking; be able to sequence (think about things step by step); be able to use pretend play; and be able to connect thoughts and feelings (Perry, 2009; Perry & Hambrick, 1998). Unfortunately, the brain's cortex develops more slowly in abused and neglected children. Even for a child to benefit from behavior modification, he or she must be able to connect behavior with consequences. For this reason, right-brain, body–mind, expressive and emotion focused interventions are useful for children with delayed language and processing.

Elementary-age traumatized children often need collateral interventions at school to help them reduce stress within an educational setting. Some become agitated, hyperactive, or withdrawn when feel overwhelmed by school demands. They are bullied more often than non-abused children and land themselves in more trouble in the classroom. Due to slow processing or cognitive inflexibility, many abused children have difficulty completing work and making transitions during the school day.

Home interventions include those that increase structure and predictability, nurturing family rituals, and emotional safety. The therapist can also teach the parent to engage the child in special bedtime activities, since bedtime is a time of high arousal for many abused children. Caregivers can use calming activities such as yoga, singing bedtime songs, and reading attachment-based bedtime stories.

Efforts of caregivers and therapists may at times be well intentioned but misguided, usually when caregiver expectations and therapy activities do not match the child's developmental competencies. A case example follows:

An abused hyperactive eight-year-old boy was placed in his fourth foster home. He had poor eye contact and could not control his moods. His communication skills were at a the level of a four-year-old, while his social development was at the level of a two-year-old. He often became easily agitated and aggressive when he thought someone was going to hurt him. He had witnessed the abuse of his mother, brother, and sister.

His foster parents set up a behavior modification plan where he got a card for every negative behavior. The cards resulted in extra chores. He got lots of cards every day, and did many extra chores, but this did not change his behavior. The intervention failed.

This little boy did not connect his behavior to the consequences because he had poor verbal skills and delayed executive functioning ability. The treatment team suggested that the foster parents start using attachment-based interventions and child-directed play therapy type activities. Once they set expectations as they would with a toddler (his approximate level of social development) and treated him like a younger child, the boy made good progress.

1.7.4 Trauma Therapy with Caregivers and Teens

Traumatized pre-adolescents or teens may present as overly withdrawn, angry, sexually-precocious, socially regressed (play with younger children), or begin using drugs or alcohol—especially pain medication, anxiolytics, and marijuana—in order to avoid or numb emotional pain. Each formerly abused child will react differently as puberty approaches. Most feel alienated and different, and the chatter of classmates can seem trivial and unimportant when compared to their own experiences. Abused children sometimes report that it seems as if others can read their minds or are able to *tell that they have been abused*. Some realize for the first time the truly sexual nature of what happened to them in the past. A subset of formerly abused teens will show strong interest in pornography to the detriment of normal peer relationships or behave in a sexually explicit manner with peers or younger children. Around puberty, many abused children experience shame, alienation, and depersonalization. They assume that adults judge them or blame them for what happened if those adults do not talk with them about their feelings, since teens often blame themselves for what happened in their families. Some adolescents become very depressed, neglecting hygiene and avoiding bathing, as if to avoid touching their bodies or to keep others at a distance. Others start having panic attacks or high levels of anxiety that disturb sleep.

Adolescent trauma work needs to include family or caregiver involvement as well as a clear contract with the caregiver to allow for the teen's privacy and some degree of non-shared, confidential communication with the young person. Adolescents need increasing freedom to become more autonomous; nurture for attachment development; and structure, for safety and boundaries. The caregiver will be encouraged to give the teen as much privacy and control over his or her decisions as possible at home. The caregiver will also be advised to build in one-on-one time and not allow the teen to become too withdrawn or isolated. With adolescents, the therapist serves in the role of consultant, supporter, and mediator and helps the caregiver and teen communicate openly, share feelings and thoughts about the past, and identify goals. The teen needs outlets beyond the family to build autonomy, gain competence, reduce isolation and ensure access to appropriate resources for adolescent development. Adolescents need to address their attachment issues and core relational schemas in therapy in order to develop a positive self identity, so that they might become able to regulate affect and avoid repeating the interpersonal patterns of their parents. As they separate and individuate, they also need to experience nurture and must be free to depend on a consistently available attachment object, sometimes for the first time.

1.8 Faulty Interpersonal Schema Development

Abused or neglected children, and adults who were abused or neglected as children, develop faulty interpersonal schemas. These are deeply held core beliefs that guide decisions and behavior which relate directly to unresolved attachment and trauma issues and are intertwined with strong emotions about fear of abandonment. Schemas that arise out of abusive or neglectful relationships are easily triggered by cues that signal danger (activate a trauma reaction) or ones that activate the Attachment Behavioral System (ABS).

1.8.1 Development of Schemas through Faulty Attachments and Trauma

When the person that is supposed to *love you (best and most)* is the one that hurts you, you start to question your value, worth, and *lovability*. Children are egocentric and believe that they are the source of parental unhappiness. They blame themselves for family conflict, and their parents may do little to contradict that belief. Children believe they must *be good (if not perfect)* to make themselves more lovable.

Children develop core schemas out of what they hear adults do and say as well as what they *experience* early in life. Young children are dependent on adults for survival, and they are not developmentally or cognitively capable of challenging parental beliefs; thus they accept parental beliefs as facts.

There are many ways in which children develop faulty relational schemas. Their caregivers promise that things will change ("I'm so sorry, I don't know what got into me . . . I'll never hurt you again . . ."), yet too often the pattern of violence repeats itself. They watch parents threaten to leave, slam doors, throw things, and hurt one another but are told to "be nice."

If children are unfortunate enough to get between two adults engaged in a fight, they learn that their efforts have no impact and that they are helpless. They hear one of their parents making excuses and minimizing the other's unacceptable behaviors ("He's had a hard life . . . He doesn't mean to . . . He doesn't know how loud he gets . . . He's better than he used to be . . . You know how men are . . . It could be worse . . . He's not all bad . . . He can be really nice sometimes . . . He loves me in his own way . . .").

Children may be expected to apologize to their abusive parents ("Tell your father you're sorry for what you did . . . Go to your room and come out when you're ready to apologize . . . What kind of child talks to her father that way—say you're sorry!"). They learn that men (who are often the dominant partners) have the *right* to be in charge and control others ("I'll give you a piece of my mind . . . I'll give you something to cry about . . . Shut your mouth and do what I say . . . I don't care WHAT you think!"). They learn that adults *can't* control themselves when they are angry ("I don't know what came over me . . . I can't stop myself . . . I've always been this way . . .").

Many children hear parents talking conditionally about love ("If you don't do what I want, then . . . I'm going to leave unless you . . .") and blaming others for their own behavior ("Don't make me lose my temper . . . If you hadn't said that, I wouldn't have . . ."). They are exposed to denial and rationalization ("Deep down, he's a good man . . . He used to be a lot worse—it hardly ever happens any more . . . My mother had it worse—he's not so bad . . . Love is a fairy tale, why expect more? I can tell he doesn't really mean it . . . He has nowhere else to go— someone has to take care of him . . . I can't abandon him . . .").

Physically or sexually abused children learn that their bodies are not their own and that unwanted touch comes without anyone asking permission. A child may be asked to do things to adults or expected to watch sexual activity. Such an individual may later have difficulty with touch boundaries, not understanding that touch is personal and that everyone has the right *to refuse*.

Children often learn about dependence and *learned helplessness* through their mothers' voiced attitudes about intimate partner violence (IPV; "When you make your bed, you lie in it . . . We don't have anywhere else to go . . . I'll never be able to leave . . . I've tried before and he always comes back . . . What else can I do?"). A child may think it is *normal* for a woman to experience IPV one night (after which she kicks him out again *for good*) and the next night engage in passionate makeup sex following her partner's *heartfelt apology*.

Some children are taught that staying with an abusive partner is a mandated religious practice and evidence of faith. ("Divorce is a sin . . . A Godly woman honors and obeys her husband . . . I married for better or worse . . . My husband is the head of our household . . . My pastor says it is my duty to stand by him and help him change . . . My husband says he is sorry and I am supposed to forgive him . . . Staying in my marriage is God's will . . ."). These children may come to question what sort of God would sanction IPV, but they believe what they are told and sometimes even feel guilty for wishing that Daddy would leave.

1.8.2 Common Schemas Related to Trauma and Attachment

Our early experiences, for better or worse, prepare us for our later relationships. In my work with adult victims of partner violence and with abused pre-teens or teens, I have observed that some begin to use drugs or alcohol to decrease arousal and avoid painful emotions while others engage in self-harm. Many of their core schemas stem from early attachment strategies that were needed to survive but are no longer adaptive.

To identify core schemas with children, adolescents, and adults in trauma therapy, it is helpful to explore the meanings and beliefs in their trauma narratives. The list below includes some core schemas and related beliefs that begin in childhood following abuse or neglect and are carried into adolescence and adulthood.

Schema: I am not lovable (Attachment-Related)

No one will ever love me.

I don't deserve to be loved.

How can anyone love me when my own parents hurt me?

I'm a bad daughter/son.

I have to help out, take care of others to earn their love.

I am stupid, ugly, weird, different, etc.

I am not good enough to hold onto someone I love.

Schema: I am Powerless (Trauma—Power and Control)

I have no rights and there's nothing I can do.

I'm going to get hurt if I do what I want to do.

I'm going to get hurt if I say what I want to say.

I need to play it safe (don't make waves, don't rock the boat).

Others are in charge.

Don't "talk back" (authoritarian parental control).

Don't think—talk—feel (safer that way).

I am trapped.

Schema: I am Worthless (Abuse-Related Victim Thinking)

Nothing I can do will get others to pay attention to me.

I don't deserve to ask for anything for myself.

No one cares what I think/feel.

I am insignificant.

I am *less than* (someone else).

I am invisible.

I don't matter.

It doesn't matter what I think.

Schema: I Am Helpless (Dependency and Attachment Needs, Learned Helplessness)

I can't survive without him.

I can't . . . escape pain, take care of myself, get away, or live on my own.

Being abused is better than being alone.

I can't survive on my own.

He's all I have.

If I don't put up with it, I will end up alone.

If I try hard enough I can earn his/her love.

If I tell family secrets, I will lose their love and be sent away.

People that love you always hurt you.

Schema: I Am a Failure (Trauma-Related, Self-Blame)

I am a bad person.

I deserve punishment.

I'm stupid and incompetent.

I mess up everything I do.

I screw everything up.

I am never good enough.

It's my fault.

I must have done something to make him/her mad.

I'm a loser.

During the course of trauma-informed treatment, the therapist is likely to hear one or more of these themes in the language of parents and children. It is important to challenge the beliefs by helping the child and caregiver see that they are not based on *fact* but are instead conclusions drawn about why and how they endured life experiences. Trauma-focused therapy stories are very helpful in illustrating core schemas and provide suggestions for alternate views.

Parallel trauma-informed treatment may be offered to the caregiver when cross-generational abuse and related beliefs or schemas interfere with the child's trauma recovery or contribute to unhealthy relationship patterns in the home. This type of treatment is often needed to help the caregiver gain the experience of being in a sensitive, consistent relationship (with the therapist) and develop new attachment strategies in his or her own adult relationships.

CHAPTER 2

USING NARRATIVE, METAPHOR, AND TRAUMA-FOCUSED STORIES IN TRAUMA INTERVENTION

2.1 The Power of the Narrative

Storytelling is an ageless tradition, and metaphorical and therapeutic stories have long been used in therapy with children and adults (Burns, 2005, 2007; Gardner, 1971; Kopp, 1995; Le Guin, 1968; and Pernicano, 2010a and 2010b). Native American tales and Aesop's Fables teach lessons with memorable themes, and TV miniseries such as *Roots* or movies such as *Schindler's List* or *Lincoln* preserve and pass on important history to the next generation. Works of fiction such as *The Adventures of Huckleberry Finn* or *Winnie the Pooh* develop memorable characters for lessons in life, while cartoons such as *Pearls Before Swine* or *Doonesbury* feature characters who offer social commentary.

As we continue to learn more about neurobiological pathways and right-brain contributions to trauma and attachment, we better understand the ways in which stories have the capacity to open up right-brain processes, activate sensory memories, trigger strong unresolved emotions, and stimulate the "aha" of insight that propels behavior change. Stories lure listeners powerfully toward identification; seemingly innocuous, they stir deeply, allowing clients to bond with a caring therapist and rebuild trust in others. They conjure up feelings about family and self which have long been avoided, and bring the past into clear focus. They allow a distressed individual to process and make sense of traumatizing events, wipe the slate clean, and move forward.

Stories are generally used adjunctively in treatment for psychoeducation or intervention. They spring-board the client to see, feel, and sense similarities between the story and the client's situation, and they introduce story themes, characters, affect, cognition and problem solving. Stories seed possibilities and new ways of looking at things, and the emotional identification with story characters triggers memories of past relationships with abusive others. Stories address barriers to change and suggest solutions, some of which are processed non-consciously and others that relate more directly to thinking and behavior. At times, a therapy story may serve as the guide for a goal-directed task such as trauma narrative work.

2.2 Story Development and Use (Case Examples)

Therapists sometimes believe that they must rely on someone else's stories. While doing so can certainly be a time-saver, any therapist can learn the art and skill of therapy story development. This author's stories have been conceived mostly through direct interactions with clients and their children. The stories in this section have been de-identified for the sake of privacy, and in some cases descriptions of the real families have been merged or changed. The core issues have been preserved, however, and the client metaphors retained.

Trauma-related therapy stories are useful for psychoeducation and for introducing and carrying out treatment interventions. Typical psychoeducational topics include post-traumatic stress disorder (PTSD) and symptoms of trauma, how memories are triggered, justification for doing a trauma narrative, parenting concepts such as attachment, the impact of IPV, the dependency of children, the elements and stages of change, and cognitive behavioral concepts such as the connection of thoughts, feelings, and behaviors. Adult psychoeducational stories also include material about caregiver blind spots, child attachment needs, child development, parenting behaviors, safety factors, decision making, and intimate partner violence.

Therapy intervention stories guide the trauma narrative process, provide material for guided imagery, help clients weigh risks and benefits of change, promote part-self integration, lead to safety planning and family discussion, reduce avoidance, and help the client begin to heal from within. The impact of therapy stories is both cognitive and emotional, some metaphors hypnotically going in the *back door* to tap into right-brain emotional and sensory processes. It is often during the reading of a story or in the weeks following this that a family, child, or caregiver experiences a breakthrough, gains and acts on new insight, or experiences emotional growth. Attachment (sensed safety, love, and felt security) develops in the right-brain limbic areas, particular in the amygdala, and therapy stories seem to have the power to emotionally trigger interpersonal awareness and relational change.

The themes and characters in therapy stories are created to have specific parallels to the client's life. It is important that the stories, their characters, and the dialogue be somewhat exaggerated and ludicrous so that the reader can see the *tall tale* (*charicaturological*) aspects and not feel threatened or defensive. The stories also need to be relatively ambiguous so that they may be applied to a broad audience and for multiple purposes. For example, self-destruction is commonly depicted by a moth drawn to a flame, but the story might be used with juvenile sex offending, adolescent substance abuse, clients with eating disorders, and children that steal, all of whom have compelling urges and need to weigh risks and benefits of acting on those urges.

Stories have the capacity to provide some intellectual and emotional distance to elusively pull the reader into identification with the character. The child character in the story can be a teaching character (empowered to give advice to a short-sighted adult) or the client character that turns to a friend or helper (therapist role). It is good to add humor, since this counters anxiety and reduces guardedness while the story is read. Humor helps us laugh at ourselves as we realize our similarities to the story characters and accepting our limitations in the context of universality. The advice given in a story can be a bit understated and should not be judgmental, preachy, or *teachy*, allowing the client to save face and acknowledge the problems in his or her life without shame or embarrassment.

During the early phases of treatment (pre-contemplation, contemplation, and preparation) within Prochaska and DiClemente's Transtheoretical Stages of Change (1982), therapy stories suggest the possibility of a new way of thinking about things and may even propel the client into the next stage of change. Stories can orient clients to the therapy process and introduce issues that are common during early trauma work including avoidance, denial, and the importance of talking about trauma. Client psychoeducation at this stage is about the nature of abuse as well as trauma-related symptoms. The early chapters in the Child's Guide are consistent with these topics.

Later in treatment, the therapist will use stories where the story character faces a problem like the child's, such as fear of the dark, depression, or obsessive compulsive symptoms. The child may be experiencing bad dreams or flashbacks and feel helpless, or may be struggling with a parent that keeps returning to an abusive partner. At this stage the treatment is more specific and focused, including tools for intervention. Stories during the Action stage of change focus on the process of change as well as attitudes, thinking and behaviors which get in the way of lasting change. The Child's Guide moves into more sensitive material in later chapters after providing a good overview of trauma symptoms.

The focus of stories for psychoeducation and treatment still later in treatment moves to relapse prevention and safety, to help a child and his or her caregiver articulate a clear safety plan and transition to aftercare services. Stories at this phase discuss specific issues that place a family at risk of further abuse or neglect, such as IPV, exposing children to sexual material, parental risk-taking behavior, poor supervision, role reversal, substance abuse, and unhealthy adult relationships.

In the next section, the author discusses the origins of some of her stories and characters to illustrate the ways in which therapy stories are co-created based on client treatment needs. Each story propelled the client toward an *"aha"* and resulted in significant therapeutic movement.

2.3 Co-creation of Therapy Stories

2.3.1 By Theme or Problem

A therapy story for a child needs to run parallel to the child's problem and fit his or her stage of treatment. The story introduces a character that feels and thinks much like the child and is trying to cope with a similar dilemma or one that will remind the child of a parent or perpetrator. If the main character will be an animal, it needs to have characteristics that *fit* the presenting issue and create a *helpful* response set in the child. The character's problem has to be significant so that there is a strong need for problem solving. For example, an eagle should not be afraid of flying, and an obsessive compulsive frog would soon starve if he could not eat flies without washing them. A peacock can easily be seen as a show-off, and there is a perceived aggressive energy to dragons, lions, and alligators. The child character can be a victim or the person in charge that offers wise advice. Either approach can be helpful when the client perceives him or herself as a victim and needs to develop self-efficacy. A perpetrator character has one or more of the characteristics of someone that hurt the child: dangerous behavior, untrustworthiness, selfishness, arrogance, self-centeredness, cruelty, or disregard for others. The action of the story will remind the child of something he or she experienced.

This author often *breaks the ice* by teaching a hybrid *Squiggles Game* to a child and caregiver. The game as carried out by the author is a combination of Winnicott's Squiggles Game (1953), Richard Gardner's Mutual Story Telling (1971), and Thematic Apperception Test (TAT, Murray) instructions and interpretation; the story must address what has happened before the picture, what is happening now, how it turns out in the end, and what the characters are thinking, feeling, and doing. In this game, the therapist closes his or her eyes and makes a simple squiggle (with a dry erase marker, making a simple line without lifting the marker) on a dry erase board. The therapist then asks the child to draw a picture, using the squiggle as part of the picture. After the child finishes the drawing, the therapist may comment on the drawing (ask what it is if needed by saying "tell me about that") and then asks the child to tell a short *once upon a time* story about the picture.

The therapist must listen carefully, as the child often introduces one or more important themes, thought patterns, or emotional responses, such as projected wishes or feelings, experienced helplessness (being overpowered by forces of nature or a malevolent character, victimization, etc.), a wish for superpowers (to overcome helplessness), or aggressive retaliation. The main character in the story may be described as isolated and not able to find or ask for help. Some children need guidance during their stories with a "what happens next?" It is OK to ask open-ended questions such as those asked in the Thematic Apperception Test, such as "What is he or she feeling?," "What happened?," "How will it end?"), but it is important not to lead or suggest. The therapist praises the child whatever the drawing or story and then *turns the tables*, asking the child to make the squiggle while the therapist does the picture and story. The therapist offers a story that includes a meaningful issue or theme for the child's treatment, introduces a small change, or mirrors one or more of the themes in the child's story. The change can relate to the feelings, outcomes, ability to get help, etc., or the therapist may offer a possible solution or way of thinking about the problem. Sometimes a therapist's story becomes an interpretation of the child's story or family situation. Over time, the back and forth stories allow the therapist to model appropriate solutions, seed other ways of thinking about problems, and assess progress in the child's inner world. This author takes a photo of the child's drawing on a cell phone and later downloads the photos into the computer. This allows for later printing of the child's therapy work and is a lovely *gift* at the time of termination, to show process and progress across time.

For example, a young boy, new to treatment, really *took to* the game-like quality of Squiggles. His early stories were about characters that were *different* in some way, each lacking self-acceptance. The *Fuzzy Boa* story helped this client understand that someone can be *different* yet still valued.

Sometimes a Squiggle story is profoundly related to the child's own trauma and emotionally intense. This author's story, *Bear of a Different Color*, arose out of such a Squiggle session. A young girl that had been sexually and physically abused in several prior homes avoided talking about her past abuse. She had expressive language and social delays and dealt with her anxiety through avoidance, agitation, and obsessive compulsive symptoms.

One day during a non-therapy Squiggles play activity with this author, she drew a large black circle then scribbled it in with black marker, put red blotches throughout and a rectangular red platform in the center. As the therapist asked "what happened next?", she told her story and kept adding to her drawing. She announced the black area was a pit, then drew a black tangled scribbled path to the pit and said that a small brown bear had walked into the woods on the path and had fallen in the pit. She added a sign that said "Danger, Keep Out" and guards who were sleeping, and said that black goop was in the bottom of the pit. She said that the bear broke his leg at the bottom of the pit, cried for help, but no one came. The red platform was where he landed. "If he didn't land there [a trampoline], he would have died. Those other red things are the hearts of others who died. If he falls in again, he will die." She then had a deer rescue the bear. His broken leg healed but he was now a black bear, covered in goop from the bottom of the pit.

We talked about the poor bear, how awful it was that the guards fell asleep, and that the mother of the bear did not know where he had gone. We were so glad he was rescued but talked about how long it might take him to heal. She said that the bear was not happy he turned black—he wanted to be a brown bear again. At that point, she abruptly got up and left the office to go back to the group home milieu.

The client was sending a clear message—she was ready to talk about her trauma. This author needed to write the rest of the story. It needed to be a trauma narrative, to inspire the little girl to talk about her own trauma. It also needed to point to healing, to help the brown bear get black again. The story also needed a helper, as the bear did not need to go through the healing alone. The therapist went home that night and wrote the story. What elements to include?

The things that went wrong that led to the fall
The responsibility resting in the hands of the guards
The pain of the bear and the fear that no one would come
The relief of being rescued
The CHANGE inside and out of falling in the pit
The trip to a healer with a caring friend
The process of healing explained to the bear
The idea that changes take time
The need to TELL the story to heal inside and out
The reality that talking about trauma is painful
The fact that no one needs to go through that alone
The eventual healing and sense of personal competence for having been brave

The next day, this author asked the little girl and her therapist if they would like to hear a story. We had agreed on an intervention to follow if the story went as planned. The child agreed. As I started the story, the child started to rock frantically and turned red in the face. "That's MY story!" she said. She added, "Don't leave him black!"

I reassured her that the bear would become brown again and read the story. She was rapt. She became anxious off and on and asked questions, but was very engaged. In the story, the bear talks about the trauma in order to make the black goop come clean, inside and out.

Then her therapist asked her if she would like to work on her problems like the bear. Surprisingly, she agreed. They went upstairs to do a body tracing and the girl used a black marker to put on her body all the places she had been hurt inside and out, even her heart, since everyone knows that a broken heart is part of family trauma. Her therapist showed her a large bottle of Wite-Out® and told her that each time she talked about a black area, she could then paint over it with the correction fluid and make it go away, like the bear.

About an hour later, the child came running downstairs with her rolled-up paper and proceeded to show everyone her drawing. She was excited and proud of her work. "Look," she said. "There is my arm, and my butt, and my leg, and that V is my vagina. He hurt me there too, you know."

This little girl who had avoided trauma narrative work for months now had the inspiration and courage to begin that work in a manner that activated her emotions and gave her a sense of competence.

In addition to addressing specific themes or problems, stories can lead to character identification, offer metaphors that symbolize family patterns of interaction, indicate blind spots, address avoidance, help clients see something from a new perspective or become better aware of interpersonal difficulties. A story can provide a metaphor to trigger self awareness (*The Monster Within, Safe Place to Call Home*) or offer suggestions for problem resolution (*Gold in the Desert*). Some examples follow that will help the reader better understand where ideas for stories come from and how they may be used within different types of treatment.

2.3.2 Stories to Address Diagnostic Issues or Symptoms

For straightforward CBT treatment and symptom reduction, the story's character suffers from symptoms of a particular diagnosis and the story itself includes elements of evidence based interaction. The character in *The Grounded Eagle* has a phobia of flying, but through coaching and exposure he becomes capable of behavior activation and successfully takes to the sky. The Bassett Hound (good depressive character) in the story *The Black Cloud* is able to connect thoughts and feelings to behavior, and he learns self-control over his black moods, obviously represented by the cloud that follows him around everywhere he goes. *OCD Frog* is a beloved character to children with obsessive compulsive symptoms. In addition to psychoeducation about the symptoms of OCD, this story presents an intervention of guided imagery for exposure and response prevention.

2.3.3 Stories for the Purpose of Character Identification

There was a particularly tough bunch of parents in parent group at one point, and they spent a lot of time blaming others for their problems. One of the more verbally abusive fathers loved dogs but demonstrated little empathy toward his children. I wrote a simple story about *Lucky the Junkyard Dog* with a variety of characters that might have been in these parents' lives growing up, and also as a way of introducing a main character that would elicit empathy. The goal was to help the parents identify and tease out how their behaviors resembled those of the story characters: Lucky the victim; Lucky's mother, who neglected him and his siblings; the mean junkyard manager who abused Lucky; the nice man who rescued Lucky; the nice man's wife who nurtured Lucky; and an angry man in the neighborhood whose loud voice triggered a flashback in Lucky.

The therapists read the story in group, and comments flew from the group. "Sometimes I'm like Lucky and sometimes I'm the mean man," said the one father. "I was kicked a lot too when I was growing up." "I think I'm a little like all the characters," said a troubled mother. "When I'm in a good mood, I'm more like the nice man's wife, but when my husband threatens me, I feel like Lucky." Each parent weighed in as the group began to deal with cross-generational abuse issues and how their own abuse impacted their parenting behavior.

Trick or Treat was a Halloween story written for a family whose mother repeatedly returned to her dangerous, mentally ill partner and exposed them to serious violence. It seemed likely that her teenage children would notice the similarity between their mother and the mother in the story. The themes in the story were about exposing children to danger and making promises that were not kept. The *front door* approach had not worked with this mother: she could list all the reasons she should not go back to her ex; she could identify the ways in which her children had been harmed by their dad; and she could understand the impact of violence on her and her family. Her insight, however, was very left-brained and her needs were very right-brained and attachment-driven. She was continuing to try to meet her own needs for security and attachment at an emotional level and disregarding safety. Her sense of self was very *young*, and she did not feel *worthy* of kind, loving behavior. She had learned to engage in caretaking attachment strategies with the adults in her life while growing up and had learned to expect little for herself. The author selected an innocuous setting (a Halloween neighborhood *haunted house)* and a particularly creepy, malevolent man who invited the family to join in with his *fun* year after year. The mother in the story wanted to believe that the man had changed and was blind to the ways in which the haunted house scared and hurt her children.

After reading the story as a family, with eyebrows raised and knowing smiles, one of the teens said, "Mom, that's like us and the man at the fun house is just like Dad. You keep going back over and over even though we tell you we don't want to. You promise to keep us safe, but we can't trust you." The story led to a frank discussion of family safety and the mother used the story in her individual treatment to discuss what prevented her from setting better limits with her partner.

2.3.4 Stories to Introduce a Symbolic Metaphor

A client may use a powerful metaphor during a session, and this type of language holds meaning. Using the client's metaphor personalizes the story and increases the impact. One family engaged in many heated arguments. Their middle child often split family members through manipulative triangulation and stirred up crisis. When confronted, she would blame the others and become emotionally upset. She often used the words *full of shit* in describing her family interactions. A metaphor was needed to show the family their *hit and run* patterns of interaction and offer alternative solutions to the *crisis mode* entered into every time this girl became angry and sought attention.

Poop in the Barnyard was written as a metaphor for this family's style of interaction. Poop is a particularly strong and enjoyable metaphor for children, especially for young abused boys. The main character was created to be headstrong and reactive. In this story, a pouting, sullen girl retaliates toward the barnyard animals after stepping in their poop. She flings poop at them rather than cleaning up the barnyard and caring for the animals. The family members chuckled as the story was read, each recognizing their interaction patterns. They gave examples of flinging poop and adopted the story's metaphor as their family's cue to stop being verbally aggressive and start expressing feelings more directly.

One of the best metaphors ever was provided by a woman who was dependent on pain and anxiety medication. She had a long history of abuse that began in childhood and continued into adulthood. She recounted episodes of life-threatening severe intimate partner violence. She was easily triggered into childlike states of fearfulness/dependency as well as volatile angry, verbally accusatory states. Her children were developmentally delayed and her preschool son tried to comfort her when she was upset, quite frightened by her behavior. We became aware that when she made a mistake or felt *bad, punished or wrong*, she dissociated into a childlike state of helplessness. She gradually stabilized, and we started to address her vigilance. She laughed and said, "I'm looking for land mines." The therapist smiled and replied, "Yes, but you are looking for them in Disneyland." The story was written and read to her at the next session, and it provided a very good tool to help her understand PTSD. It was a good way to introduce techniques to reduce her arousal, help her question core schemas, pay attention to trauma triggers, and build coping skills.

2.3.5 Stories to Point Out Blind Spots

Parents in our program have many blind spots, including a lack of awareness of children's needs for close supervision. One young mother did not understand that her children's bids for attention were normal signs of developing attachment. She complained that her baby woke her up too early and should be content to stay in the playpen until the client was ready to get up. The story needed to be humorous, since this mother became quickly defensive with direct confrontation, and the main character had to be both likeable and objectionable. Her behavior had to be due more to lack of experience and familiarity with children than to intentional neglect. *Velma Crowe's Sticky Situation* was written, tongue in cheek, about a bird that was not prepared to become a mother. Her lifestyle interfered with caregiving behavior and she had unrealistic expectations for her babies. The story was laughable, yet the mothers in the parenting group found themselves remembering and talking first about how they were parented and then how they carried on some of the same practices with their children.

A second blind spot commonly seen is risk-taking exposure of children to adult relationships, especially with questionable men. Another mother in the program tended to be overly friendly with men, including strangers and her abusive ex-husband, and she did not understand the risks for her and her children; in fact, she took her children to visit their father not long after they had witnessed him assaulting her. The same mother was very protective of her children around dogs, staying close to them when a dog was present. The story entitled *Does He Bite?* triggered dissonance and provided a *wakeup call* for this mother.

2.3.6 Stories to Reduce Avoidance

The ostrich story, *Hidey Hole*, was developed to help a family begin talking about and processing past trauma that the family had avoided. The mother and her daughters began crying any time the sensitive issues came up. For this family, the author needed a story with a theme of avoidance that would initiate conversation about this topic. The main character was an ostrich that put his head in a hole on a railroad track and ignored the train that was coming. The story showed the character's wish for a more stress-free life and that his behavioral solution presented a risk to his safety. The bottom line was "what you don't see can hurt you." The family members, none of whom had finished high school, read the story together, passing around the book. Then the family used mural paper to draw a railroad track. The oldest daughter suggested they draw holes on the track, one for each family member. The therapist suggested that each family member write in her hole the three things that were hardest to talk about. The issues in the holes included: mom having been in jail; grandma's death; mom's drug use; the children going into foster care; one daughter's sexual abuse; and the oldest daughter's drug use. The ice was broken and the unspoken issues were now *on the table*.

2.3.7 Stories to Offer a New Perspective

The women's relationship recovery group (IPV and co-dependency) had been avoiding personal disclosure for several weeks, and the group leader was having trouble directing them into more personal sharing. One mother in the group had allowed her baby's father to live with her even though they had broken up. He relied on her to feed him and did not contribute financially to the household. The mother felt sorry for him and was afraid that he would end up on the streets if she did not take care of him. The author wrote a story, *Don't Let the Leeches Suck You Dry*, and the women's relationship group read it together the following week. This story was written with the *gross factor* in mind, using a metaphor that would elicit a strong emotional *yuck* response. The main character was created to be someone with blind spots about relationships with *leeches*. The women talked about codependent behaviors with their partners and their fears of abandonment. Soon after that group, the one mother came to the author and said, "Can I ask you something? Well, can you tell me how to get rid of a leech?" The story's metaphor had stayed with her, and she was able to apply the concepts to her partner. Not long after, she asked him to move out and said, "I figure he'll find someone else—there's always another blood supply once I cut him off."

2.3.8 Stories to Introduce Therapy Elements and Treatment Structure

A toddler was brought in for outpatient treatment by her caregiver at age two. At age 18 months, she had witnessed the shooting murder of her mother and had stopped talking for the most part. She was afraid to sleep alone, had horrible nightmares, whispered about *bloody hands* and a gun, and shook in the therapist's office. Trauma affects brain areas that impact memory, language, verbal processing, and mood regulation. The author wrote a toddler story that could be used across a number of sessions with this child and her grandmother with the goal of anxiety reduction and increasing caregiver–child nurturing behaviors. The story about *Little Butterfly and the Bad Thing* depicted a butterfly whose wings no longer worked (using the theme of incapacitation) after seeing something so bad that it scared her speechless. She needed to return to the cocoon (regression) until her wings grew strong again. In the story, Little Butterfly also drew pictures with a healer and had a spider wrap them up and place them in her web.

This little girl had experienced an acute trauma, and after reading the story to the grandmother and child, play therapy was set up to help her regulate her arousal, give words to her experience (trauma narrative), wrap up the anxiety, and build a strong attachment with her grandmother. A therapeutic story and play intervention were used in which they spoke words that came into her dreams and scared the girl ("gun," "blood," "bad daddy," etc.), drew pictures together, then wrapped them up in cocoons and put them on a large spider web in the therapist's office. As they wrapped up the bad memories, the girl started to speak up and whispered less. Then they made a cocoon (sleeping bag) for the girl to use at home so that her grandmother could carry and nurture her until she was ready to come back out. They noted steady improvement in the girl's sleep and behavior as she engaged in weekly play therapy. Her improvements were evidence that brain integration was occurring and that the impact of the trauma would be lessened.

The next three sections of the book are sets of therapy stories that may be used with children, caregivers, and families in psychoeducation and intervention. But the author hopes the reader will not stop there. Clients respond powerfully to their own metaphors and stories; and although not everyone is a writer, anyone can become a storyteller.

In sum, when using the stories, the following format is recommended:

- Select a story that matches the purpose of the treatment session and phase of treatment (for example, psychoeducation about PTSD, trauma narrative, mood management, seeking safety). The stories are organized in chapters that parallel the steps of TF-CBT. Consider whether the client is in Pre-Contemplation, Contemplation, Preparation, Action, or Maintenance/Relapse Prevention. Some stories help move the client to the next stage of change.
- Read the story with the child and/or caregiver. If the child is able to read, take turns reading.
- After reading the story, wait for whatever comes up spontaneously before using that information to go deeper into the client experience. Link the story to the child's life, experience, feelings, etc.

- Ask questions to clarify the child and/or caregiver's thinking or feelings about the story and characters: "Why do you think this happened?," "What advice do you have for the character?," or "What do you think led to this?"
- Go through a section of the Child or Caregiver Guide with the child and caregiver.
- Move into a planned treatment activity (TF-CBT, ARC, Trauma Play Therapy, Expressive Intervention) that follows from the story or client's response to the story; and addresses a theme, schema, or feeling from the story. A plethora of handouts is available for use in treatment at www.psychology-tools.org.
- For homework, assign material from the Child and Caregiver guides. Provide discussion questions and tasks for coping skill practice as well as in-home therapy interventions that run parallel to the story themes.

The stories are organized under the PRACTICE format of TF-CBT; they may, however, be applicable to one or more phases of treatment and re-visited as old issues re-emerge due to new triggering.

PART II

THERAPY STORIES TO USE WITH CHILDREN

CHAPTER 3

PSYCHOEDUCATION

Story 1: Trauma Triggers

Purpose(s) and Goal(s): ☒ Psychoeducation about vigilance and acute stress, the concept of trauma triggers and arousal, the need for stress-management. ☒ Treatment Intervention: read story before practicing relaxation and stress management.

After you have gone through a trauma, you can be *triggered* by things that remind you of the trauma. Those triggers can set off fear and make you feel as if the bad thing is happening all over again. You can learn what sorts of things trigger *you* after abuse. Then with the help of your therapist you can figure out things to do to prevent a Trauma Stress Response (chain reaction). This story is about a weatherman who is triggered by bad weather after a damaging tornado.

The False Alarm[1]

It was a gray and windy day. A light rain was starting to fall.

"Beeeeep! Beeeeep! Beeeeep!" went the radio. It was a weather alert.

"A tornado warning has been issued by the National Weather Service. Please take cover. This is not a test, I repeat, there is a tornado in your area."

"Beeeeep! Beeeeep! Beeeeep!" went the radio. Outside, the tornado siren blared, "ENHHHHHHHHHHHHHH" as if to say, "Take cover!".

A few weeks before, a large tornado had touched down without warning. The sky had turned black as night and hail had pounded down. Lives were lost and homes destroyed in the terrible storm.

A boy on his bike heard the siren. He got off the bike and quickly took cover in the library. His heart was pounding in his chest.

A mother heard the siren from the laundry room. She, her children, and the dog took cover in the basement.

Some office workers heard the siren. They huddled together in a large stairwell.

A few minutes later, the siren stopped. The radio announcer said, "Ladies and gentleman, I'm sorry for your trouble. There is **no tornado** in your area. This has *not* been a test. This has been a *false alarm*."

"Are you kidding?" exclaimed the boy in the library. "This is the third false alarm in the last week!"

"What is going on?" asked the mother. "Is this someone's idea of a sick prank?"

A man in the office stairwell was angry. "I'm going to report this to the National Weather Service!"

The boss at the radio station put his head in his hands and groaned. Then he went into the room where the weatherman worked. The boss said, "That was your third false alarm in a week."

A small man with wire-rimmed glasses was sitting at a desk. The office was filled with weather maps and radar equipment. The weatherman was trained to notice signs of bad weather. He had machines that informed him about rainfall, wind speed, and air pressure. It was his job to spot a severe storm, figure out when it would arrive, and then warn the people.

In a firm voice, the weatherman replied, "Better to be safe than sorry."

"What did you say?" asked his boss.

The weatherman repeated, "Better to be safe than sorry. I missed the tornado that touched down a few weeks ago. I didn't send out a warning and people got hurt. It was my fault. I can't **ever** let that happen again."

He added, "I've been having bad dreams and *freaking out* about what happened, so I *turned up the* radar. Now the radar goes off if the wind picks up. The radar goes off if the sky turns gray. And it goes off if heavy rain starts to fall. I send out a warning when the radar goes off."

"You *turned up* the radar?" asked the boss. He could not believe what he was hearing.

"Yes," said the weatherman. "I don't want anyone else to get hurt on my watch. It's better to be safe than sorry."

The boss scratched his chin and said, "You are the best weatherman we have. It wasn't your fault people got hurt in the storm. That tornado touched down in five places, and no one saw it coming."

"That's true," said the weather man. "No one saw it coming."

The boss added, "You are being triggered by bad weather. It reminds you of the tornado. But people are upset by the false alarms. A thunderstorm is just a thunderstorm. A tornado warning is meant for a real tornado. You need to stop freaking out at every sign of bad weather. I want you to turn the radar back to normal; then let's get you some help."

The weatherman reached over to his weather equipment and turned the radar down.

His boss was right. Bad weather triggered his memories of the tornado. But a thunderstorm is just a thunderstorm. A tornado is a tornado. He needed to get help—to calm down and not overreact to triggers. After all, you need to save your *warnings* for the real dangers in life.

THE BOTTOM LINE: Turn Down the Radar!

Food for Thought Questions:

- What were the triggers that caused the weatherman to *freak out* (the sounds and sights that made him worry there would be another tornado)? _____
_____

- Why did he turn up the radar?_____
_____

- Abused kids freak out at things that remind them of the abuse. These things are triggers. What are your triggers (sights, sounds, places, people that make you think you might get abused again)?_____
_____

- List two or three things you do or feel when you think someone is going to hurt you: _____
_____
_____

- List two or three facts that *prove* you are safe now from abuse: _____
_____
_____

- Give an example of a real threat of abuse (danger) and a false alarm? _____
_____

Story 2: The Impact of Trauma

Purpose(s) and Goal(s): ☒ Psychoeducation about PTSD, trauma symptoms, trauma triggers. ☒ Treatment Intervention: with families, parents (group or individual) as a lead-in to discuss abuse history and how trauma impacts family members. Elicits memories about physical and emotional childhood abuse and allows caregivers to empathize with child victims.

Lucky's story was written to help kids and caregivers understand and talk about trauma. This story gives an example of Freak Out, Freeze, Flight and Fight and points out that it takes time and loving care to get over abuse.

Lucky the Junkyard Dog[2]

Lucky dreamed of living in a home with a soft bed, a kind master, and a big grassy yard. But Lucky lived with his three little brothers and sisters in a dark alley. They were homeless and hungry. Lucky was a good big brother. He took care of his little brothers and sisters as best he could, and went hunting for food every night. He growled at anyone that came too close.

Of course it was their mother's job to take care of them. But she ran around with her friends, and there was never enough food to go around. Sometimes when she was in a bad mood she barked, "Shut up! You're getting on my last nerve and I need some peace and quiet!" When she got mean like that, the puppies put their tails between their legs and hid.

One day a big man came into the alley. He tossed a rope around Lucky's neck. Lucky growled at the man, who kicked him hard in the side. Lucky yelped in pain and tried to nip the man in self-defense.

The man threw him into the back of a red pickup truck and drove off. They ended up at the junkyard, where the manager needed a good guard dog.

Three years later, Lucky was still a junkyard dog. The mean junkyard manager kept Lucky on a heavy chain. He thought it was funny to tease Lucky, and would hold out a juicy steak bone. When the hungry dog went for it, the man laughed and pulled the bone away. The man often cursed at Lucky and kicked him in the side. Too often, Lucky went to bed hungry.

Lucky could never tell when the man would be mean. When he heard the man coming, Lucky whimpered and hid. When the man came near, Lucky growled and put his tail between his legs. Lucky shivered and shook when the man started to shout or curse. Lucky never felt safe— sometimes he wished he had never been born.

One day, a big four-wheel drive pulled in with a load of junk. A man started unloading and saw Lucky laying there. Lucky eyed the man with caution, his nose tucked between his paws.

"Hey, good buddy," said the man. Lucky growled and backed away. The man saw cuts and bruises on the dog and came a little closer.

"What happened to you? Your ribs are showing—are you hungry? I have a burger in my truck—would you like it?" He sounded concerned.

The man went to his truck and came back with a McDonald's bag.

"Here you go," he said as he tossed Lucky the burger. Lucky lunged at the treat and gobbled it down.

"You're half-starved," said the man. "No one should treat a dog like this."

When the junkyard manager came back, Lucky growled and slunk away with his tail between his legs. The man raised his leg to kick Lucky, and the nice man said, "Stop! It's against the law to beat and starve a dog."

The nice man went on, "I think I'll just take that dog with me. Or I could call the authorities. So what is it? The dog goes with me or I make that call?"

The junkyard man unchained Lucky and put him in the man's truck. He sneered, "You'll be sorry. This mutt has no love in him, just meanness."

"We'll see about that," said the nice man as he drove off.

The man drove Lucky to where he lived, a nice house with a big grassy yard. Lucky ran inside and hid in a corner when the man opened the door. When the man came near him, he growled. Lucky expected him to shout, curse, or hit.

Lucky didn't trust the man or his wife. Not even when they gave him a soft bed with a thick blanket. And fed him treats like steak and liver bits. And spoke in soft voices. And kept his food and water dishes full.

The man gave Lucky a red ball and took him out to play. At first, Lucky thought the man might throw the ball *at* him and hid under the deck. But one morning he ran after the ball.

The man laughed and said, "Good boy!" He wagged his tail a little at their praise.

After a long time, Lucky figured out that the man and woman were *really* nice. They weren't faking it, and they weren't going to hurt him.

Then one night, the man held out a juicy steak bone.

Lucky almost growled. Somewhere in his memory was another man holding a steak bone.

"It's OK, Lucky. Come get the bone," said the man in a kind voice.

Lucky moved toward the nice man, one slow step at a time. He grabbed the bone in his mouth and ran away with it so that man couldn't hit him or take it back.

"That's the other man," thought Lucky, "but it's hard to forget."

Lucky started letting the man's wife pet him at night before bed. She stroked his scarred back and told him, "You sweet dog. We are glad to have you in our lives. We love you!" Lucky liked her touch, and he rolled over to let her pet his belly. Lucky started feeling safe and loved.

One evening the man took Lucky on a walk around the block. It was one of Lucky's favorite things to do. All of a sudden, Lucky heard a very loud voice. A big angry man was standing in a driveway shouting into his cell phone. *Instantly,* Lucky's tail went between his legs and he started to growl. The loud voice scared him— he shivered and started to shake. Lucky tried to run, but his owner held him firmly by the leash.

"It's OK, Lucky. Sit! Stay!" said his owner in a quiet firm voice. "You still think something bad might happen, but I will keep you safe. I won't let anyone hurt you." He stroked Lucky gently on the head and talked to him until he stopped shaking.

Then Lucky's owner spoke to the big man in a steady voice. "You scared my dog. If you're going to talk like that, take it inside."

The angry man scowled but went in the house and closed the door.

After Lucky's owner walked him home, Lucky was still scared. He ran under the deck in the yard. He felt like growling or biting. Somewhere in his dog memory, he remembered a loud mean voice with kicks and hits, and he could almost taste the old pain and fear. That night, he refused to eat and slept outside.

The next morning when they let him in, Lucky pooped and peed on the carpet, which was something Lucky had never done before.

"I'm in trouble now," thought Lucky. "I'm a bad dog—they will send me away."

The man and his wife did not send him away. They didn't even yell at him.

They just said, "Lucky, this is something that happens when a dog has been abused."

His family knew that it takes awhile for a dog to get over abuse. Lucky's accident on the carpet was just a rough spot, like a bump in the road.

"Let's clean it up and go take a walk," they said.

On the walk, Lucky pooped and peed in all the right places and his owner said, "Good dog! I knew you could do it!"

Nothing bad happened during that walk—or the next one—or the one after that.

Lucky's family was patient, because bad memories last a long time. They helped him learn coping skills to calm down when something startled him. They used quiet voices and petted him a lot. They took him to the dog park so he could hang around other dogs and run off his stress.

Lucky's family loved him, and he was there to stay.

And every night, as they watched TV, ate popcorn, and fed Lucky dog treats, they said, "Lucky, we are so glad to have you in our lives!"

And every night, right before bed, Lucky rolled over on his back, bared his belly and whined for just one more petting, please, as he thought, "This is as close to Heaven as it gets!".

THE BOTTOM LINE: Healing Takes Time!

Food for Thought Questions:

- Why was Lucky still scared after he moved to a safe home? _____

- List examples of Freak Out, Freeze, Flight, and Fight in this story. How were these behaviors protective for Lucky (to keep him safe)?_____

- How are you like Lucky?_____

- What three things helped Lucky the most to get over his abuse? _____

- Do you ever feel like snapping at someone? Give an example. _____

- List the characters in the Lucky story. Next to each name write who (in your life) would play this part if you acted out this story as a play? Hint: the family member or other person should have something in common with the Lucky character and remind you of that character._____

- If you had a magic wand, what three things would you change that would help you get over your abuse?_____

Story 3: Repeated Exposure to Abusive Behavior

Purpose(s) and Goal(s): ☒ Psychoeducation for caregivers about domestic violence and exposing children repeatedly to traumatic or high stress situations. Helps caregivers understand the ways in which children are harmed by lack of protection. ☒ Treatment Intervention: to be used in family treatment with adolescents and caregivers or in a parent session to discuss lack of protection. This story is particularly helpful in situations where there has been intimate partner violence.

It is not good for kids to go through violence even once. This story was written for a family that had gone through domestic violence many times. The three children had witnessed their dad hurting their mom (over and over), and each time she left him she ended up going back. Adults sometimes want to believe that someone has changed and they give that person another chance, even though the person has not changed. Abusers don't deserve another chance until there is evidence (facts) that show the person has changed. The story helped the family talk about what they had gone through in the past.

Trick or Treat[3]

It was Halloween night and the moon was full. A mother dressed in a black witch's costume held the hands of her two children. The smallest child was dressed as a clown, the older as a Ninja. Their breath smoked in the cold air. They shivered at the sight of what lay just ahead. It was a large, creepy-looking house with orange candles flickering in each window.

The mother said, "Let's go there next," pointing at the creepy-looking house. A sign said, "Haunted House."

"No way, Mom," said the smaller child, pulling back. "I'm not going in the Haunted House this year. I can't believe you would ask us to go back there after what happened last year."

"Nonsense," said the mother. "It was not *that bad* last year. I know it was a little scary, but we should give it another try. After all, Halloween only comes once a year."

"Mom," said the older child, "Every year we say we don't want to go in the Haunted House. And every year you tell us it won't be as bad this year. And every year it turns out to be at least as bad—or even worse."

The Clown's nose wrinkled up with disgust. "Remember the worms last year? Mom, you told us they were just sour candy and to eat them. They turned out to be real worms! They made me puke!"

"Well, they didn't *look like* real worms in the dark," answered the mother. "And they didn't taste *that bad*. The man at the Haunted House promised not to do the worms again."

The Ninja argued, "Every year he makes promises—but he doesn't keep them. And he's *really* mean. His torture chamber had real torture. He put me on a rack and stretched me until I cried!"

The mom grew silent. She remembered her daughter crying on the rack in a dark room. But she quickly pushed the memory down and regained her perky attitude.

"No pain, no gain, I always say."

"A Haunted House shouldn't have things in it that *really* hurt you!" retorted the Ninja.

"I know, I know," replied the mother. "And I didn't want you to get hurt. But the man said he was really sorry for hurting you last year. He promised not to do it again. Can't we give him another chance?"

The children didn't trust the man to keep his promise. But they loved their mother and didn't want to disappoint her. They knew how much she loved Halloween. So they followed her to the house . . .

As they stepped on the doormat, a deep scary voice said, "Welcome to the Haunted House. Enter at your own risk." The Clown and the Ninja grabbed each other's hands and huddled together.

"Creak," went the front door as it opened. The family crept inside the dark house. "Slam!" went the front door as it closed behind them.

A man appeared out of nowhere. His face was lit up by a glow-in-the-dark vampire shirt. "Happy Halloween," he said as he held out a tray of chocolate chip cookies.

The Clown cautiously took a cookie and took a bite. "OMG!" the child shouted and spit out the bite. "What is in this cookie?"

"Oh chocolate chips and just a little dog food to add crunch." He paused. "But the plate was under my hamster cage, so I hope nothing fell on the cookies." He raised his eyebrows and smiled.

"Mom, the bad stuff is starting already. We need to leave," said the Ninja.

"Sweetie," said the mother. "It was an accident if anything fell out of the hamster cage on the cookies—not his fault at all. Let's go through the rest of the house.

One room at a time, the family made their way through the Haunted House. The children were really nervous, because they didn't know what was coming.

The next room had a bowl of fake cut-off fingers made out of cookie dough and red food coloring. The children looked them over carefully. The Ninja picked one up and took a bite. "Mmmmm, this tastes good!" she said in surprise.

"See," said the mother. "That cookie is just fine." They all munched on cookies as they moved on to the next room. That room held a plate of sparkling witch-hat cupcakes. Just as they entered the room, all three had a sudden need to use the bathroom.

"What did you put in the cookies?" the children asked the man as they raced off.

"Oh, that must be the Ex-Lax," he said with a snicker and a mean smile.

The children grabbed their mother by the hand and pulled her toward the front door. "Mom, we're leaving now and we are *never* coming back. How many times do you have to put us through this before you understand it's not going to change?"

"OK, we can leave," said their mother. "Before we go, let me eat one of these sparkly cupcakes."

The man sneered and said, "Eat a cupcake at your own risk. The cupcake sparkles are fragments of my favorite wine glass. Nothing sparkles quite as nice as shattered crystal."

The mother gasped. She exclaimed, "My children were right. You can't be trusted. I talked them into coming back to your Haunted House. I gave you another chance. You promised not to do mean things this year."

"That's true," he said slyly. "I did promise. But I didn't promise to *keep* my promise . . . And I never asked you to trust me."

At that, the family left the Haunted House and went straight home. The mother made hot chocolate for her children and then sat down in the family room to talk with them.

She said, "I let you down. I shouldn't have trusted that man. I wanted to believe that he had changed. And each time we went back, it was clear that he had not changed. You could see it, but I was blind. I saw what I wanted and hoped to see."

The mother added, "I will not take you back there next Halloween or any Halloween after that. There are better and safer places to spend our time as a family. You might not believe me yet, but I will show you that I mean it. I am sorry I kept putting you through that fear and pain. Please forgive me."

"Of course we forgive you. But how can you be sure you won't take us back there?" asked the children. Sometimes their mother had trouble following through.

"I am sure. That man is not going to change. And it's my job to keep you away from him."

The children sighed in relief. Perhaps their mother finally understood that her desire for Halloween fun was not as important as their safety. Time would tell.

THE BOTTOM LINE: The Treats Aren't Worth the Tricks!

Food for Thought Questions:

- Give an example of a time a grownup did something that put you in danger._____

  _____

- Give an example of a time a grownup didn't listen to your feelings or concerns about violence or abuse._____

  _____

- How are you like the children in this story?_____

  _____

- Who in your life promised to change but kept doing the same old thing?_____
  _____

- Describe promises that someone made to you or to a family member and how they kept or broke those promises._____
  _____

- What is the evidence that the Haunted House man has not changed? _____
  _____
  _____

- Give the mother in this story some advice._____
  _____
  _____

- Pretend it is three years from now. List some things that you think would be evidence (facts) that the man had changed._____
  _____
  _____

- What would be evidence or facts (behaviors, thinking, and moods) that someone in your life has changed?_____
  _____
  _____

Story 4: Avoidance

Purpose(s) and Goal(s): ☒ Psychoeducation about avoidance behaviors. ☒ Treatment Intervention: with individuals or families to identify avoided issues.

There was a family that did not know how to talk about important things that had happened in their family—things like drug abuse, jail, death, and child abuse. They had strong feelings about those things but pretended that everything was OK when it was not. Ignoring the bad things made them really stressed. The story that follows helped them talk about what they were avoiding. Talking about the bad things was not as bad as they expected and helped them start to get over what had happened in the past.

The Hidey Hole[4]

Ozzie Ostrich loved to play outside, like most other ostriches his age. He really loved climbing the small hill up to the train tracks and then standing on them. He could see for miles around when he was up there; he felt like king of the hill!

Of course, Ozzie's mother had told him over and over, "NEVER stand on the railroad tracks. They are dangerous and you could get hurt." He did not mean to disobey his mother, but it was a hard decision; should he do what his mother said or enjoy how he felt when he was on the railroad tracks?

Ozzie knew that trains were dangerous, but he always got out of the way before the train got too close. As he stood on the tracks, he could hear the train whistle.

First, far off in the distance. "Whoo-whoo!" The whistle got louder and louder as the train got closer. *"Whoo-whoo!"* Ozzie felt the tracks rumbling through his tennis shoes, and the train got even closer. "WHOO-WHOO!" He knew it was time to jump when he saw the wheels turning.

One day when Ozzie was playing on the tracks, he saw a hole. It was right in the middle of the tracks.

"I think my head would fit inside that hole!" thought Ozzie. So he stuck his head down inside the hole—it was a good fit. It was also dark, quiet, and peaceful.

Ozzie whispered, "I like it in here. It's quiet, and I can forget about my problems."

Ozzie started going to the tracks every day. Sometimes, he played king of the hill on the tracks. But when Ozzie had a bad day, he stuck his head inside the hole, just for a little peace and quiet.

Then Ozzie had a really bad day. He had an argument with his best friend Fred, and he got a bad grade on the spelling test. After school, Ozzie wanted to get away from it all. He ran over to the train tracks as fast as he could.

Before he stuck his head in the hole, Ozzie looked down the tracks to check for trains. Unfortunately, a train was coming. It was still far off in the distance; perhaps a couple of miles. It seemed to be moving slowly. Ozzie could faintly hear the whistle blowing. "Whoo-whoo!"

He thought, "I have time to put my head in the hole, just for a minute."

So Ozzie put his head in the hole. It was dark, quiet, and cozy. He breathed a sigh of relief. He couldn't hear the train whistle from inside the hole. Ozzie decided to pretend that the train wasn't coming.

Ozzie thought, "Can't see the train—the train's not coming! Can't hear the train—the train's not coming!" He said this over and over. He said it so much that he started to believe it!

And when the tracks began to rumble, Ozzie did not get off the tracks.

His friend Fred had come over to "make up" and saw Ozzie standing on the tracks. Fred saw the train getting closer and closer. Fred hollered, "Ozzie! Get off the tracks!" Of course Ozzie's head was inside the hole and he did not hear Fred hollering at him.

Fred knew he had to do something fast or Ozzie was going to get hit by the train. Fred dashed across the street and ran up to the tracks. He pulled Ozzie's head out of the hole and yanked him off the tracks right before the train zoomed past. Ozzie felt the wind blow his feathers and heard the train's "Whoo-whooooooooo!" as it whizzed by.

Ozzie and Fred were red in the face. Their hearts were pounding! Ozzie realized he had nearly been killed. He said, "Whew! That was a close call! I'm never going to do THAT again."

"Exactly what **were** you doing?" asked Fred.

Ozzie replied, "I couldn't see or hear the train, so I pretended it wasn't coming."

His friend Fred exclaimed, "That was the stupidest thing I've ever seen! You're lucky I came by when I did!" Fred added, "You need to keep your head above ground and your eyes wide open at all times!"

Ozzie thanked his friend over and over, and the two of them went to play in the park.

Later that day, Ozzie had a "guilt attack" and told his mother what he had done and what had happened. His mother grounded him for a week. "I want to be able to trust you and know you're safe," she said.

"I know, Mom," said Ozzie. "I'll keep my head above ground from now on!"

THE BOTTOM LINE: What You Don't See CAN Hurt You!

Food for Thought Questions:

- How are you like Ozzie?_____

  _____

- What was Ozzie avoiding when he put his head in the hole?_____

  _____

- List other things Ozzie could do to cope with his stress._____
  _____

- What things (from your past) do you or family members avoid talking about?_____
  _____

- Do you ever *pretend things are OK even when they aren't?* Give an example._____
  _____

- Draw a train track. Put a hole on it for each family member. Write each family member's name by one of the holes. Inside the hole or next to the track, write things that each person has trouble facing or avoids talking about. As a family, talk about why you avoid these things. Ask, "What is the worst thing that can happen if I talk about this?"

Story 5: Trauma Narrative

Purpose(s) and Goal(s): ☒ Psychoeducation about the personal experience of trauma, feeling damaged, healing on the outside but still experiencing pain on the inside (the lasting nature of some trauma symptoms), the need for and process of treatment, the need to tell the trauma narrative story, hope for change after telling the trauma narrative. ☒ Treatment Intervention: for PTSD and Trauma Narrative. The story is to be read prior to trauma assessment and trauma narrative work in individual treatment. It can clarify the nature of trauma, prepare the child for the trauma narrative process, and lead smoothly into trauma-informed intervention. The story will also help the caregiver understand the need for a child to talk about the trauma, to listen to the child, and experience empathy.

Telling your abuse story is part of the *cure* for PTSD, but many victims of abuse don't do it because it is so hard. A little girl in the group home didn't know how to talk about her abuse; in fact, she avoided speaking about it and hid under tables and put blankets over her head instead. These things did not help her get over her abuse. She came up with the idea for this story and it helped her talk about what happened in her life. It is also a good story to help kids understand PTSD and the Trauma Narrative.

Bear of a Different Color[5]

Bear Bear, a small, black-colored bear, frowned. "I should be happy," Bear complained in a grouchy voice. "I should be happy to be out of the black pit. But noooooo, I'm still not happy."

The black pit that Bear was talking about was on the other side of the forest. Bear had taken a walk in the woods without telling his mother where he was going. It had been getting dark, and he took the wrong path. Bear had also missed the warning sign that said, "Danger, black pit ahead!" He didn't read very well, and it was too dark to see the sign.

"What about the guards?" you ask.

That's true—there were two guards posted in front of the pit. They were supposed to stay awake and alert. But they fell asleep and did not warn Bear of the danger ahead. So Bear did not see the pit and fell in. When Bear hit the bottom of the pit, black, nasty, sticky, smelly goop splashed and covered Bear from head to toe.

"Please help me, somebody—anybody!" Bear cried out in pain from a broken leg for several long hours.

Bear hurt all over. Finally, the guards woke up and heard Bear's cries. They helped him out of the pit and called an ambulance.

Bear's broken leg healed, but no one knew how to remove the black goop. The goop was an awful reminder of the fall. Bear wanted to "come clean."

Bear's best friend, Brown Squirrel, heard Bear complaining. Squirrel scrambled down a nearby tree trunk. With a large acorn in his mouth, Squirrel ran to Bear and asked, "Mwass wongh?"

Bear said, "Squirrel, with that acorn in your mouth, I can't understand what you're saying."

Squirrel smiled, spit out the acorn, and said clearly, "What's wrong?"

Bear replied, "I'm having bad dreams and I'm scared all the time. I want my old life back. I used to be a happy, brown bear. Well, now I'm not brown and I'm not happy!"

Squirrel wrinkled up his bushy brow and said, "So that's what's wrong, Bear. The fall into the pit changed you. You want to be brown and happy again. Let's go to the Recovery Center. It is a healing place. Maybe they can help you."

It was a long walk to the Recovery Center. When they arrived, Squirrel said, "Go ahead and knock, Bear."

Bear knocked sharply on the broad wooden door. The door opened.

"May I help you?" asked a kind voice.

"Yes," said Bear. "My name is Bear, and this is my friend Squirrel. I fell in the pit on the other side of the forest—the one where the guards sit day and night. I got covered with black, sticky, smelly goop. My friend thought that you might be able to help me."

"Hello, Bear and Squirrel," said the person. "Please come inside."

Bear and Squirrel went inside. The Recovery Center smelled nice and looked a little like a health spa. There were colorful flowers and soft music.

"I hear the sound of ocean waves," exclaimed Squirrel.

"Look Squirrel!" said Bear. He pointed to a big hot tub in the middle of the room. It had purple bubbles bubbling on top. There was a pile of soft spa towels to dry off with.

"Let's sit down and talk," said the person who invited them in. "I am a Healer, and I know about that awful pit. Children get hurt when the guards fall asleep. It is a terrible thing indeed. Sometimes, children are at the pit's edge before they realize the danger. Then it is too late. It's good you survived, because many do not."

Bear told the Healer, "I'm glad I survived, but I want to be brown again. I want it more than anything else in the world."

The Healer replied, "I can help you get rid of the black goop, but it's not an easy cure."

"Does the cure hurt?" asked Bear.

The Healer answered, "Yes, but not as much as falling in the pit. The healing takes time, so you can't be in a hurry. I can help you if that is what you want."

"Yes," said Bear and Squirrel at the same time. "Please help!"

The Healer said, "Come. You must soak in the hot tub to wash off the black goop."

So Bear got into the hot tub with all the purple bubbles. It was very uncomfortable on Bear's sensitive skin—enough to make the little bear cry.

"I'm sorry, little bear," said the Healer. "I know that the healing waters hurt at first."

Bear sat in the tub, and Squirrel sat right there next to Bear, offering his paw to hold. Bear said, "Thank you, Squirrel. I'm glad I don't have to go through this alone!"

"It's OK, Bear," said Squirrel. "You're worth it!"

The hot solution bubbled around Bear and soaked deep down through the black goop into Bear's skin. Little by little, it washed Bear clean. Then the Healer helped Bear out of the tub and offered a soft towel. After Bear dried off, the Healer gave Bear a nice-smelling lotion for his tender skin.

"Can I look in a mirror?" asked Bear. The Healer led Bear to a mirror. Bear was now a lovely golden brown color. He looked in the mirror, and frowned.

Bear said, "I can see that the black goop is gone and I'm brown again. But I still don't feel happy. I don't want to complain, but the hot tub didn't fix that."

The Healer said, "When you fell in the pit, you were so shocked and scared that you gulped in some black goop. Getting rid of the black goop on the outside doesn't get rid of the black goop on the inside."

"Inside me?" asked Bear with horror. "How can I get rid of something bad inside me that I can't even see?"

"You need to go through a second type of healing," the Healer said.

"I'll do whatever you say," said Bear.

The Healer told Bear, "For the second type of healing, you need to tell your story."

"My story?" asked Bear. "What do you mean?"

"You know," said the Healer. "The awful story of how you fell in the pit—how the guards didn't keep you safe; how you felt when you were falling and knew you might die; how you landed in the black, smelly goop and broke your leg; and how scared you were when you thought you would never get out of there alive."

Bear argued, "I *won't* talk about the fall or the pit. I spend almost every waking moment trying *not* to think about falling in the pit. Talking about it would make it even worse."

"Well," said the Healer, "That's the only way to heal *inside*. As you tell your story, the telling dissolves the black goop. Then you'll stop having bad dreams and stop thinking about falling in the pit."

Bear thought hard, weighing the options. Maybe it would be worth it to tell the story of falling in the pit. Bear really wanted to get rid of the black goop.

Bear said, "I guess I'll talk about what happened to me. I don't really have a choice."

"You always have a choice," said the Healer.

It was true. Bear had a choice.

So Bear sat down with the Healer in a private corner of the room. The Healer said, "When you are ready, Bear, start at the beginning, and tell your story. It's OK to start and stop. Just get it all out, a little at a time."

Bear told the story of the fall in the pit, one memory at a time. For Bear, it was awful to think and talk about what had happened, and he wondered whether the tears would ever stop. But he stuck with it, and day by day, spot by spot, the black goop inside disappeared. Bear could feel the healing taking place. The tears finally stopped, and Bear felt relief.

Then one day, Bear said to the Healer, "I have stopped having bad dreams about falling in the pit. I can think about that time without my heart pounding. The memory has even faded some, and I feel better."

The Healer replied, "That's good to hear. The black goop left a few scars but it is pretty much gone. You have been very brave, and I am proud of you. I think it is time for you to move on."

"Hip, hip, hooray!" shouted Squirrel and Bear at the news.

"By the way," added the Healer, "We built a high fence around the pit and put in an alarm system. The forest should be a lot safer now for children."

"Thank you for your help," said Bear. "It means a lot!"

Bear hugged the Healer and left the Recovery Center with Squirrel. As they walked home, they saw the sun shining through dark rain clouds. A large rainbow appeared in the sky.

"Maybe that rainbow is a sign," said Bear to Squirrel. "A sign that better times are ahead."

"I'm sure that's so," said Squirrel, "And you deserve it!"

"Thanks," said Bear. "I couldn't have done it without you."

THE BOTTOM LINE: Heal Inside and Out.

Food for Thought Questions:

- Why did Bear get hurt? _____

- How come Bear didn't feel better on the inside after the black goop was washed off on the outside?_____

- How is the black goop like what happens after trauma?_____
  _____

- Why was it important for Bear to tell his story of falling in the pit?_____
  _____

- How are you like Bear?_____
  _____

- How old were you when you first *fell into the pit*?_____

- How many times have you fallen into the abuse pit?_____

- Did you get hurt inside, outside or both?_____

- Who is a Squirrel friend in your life? How does this person stick by you?_____
  _____

- What are you doing now to be safe so you don't fall in another *pit*?_____
  _____

Bear Body Drawing

- Draw an outline of your body on a big piece of paper. Put a red heart where your heart would be. Mark the body in black where you were hurt, inside or out. This can be your heart (feelings) or your actual body.

- Which of these black areas is hardest for you to talk about? _____
  _____

- On your body drawing, number the black areas from hardest to easiest to talk about.

- With your therapist's help, pick the area you want to talk about first. It should be a memory that bothers you and makes you feel bad. On a scale from one to ten, say how bad you feel about that memory. One is really OK, ten is really bad. When you have talked about it (told the story), paint over it or white it out and celebrate being brave! Now say how bad you feel about that memory, again from one to ten.

- Keep picking black spots to talk about with your therapist and caregiver. You do not have to do this all at once. You might consider writing about each black spot before you talk about it.

Story 6: Self-Blame

Purpose(s) and Goal(s): ☒ Psychoeducation for children and teens about self-blame or guilt following abuse. ☒ Treatment Intervention: to be used with children or adolescents who blame themselves and feel responsible for the abuse. The story can also be used with caregivers who are holding the child responsible for what happened.

Many victims of abuse later blame themselves for what happened. They feel guilt and remorse and start to obsess about how it happened and their role in it. They regret not escaping or saving siblings from harm. They do not accept that they were children and could not safely escape what happened. The next story is a follow-up to *Bear of a Different Color*.

Bear's Self-Blame Game

"Falling in the pit was a very STUPID thing to do! I can't believe I did it! I got hurt, I worried my mother, and my friend Squirrel had to go with me to the Healer," fussed Bear Bear, as he hit himself in the head with his small brown paw.

You might remember Bear from the story *Bear of a Different Color*. In that story, Bear fell in a dark pit and went to a Healer with his friend Squirrel to tell his story and get over the trauma of the fall.

Ever since he came back from the Healer, Bear kept going over and over in his bear brain all the mistakes he had made the day of the fall and how he was *stupid for letting it happen*. He had healed from the trauma and felt better inside and out, but he still blamed himself for what had happened. Sometimes his blame and worry kept him awake at night—he was mad at himself and kept thinking about what he could have done to prevent the fall. He just *knew* he could have prevented it if he had really tried! He felt guilty for making his friend Squirrel and his mother upset. When he did not sleep well, he was very grouchy the next day. He snapped at others and sometimes fell asleep during the school day.

One morning, Squirrel was sitting by Bear, cracking nuts and eating breakfast. Bear was tired and grouchy. Squirrel said, "What's up?"

Bear said, "I came up with a list last night when I couldn't sleep. It's *Five Things I Did Wrong That Caused My Fall*—five reasons why I need to feel guilty and blame myself for falling in the pit. It was my own fault that I fell in the pit and worried you and my mother. Do you want me to read the list?"

Squirrel said, "Bear, by now you should know it was not your fault that you fell in the pit. The Healer helped you get over the fall, and a large fence was put up around the pit. There's nothing left for you to worry about. So yes, tell me the five things. I don't see why you should blame yourself for the fall."

Bear declared, "It *was* my fault, and you will see why when I tell you the five things. Number One: I disobeyed my mother and went for a walk in the woods by myself."

Squirrel answered, "Well, it's true that you made a mistake in not obeying your mother. But all little animals disobey their mothers sometimes. They want to do things their own way or be more independent—most of the time they don't get hurt. It is sad and unfortunate if you get hurt. You did not understand that the woods could be dangerous or that there was a pit deep in the woods. Where was your mother the day you took the walk?"

"I don't remember. She was probably watching TV, taking a nap, or talking on her cell phone."

"Well," said Squirrel. "It was her job to keep track of you and know where you were. Little animals can quickly get into trouble without meaning to, so mothers have to watch them closely."

"Let me tell you Number Two," said Bear. "I did not pay attention to the sign at the path that led into the woods. The sign said, 'Caution' and warned of the pit ahead."

"Silly Bear," said Squirrel. "You didn't know how to read. It was not your fault that you ignored the sign."

"OK," said Bear, "You got me on that one. Number Three: I should have turned around and gone back home when it started to get dark."

"That is true," said Squirrel. "It is not safe for anyone to walk in the woods after it gets dark. You probably thought you had plenty of time and didn't realize how quickly nighttime would come."

"Yes," said Bear. "I thought I had plenty of time to run back home, but before I knew it, I could not see where I was going. Number Four: I should have woke up the guards that were sleeping by the pit."

"No," said Squirrel. "Waking them up was not your responsibility. The guards had a job to do and they did not do it. They are supposed to stay awake on their shift. It is not *your* fault that they were sleeping and it is not your fault that you got past them."

"I didn't think about it that way," said Bear. "Number Five: It was my fault that I ignored the 'Danger' signs at the edge of the pit. I went right past them and fell in. I should have seen what was coming."

Squirrel disagreed. "It was dark out by then and hard to see the 'Danger' signs. You could not really see or know what was coming. And remember, you did not know how to read. You were too little. It is not your fault you fell in—it was an accident."

Bear rubbed his head with his paw. What Squirrel said was true.

Squirrel added, "Bear, it was a mistake to disobey your mother, because you were too little to go in the woods alone. And you did not go back home when it started getting dark, so that was a mistake, but those two mistakes did not *cause* your fall in the pit. You did not know how to read (the warning sign), you did not realize there was a dangerous pit ahead, and you were all alone in the woods. The fall happened because your mother was not keeping a close eye on you that day, and the adult guards fell asleep and did not protect you from the fall."

Bear said, "OK, I get it. And frankly I am very relieved. But I still feel so stupid for making those two mistakes!"

Squirrel was very wise. He said, "Bear, everyone makes mistakes. When you make a mistake and are sorry, you wipe the slate clean and get another chance. Even criminals get to wipe the slate clean after they serve their time. Only the very worst criminals get sentenced to life in prison. You need to forgive yourself and move on with your life. Even if you made a couple of mistakes the day you fell in the pit, you do not have to feel guilty forever."

As you know, we sometimes blame ourselves for things in our lives that are beyond our control. If you worry like Bear about things that were not in your control, I hope you will let go of them and move on. You will be glad you did.

THE BOTTOM LINE: Stop Playing the Self-Blame Game!

Food for Thought Questions:

- How are you like Bear? _____

- Why did Bear think it was his fault that he fell in the pit?_____
_____

- Whose fault was it that Bear fell in the pit?_____
_____

- How is a mistake different than an on-purpose *bad* behavior?_____
_____

- How do you feel when you make a mistake?_____

- What can Bear do to forgive himself and move on?_____
_____

- How can Bear's mother help him forgive himself and move on?_____
_____

- Name one thing you feel guilty about or blame yourself for:_____
_____

- Name mistakes you might have made in this situation:_____
_____

- Name things in this situation that were outside your control or not your responsibility:
_____
_____

- Who could help you or look out for you in this type of situation?_____
_____

- What can you do forgive yourself and move on?_____
_____

Notes

1 From *Outsmarting the Riptide of Domestic Violence: Metaphor and Mindfulness for Change,* by P. Pernicano, 2011, Lanham, MD: Jason Aronson. Reprinted and adapted with permission.

2 From *Family-Focused Trauma Intervention: Using Metaphor and Play with Victims of Abuse and Neglect,* by P. Pernicano, 2010, Lanham, MD: Jason Aronson. Reprinted and adapted with permission.

3 From *Outsmarting the Riptide of Domestic Violence: Metaphor and Mindfulness for Change,* by P. Pernicano, 2011, Lanham, MD: Jason Aronson. Reprinted and adapted with permission.

4 From *Metaphorical Stories for Child Therapy: Of Magic and Miracles,* by P. Pernicano, 2010, Lanham, MD: Jason Aronson. Reprinted and adapted with permission.

5 From *Family-Focused Trauma Intervention: Using Metaphor and Play with Victims of Abuse and Neglect,* by P. Pernicano, 2010, Lanham, MD: Jason Aronson. Reprinted and adapted with permission.

CHAPTER 4

RELAXATION

Story 7: Coping with Stress

Purpose(s) and Goal(s): ☒ Psychoeducation about how stress weighs you down, the need to lighten your load, the nature of responsibility for past events and worrying about the past, the concept of gratitude and blessings. ☒ Treatment Intervention: with children, adults and families for identifying and letting go of stress. This story is a good introduction to a stress-management session where the therapist uses CBT or relaxation. Story provides a good metaphor of burden bag to use in sessions.

Kids need to be able to *let go of* or reduce stress. Stress is like a *Burden Bag* that we carry around, one that weighs us down. I have put that idea in this story and I hope you will enjoy it. It was written about six years ago for a young girl in outpatient treatment who worried excessively following family trauma. She made her own burden backpack using a paper lunch bag, and then also created a blessing bag. She enjoyed acting out the story with puppets and shared what she learned with her mother, who then applied the story to her own life.

The Burden Bag[1]

One sunny day, Jack and his friends were hopping through the meadow. Jack was having trouble keeping up with the others. Jack was a young rabbit that moved as slowly as a turtle. Jack was not sick or old or physically challenged—he just moved very slowly. And even when he smiled, Jack Rabbit looked tired and sad.

As Jack and his friends hopped through the meadow, they came across an older rabbit friend who was staring at Jack. He knew it was not polite to stare but he could not help it. Jack was wearing a large, overstuffed, heavy backpack. It pulled on Jack's shoulders and sagged halfway down to the ground. It was labeled "Jack's Burdens." Burdens, by the way, are problems that worry you and weigh you down.

"Jack Rabbit," said the friend, "Why are you wearing that heavy backpack? You don't run or jump like the other young; in fact, you move slower than a turtle in mud! The backpack weighs you down. You could hop faster if you took it off."

Jack said firmly, "No. I NEVER take it off."

His older friend asked, "Do you take it off to eat?"

"No," Jack said. "Not to eat."

"What about to sleep?"

"No," he said. "Not to sleep."

"Well surely you take it off to play?"

Jack said, a little annoyed at all the questions, "I *TOLD* you I *NEVER* take it off. Not even to play!"

The older rabbit said, "I can't believe a young rabbit like you could have so many burdens."

Jack replied, "You can look inside if you want." So the wise old rabbit opened the backpack, and peered inside. There were many bags of burdens in the backpack, each bag neatly labeled with colored permanent marker.

The first bag, with a blue label, said, *Stupid Mistakes.* The second bag, with the green label, said *Rejections* (rejection is when someone you like stops liking you back). A third bag of burdens said *Family Problems.*

The older rabbit took a peek inside the *Family Problems* bag and remarked, "These belong to other family members. Why do you carry around someone else's problems?"

"I like to help out," said Jack.

The fourth bag of burdens, labeled in purple, smelled really AWFUL: *Imperfections.* The young rabbit explained, "Those are things about me that aren't perfect, like my warts, my big feet, and my crooked teeth."

The wise rabbit said, "No one's perfect. If you want to jump like other rabbits, you need to dump these burdens. A rabbit is not meant to move as slow as a turtle!"

Jack begged, "I've been carrying these burdens my whole life. I wouldn't know what to do without them!"

"It's up to you," said the older rabbit," But you might want to lighten your load."

Jack agreed that the backpack was *very* heavy and that it might help to lighten his load.

His friend said, "I know just the place to dump your burdens."

"Lead the way," said Jack.

They hopped down a rocky path and found themselves standing in front of a beautiful lake.

"Here it is—a bottomless lake" said Jack's friend.

Jack said in disbelief, "*No* bottom?"

"That's right," said his friend as he pointed. "If you throw something in, it's gone for good. And look at the sign over there."

Jack looked where his friend pointed and saw a big sign next to the lake. It read, *NO FISHING.*

"I know what you want me to do." said Jack. "You want me to dump my burdens in that lake."

"That's right," said his friend.

Jack took the backpack off and laid it on the ground.

Jack's friend reached into the backpack and handed him a burden. Jack took a deep breath and threw the burden with all his might. The burden flew out over the water and came down with a big "plop!". As the burden hit the lake, Jack saw big circles of ripples spreading out on top of the water. As Jack watched, his heart grew lighter and lighter. Eventually the burden sank below the surface.

Letting go of that first burden gave Jack courage. One by one, he threw the other burdens in the lake. Before Jack knew it, he was standing on the edge of the lake with an empty backpack.

Jack had a sudden moment of doubt. "Oh my goodness, what have I done? What will I do with an empty backpack?"

His friend said, "Throw it in too."

So Jack threw his backpack into the lake and watched it sink. He felt hopeful and took a quick hop forward.

Jack thanked his friend and hopped home to tell his mother about his day.

"That was a good choice, Jack. I'm proud of you," she said, smiling.

"Mom," said Jack, "I'm a little worried that sooner or later I'll go back to my old habits of collecting burdens."

His mother replied, "I think you need a new backpack!" She went to the closet and came back with a new backpack. On the front pocket, it said, *Blessings.*

"What are *Blessings*?" asked Jack.

"Blessings," replied his mother, "are good things, like carrots and lettuce and making new friends. When you notice a blessing during the day, stuff it in this bag. At the end of the day, you can count your blessings."

"I like that idea," said Jack. "But what if I have a bad day and start collecting burdens again?"

His mother answered, "If you start to collect burdens again, the lake is a good backup plan. After all, you're *only rabbit.*"

In case you did not know it, that's rabbit for "You're only human." It's what you say to someone when you want to remind him that no one is perfect and everyone makes mistakes. So whether you are *only rabbit* or only human, do something to lighten your load. And take time to count your blessings!

THE BOTTOM LINE: Lighten your Load and Count Your Blessings.

Food for Thought Questions:

- How are you like Jack?_____
  _____

- Burdens are heavy and they cause stress. What burdens do you carry around?_____
  _____
  _____

- Do you ever carry around someone else's burdens? Give examples. _____
  _____
  _____

- Name three blessings in your life._____
  _____

- Name three things you can do to let go of burdens._____
  _____
  _____

- Describe how you plan to count your blessings every day. _____
  _____

- Make a burden backpack out of a paper lunch bag. On dissolvable paper (available at magic stores or online) write down burdens you carry around. Put them in the bag. During a therapy session, empty the bag one burden at a time and identify coping skills to deal with that burden. Then drop the burdens in the toilet and watch them dissolve. Flush.

- Make a blessings bag. Each night before you go to bed, write down or draw blessings from that day. Put them in your bag and think about them as you go to sleep.

Note

1 From *Metaphorical Stories in Child Therapy: Of Magic and Miracles*, by P. Pernicano, 2010, Lanham, MD: Jason Aronson. Reprinted and adapted with permission.

CHAPTER 5

AFFECT IDENTIFICATION AND EXPRESSION

Story 8: Letting Out Negative Feelings

Purpose(s) and Goal(s): ☒ Psychoeducation about constipation and impacted bowel following trauma, the impact of tension and stress on bowel habits, the need for daily toileting routine; also educates child about the need to talk about trauma a little at a time so as to practice coping skills throughout. Reduces anxiety about talking about what has happened. ☒ Treatment Intervention: for children who have been holding in feelings and bowel movements; or children who are afraid to talk about trauma for fear of losing control or opening up too quickly.

Some kids are afraid to talk about abuse because they think it will all come out at once like messy, smelly poop. It is OK to let out feelings slowly and talk about abuse a little at a time, though. It takes time to think about what happened to you and it takes time to figure out what you want to say about that time in your life. This story reminds kids that they can let out their feelings, and tell their story, a little at a time.

A Little at a Time[1]

Four-year-old Eleanor Elephant could not move. No, she was not paralyzed or injured. She had lived at the Louisville Zoo since she was two years old. It was a nice place with smelly straw, shady trees, and water. People came from miles around to watch the elephants walk and play, but Elly just lay there by a pool of water.

"Come on, Elly," people called out. "Get up and play. Get up and run around. Get up and squirt water on the other elephants."

But Elly just lay there.

The other elephants enjoyed their life. They lumbered around slowly, except when they got excited, mad, or very playful. But Elly did not move at all—she was too big.

Was she *fat*, you ask? Not really. She was big and round and puffed up like a balloon.

You see, Elly was full of "poop," or, in elephant terms, dung. She had held in her poop for two years. Two years of elephant poop is a lot of poop! Most people know what it feels like to hold in poop. The poop gets hard and then it hurts to go. Your belly starts to hurt and gas builds up. Eventually you can't go at all, even if you try. So you stop trying.

Elly started holding in her poop at the same time she started holding in her *bad feelings*; feelings like *fear*, *sadness*, *anger*, and *worry*. Elly didn't want her poop, or her feelings, to come out all at once in a big smelly, painful mess, so she kept it all in.

That is why Elly couldn't move. The other elephants and the zookeeper offered to help, but Elly said, "I don't want or need your help. My life is fine, thank you. My life and my poop are none of your business!"

But one day, an older elephant said, "Elly, you need to get up and get a life."

Elly admitted, "I would like to. But I'm too full of poop and can't move."

"You need to let it out, your poop and your feelings," said the older friend.

Elly said, "It will all come out at once. It will be too smelly and hurt too much!"

"Elly," replied her friend. "Don't you know that you need to let it out *a little at a time*?"

"A little at a time?" asked Elly.

"Yes," said her friend.

Elly thought, "It won't work. It will all come out at once and make a big mess."

Elly didn't want to hurt her friend's feelings by saying those things.

"OK," said Elly. "I'll try. But I might need a little help."

Elly's friend trumpeted loudly. "Heads up, Elephants—we need some help here. Elly's ready to stand up."

All of the elephants in the yard helped Elly get on her feet.

"Come on, Elly," they cried. "It's time to get moving!"

"I don't think I can do this," said Elly. "I can't walk."

"Baby steps," said her friends. "Just take baby steps, one step at a time."

Elly took a careful step forward, then another. One step—two. One step—two.

"I'm walking again!" trumpeted Elly in an excited voice.

Elly moved slowly away from the pool.

"You can do it, Elly," said the other elephants.

Elly's friend whispered, "Get ready, Elly. You'll probably start feeling things inside now that you are moving."

You might smile at what happened next.

"Faaaaaaaaaaart!" went Elly. It was a *big one*!

"Oh my goodness!" said Elly, a little embarrassed. Her face turned bright red. "Excuse me! I guess that's bound to happen as things get moving."

Elly walked around the elephant yard, with the help of her friends. She started letting her feelings, and her poop, out a little at a time. The zoo keeper came to the elephant yard to help.

"Poop—poop", went Elly. "Shovel—shovel," went the zookeeper. The zookeeper has to clean up the elephant yard, and this was going to be a big clean-up job!

It went on for four days and four nights.

Elly cried, laughed, raged, shivered, and shook as she let out her poop and her feelings, a little at a time. Her belly got smaller and smaller. Her legs grew stronger and stronger. Elly felt much better.

Many people heard Elly's story and came to the zoo to see her. People came for miles around to watch her squirt water on the other elephants. Elly waved her trunk at the people and trumpeted in a proud voice. And she kept the zookeeper so busy shoveling poop that his job was secure for years to come!

THE BOTTOM LINE: Let it Out, a Little at a Time!

Food for Thought Questions:

- How are you like Elly?_____
  _____

- What have you kept inside that you want or need to let out?_____
  _____

- What do you think will happen if you let it out?_____
  _____

- Elly let things out a little at a time. How could you do that?_____
  _____

- Make a list of things you need to talk about that have something to do with your abuse. Put the list in order from easiest to talk about to hardest to talk about. Show your list to an adult and pick things to talk about. As you talk about each thing, cross it off your list.

  Easiest to talk about: _____

  _____

  Medium to talk about: _____

  _____

  Hardest to talk about: _____

  _____

Story 9: Self-Control

Purpose(s) and Goal(s): ☒ Psychoeducation about the need for self-control in order to remain safe. ☒ Treatment Intervention: to be used with children or adolescents who engage in high-risk behaviors, defy parents, or do not see the need for self-control. The story can also be used in relapse prevention (controlling urges).

Abused kids need to have a safety plan and follow it. Their caregivers need to monitor them closely and help them understand the protective nature of a safety plan. Sometimes children make choices that put them at risk, or they let their emotions over-ride their judgment. In the next story, the boy doesn't follow his safety plan, and he places himself in danger.

Keep the Lion on a Leash[2]

Sam really liked to do things his own way. He just couldn't help it. His mother would say, "Please don't wipe your mouth on your shirt when you're eating." But Sam really *liked* wiping his mouth on his shirt. So when his mother wasn't looking, he did it anyway. Sometimes his mother caught him doing it and said, "Oh Sam, you always want to do things your own way." It was true—he was just that kind of boy.

By the way, did I tell you that Sam had a pet lion that lived in his bedroom? He got it for his birthday when it was just a baby. "That's it!" Sam had thought, "I'll call him Baby!" Sam taught Baby how to wrestle and they played together. Sam taught Baby tricks, like "beg for hotdogs." Baby purred very loudly, like a motor running—Sam could feel it on his cheek when the lion cuddled up beside him to watch TV.

As Sam grew, Baby grew, too. Soon, Baby was really *big*. His mouth was as big as Sam's head. Sam's mother said, "It's time to keep Baby on a leash. He is a wild creature and doesn't know his own strength. He will hurt you or someone else without meaning to."

"Oh Mom," said Sam, rolling his eyes. "Baby is my friend, and he loves me. He would never hurt me."

"Trust me, Sam," answered his mother. "Baby is a lion. It is his nature to hunt and attack. I want you to buy a leash today. You won't be able to control him without one."

Sam didn't want to admit it, but he was a little afraid of Baby now. Baby's teeth and claws were sharp and pointed. When Baby *roared*, he scared everyone in the house. So Sam bought a red collar and a nice strong leash, and for several weeks, Sam kept Baby on the leash.

But a part of Sam still wanted to let Baby off the leash again. He thought, "I raised Baby, and I don't think he would ever hurt me!"

So one night Sam took Baby in his bedroom. He looked Baby in the eye and unhooked the leash from the lion's collar. "Good lion," said Sam. But Baby opened his mouth and *roared* loudly. Sam backed away and said, "Stay, Baby!" Baby moved forward slowly, one step at a time, a fierce look in his eye. The hair on the back of Baby's neck stood up, his tail went up in the air, and his eyes narrowed. He looked like a wild lion! Baby swiped at Sam with a huge clawed paw and squatted down as if ready to pounce.

Sam thought, "Oops, bad decision . . ." He could see that Baby was dangerous and wild off the leash. Sam did not know what to do. Any minute now he was going to get eaten alive! Then Sam had a sudden "aha." He ran out of his room and slammed the door behind him. "*Roar*," went Baby, as he clawed at the thick door. For the moment, Sam was safe.

Sam dashed into the kitchen, opened the fridge and grabbed ten hotdogs. Baby *loved* hot dogs! As Sam ran toward his room, he saw his mother at the bedroom door. Her hand was on the doorknob.

"Oh no!" thought Sam, "Mom is going to get eaten alive!" He *shouted*, "MOM, DON'T OPEN THE DOOR!"

It was too late! Baby's head pushed out—so close that Sam's mother could feel his hot breath on her hand. She got the door closed right before the lion could take a bite out of her. Her face was very red and she did not look happy at all.

Sam's mother backed away from Sam's bedroom door and said sternly, "Sam, what have you done?"

Sam did not answer her. He opened his bedroom door a crack and threw the ten hotdogs far into the room, behind Baby. Baby headed for the hotdogs. Sam jumped into the room and quickly re-hooked the leash to Baby's collar. Then Sam commanded, "BABY, STAY!" as he tugged on the leash. Baby lay down with his head on his paws. He looked a little sad, as if to say, "Sam, I didn't want to hurt you or your mother. It is just my nature."

Sam ran over to where his mother was standing. "Mom, let me explain," he begged.

His mother shook her head "No," she said and held out her hand like a STOP sign.

"Oh boy," thought Sam, "I'm in real trouble, now."

His mother said, "Give me a minute, Sam. My heart is pounding and I need to calm down." Her face was still quite red.

When his mother had calmed back down, she said, "Sam, I know you like to do things your way. But this time, doing things your way almost got us killed."

His mother also wanted to say, "I told you so," but she bit her lip (which means she did not say it). Instead, she wrapped Sam up in a big hug.

Sam said, "I still like to do things my way, but I'll try to think first before I do something stupid."

His mother tried to hide a smile. She thought, "That's my Sam. He always likes to have his way, and that is not such a bad thing. My Sam is a boy with backbone and lots of courage."

Sam and Baby, of course, sat down to watch TV in Sam's bedroom. Sam held the leash firmly in his hand, and Baby purred to his heart's content.

THE BOTTOM LINE: Keep Your Lion on a Leash!

Food for Thought Questions:

- How are you like Sam?_____

  _____

- A safety plan is something to help you stay safe from abuse. What is your safety plan?_____

  _____

  _____

- A safety plan only works if everyone follows it. Describe a time when you or someone else did not follow a safety plan?_____
  _____

- Make a coping card for Sam. List three things he needs to do to remain safe around Baby. _____
  _____
  _____

- Sam and his mother write a safety plan for having a lion in the house. What is their plan? _____
  _____

Story 10: Anger-Control (Bullying)

Purpose(s) and Goal(s): ☒ Psychoeducation about bullying, anger management, social skill deficits. ☒ Treatment Intervention: for children who alienate or intimidate others with aggressive, bullying, or bossy behavior,

Some kids get so mad after abuse that they start picking on others. It makes them feel in control to behave in this way. They don't want to be *victims*, so they bully others. They think if they are mean enough, people will leave them alone and they won't get abused. They forget or ignore how it was to be the victim of bullying and abuse. It is important to find ways to get along with others instead of picking on them. The dragon in this story is like that. He learns self-control and stops bullying others.

The Dragon's Fire[3]

Flame was a bossy bully and had no friends. He pounded his feet on his scaly chest and shouted, "No one can beat me—I'm king of the dragons!" Of course, he was not king—his Uncle Smoky was really the king—but Flame liked to pretend he was in charge.

You would probably be scared if you ran into Flame at the mall. He had a huge, ugly mouth full of sharp teeth and when he roared, he spit out balls of orange and red fire. When he opened his mouth, you could see all the way back to his tonsils, and you could smell his bad breath.

Flame had a bad temper and loved to scare others away with his fire.

"I'll get them before they get me!" said Flame. And when he got mad, he would burn down a house or torch a tree. He burned a whole bowling alley one night in a fit of rage. Thank goodness it had already closed! He threatened, "If you don't do what I want, I'll burn your house down." He always got his way, because everyone knew what a bad temper he had.

When other young dragons saw Flame coming, they ran away. No one wanted to play with him.

One afternoon, Uncle Smoky came to visit Flame. Flame loved Uncle Smoky. Uncle Smoky played Dragon Ball with Flame, a game like dodgeball, using great balls of fire. But this visit was not to play Dragon Ball. Uncle Smoky had heard about Flame being a bully.

Uncle Smoky said, "Flame, I've been hearing some things about you. People are saying you're a bully."

"Yes," admitted Flame, "I am a bit of a bully . . . I like using my fire to scare people. I don't want to give it up."

Flame's uncle said, "You don't have to give up your fire. You just need to change how you use it. Flame, tell me how you use your fire."

Flame told his uncle about scaring people and making threats.

His uncle advised, "The *way* you use your fire is a problem. Dragon fire is for self-defense, not for picking on others. No one likes a bully!"

His uncle added, "Fire is both good and bad. You need it to survive—but you also need to control it."

Uncle Smoky looked at Flame. "Flame, tell me some good things about fire."

Flame thought for a minute and said, "A dragon can blow a little fire as a warning to scare off a dangerous giant."

"Good thinking," said his uncle.

Flame went on, "And fire is good for cooking or keeping us warm."

Flame's uncle questioned, "Now how can fire be bad?"

Flame said, "That's easy. Fire can quickly get out of control and damage or destroy things." He added, "It can also burn and cause pain."

"That's right," said Uncle Smoky, as he scratched his scaly back. Those are ways that fire can hurt."

"Now Flame," Uncle Smoky went on, "Don't you want to have friends? Do you want to get arrested for vandalism?"

"I don't want to get in trouble with the law," said Flame. "And I guess I wouldn't mind having a couple of friends." This might surprise you, but once in a while Flame felt lonely.

"No one will play with me—not even Jimmy the ugly troll or the other bullies," said Flame.

It was true; not even the bullies wanted to play with Flame, because he was the meanest, toughest bully of all.

His uncle said, "If you want to stay out of trouble and make friends, you need to stop being a bully. Use your fire in ways that help, not hurt. Control it."

Flame respected his Uncle Smoky and thought about what he had said.

During recess the next day, Flame went up to a group of young dragons.

He said, "Can I play with you?" They were scared and flew off in the other direction. There was no way they would come near him, because they didn't trust him. Who wants to get torched?

Flame saw his uncle across the street and shouted, "Uncle Smoky, how can I convince them that I want to change?"

"They will need to see new behavior," said Uncle Smoky. "Promises are cheap."

Uncle Smoky suggested that Flame learn new coping skills for getting along with others and practice those skills by acting nicer around other dragons so that they could see he was trying to change.

After about 30 days of learning and practice, Uncle Smoky said it was time for Flame to invite some dragons to play so that he could try out his new skills. So from 50 yards away, Flame called out, "Please come over Saturday. We can play Dragon Ball and I'll cook dinner."

Uncle Smoky talked to the dragons and said he would be there to make sure they stayed safe. They trusted Flame's Uncle Smoky and agreed to give Flame a chance.

That Saturday, Flame found the perfect spot to have a campfire—one that would not create a forest fire.

As his guests watched, Flame opened his huge mouth and spit out a ball of orange and red fire, **away** from everyone. The stacked wood caught fire easily! The group of young dragons put hotdogs and marshmallows on *long* sticks and cooked them to perfection. Everyone had a great time, after they got over their fear that Flame might roast *them*.

When Flame returned to school on Monday, a dragon invited him to play Dragon Ball at recess. The other dragons saw that Flame did not hurt anyone and that he followed the rules fair and square. From that day on, Flame began to make friends, and he kept his promise not to be a bully.

Flame was proud of his decision to change. He had learned to have his fire and control it, too. Once in awhile, he still got in a really bad mood and felt like torching someone. But instead of doing that, Flame went flying until he felt better. It was a dragon version of "time-out!"

Someone once said that *lighting a fire under someone* helps them change. So if you have a little fire inside you, I hope you will put it to good use.

THE BOTTOM LINE: Have Your Fire and Control It, Too!

Food for Thought Questions:

- How are you like Flame? Give an example of a time you bullied someone or someone bullied you.
  _____
  _____
  _____

- How is anger like fire?_____
  _____

- What advice would you give Flame?_____
  _____

- Make a coping card for Flame—list some helpful hints to help Flame get along better with others._____
  _____
  _____

- A bully can become a leader by working *with* others instead of *against* them. A leader is a strong, persuasive person that respects others, and feels strongly about a cause. A cause is like a charity or issue that you want to support—something like rescuing stray animals or taking better care of children. If you were Flame, what would be your cause? Make a speech as a leader to get others to join your cause._____
  _____
  _____
  _____
  _____
  _____

Notes

1 From *Outsmarting the Riptide of Domestic Violence: Metaphor and Mindfulness for Change*, by P. Pernicano, 2011, Lanham, MD: Jason Aronson. Reprinted and adapted with permission.
2 From *Metaphorical Stories for Child Therapy: Of Magic and Miracles*, by P. Pernicano, 2010, Lanham, MD: Jason Aronson. Reprinted and adapted with permission.
3 From *Metaphorical Stories for Child Therapy: Of Magic and Miracles*, by P. Pernicano, 2010, Lanham, MD: Jason Aronson. Reprinted and adapted with permission.

CHAPTER 6

COGNITIVE COPING

Story 11: Protective Behaviors

Purpose(s) and Goal(s): ☒ Psychoeducation for children about the anger and self-protection that can result from abuse. The story educates the child about the importance of turning to others for help rather than going it alone. ☒ Treatment Intervention: to be used with children or adolescents when working on safety planning and discussing relational supports.

A young boy had been physically abused by both his stepfather and older brothers. He didn't want anyone else to hurt him, so he started acting mean and tough. Soon he didn't know how to get along with others. He did not like to ask for help: that made him feel weak and dependent. This story helped him realize that asking for help was a sign of strong wisdom and a good coping skill.

Safety in Numbers

The small Clownfish, Charlie, was all alone in the ocean, and he didn't feel safe. He had been playing in the coral, having a good time. He did not notice when his school of Clownfish, including his parents, swam off. In case you do notknow it, a school of fish is not a place where fish learn things; it's a large group of fish that live and swim together.

Charlie was afraid. A shark or bigger fish might eat him alive! He wanted to protect himself but he didn't know how. He swam around in circles. "How can I be safe in this big ocean?" he thought.

An idea came to him. He decided to pretend he was a shark. It would be perfect. If he looked like a shark, the other sharks and fish would leave him alone.

So Charlie put on a really good costume. It had big white teeth that looked real. The mouth even opened and closed. It made him look like a huge, grey shark. He loved the big fin on top that sliced through the water. He felt safe in the costume, and soon he was acting more like a shark than a Clownfish.

When other fish came near, Charlie showed them his teeth and pretended to attack. He acted so mean that everyone swam away in fear. After Charlie acted mean for a few weeks, he started to feel mean.

Charlie pretended to be a shark for so long that he almost forgot he *was* a Clownfish. One day he was acting like a mean shark, and a real shark swam up behind him. The real shark knew Charlie was just pretending. He could smell the little Clownfish inside and could tell that the costume was not real fish skin.

"That stupid wimp imposter!" said the shark. "I'll just eat him up!" In case you do not know it, an "imposter" is a fake, like the Wizard behind the curtain in *The Wizard of Oz*.

The shark swam closer and closer. He opened his huge mouth, ready to attack. Just before the real shark grabbed Charlie in its sharp teeth, a huge school of colorful Clownfish swam in and surrounded him. Wow—there were nearly 500 of them!

Charlie was startled and so was the shark.

"Out of the way, you big bully," said the leader of the school to the real shark.

"We'll keep you safe," the leader told Charlie. "Quick, swim with us and don't ask any questions."

The school of Clownfish swam *as one* toward a small ocean cave. The leader helped Charlie remove his costume so that he would fit through the opening, which was too small for a real shark to go through.

Once they got inside, the leader said to Charlie, "You couldn't fool us," We knew you weren't a shark. You're one of us."

"How could you tell I wasn't a shark?" asked Charlie.

"You are what you are," said the Leader. "And that came through. It didn't really matter what you looked like on the outside—you were still a Clownfish on the inside. You need to stop being an imposter."

He added, "You know, there is safety in numbers. You are welcome to join our school."

From that day on, Charlie stopped pretending to be a shark and hung out with the school of Clownfish that had saved him. He didn't really like being alone, and it's hard to find a friend when you're a shark.

THE BOTTOM LINE: There Is Safety (and Friendship) in Numbers.

Food for Thought Questions:

- How are you like the Clownfish? _____

_____

- How are you like the Shark? _____

_____

- When do you act tough?_____

_____

- How will it help Clownfish to be part of a school of fish?_____

_____

- Do you feel safer with others or alone?_____

_____

- Who would *save or protect* you if you were in danger? _____

_____

Story 12: Coping with Depression

Purpose(s) and Goal(s): ☒ Psychoeducation for children and adolescents about the connection among thoughts, feelings and behaviors. ☒ Treatment Intervention: to be used with children or adolescents as part of CBT for depression.

Some kids get depressed after they have been abused. Depressed kids have negative thoughts and feelings, and they have trouble being happy or hopeful. Some become sad and others feel more grouchy or irritable.

The point of the story that follows is that thoughts and feelings are connected. It shows how thoughts are feelings are connected in depression. It also offers ways that depressed kids can gain control over their depressed thoughts and feelings.

The Black Cloud[1]

Barry the Basset Hound was alone in his room. Barry wanted everyone to leave him in peace, because it had been a very bad week.

"What a terrible week this has been!" moaned Barry. "I can't do anything right."

On Monday, Barry had an "accident" on the kitchen floor and his mother growled at him.

On Tuesday, Barry barked in the middle of the night and woke up his parents.

On Wednesday, Barry ate something he shouldn't (a dead mouse the cat brought home) and threw up all over the rug.

On Thursday, the dogs at school laughed at him (for about the hundredth time) for having long ears.

On Friday, Barry's dad lost his job.

Now it was Saturday. Barry's dad was grouchy, his mom was howling, and Barry did not think things would get better any time soon. Barry spent the whole day in his room, with his tail tucked between his legs.

Sunday arrived cloudy and raining. It turned out to be another bad day. On Sunday afternoon, Barry chewed the leg of his mother's favorite chair leg.

"Naughty dog!" howled his mother.

When Monday came, Barry said, "I don't want to go to school."

"You're not throwing up and you don't have a fever, so you have to go to school," replied Barry's mother.

"You are the meanest mom in the whole world," cried Barry.

"Maybe I am, but you are going to school," his mother said.

That night, Barry's mother asked about his day.

"No one likes me," Barry said. "I'm stupid and ugly!"

Barry's mother replied, "You are fine just the way you are. Go to bed."

"Nobody knows how I feel—not even you!" Barry barked at his mother.

On Tuesday, Barry woke up with an upset stomach and a headache. He threw up right after eating his dog chow breakfast.

This time, Barry's mother let him stay home from school, because he was really sick and not just "faking it." Barry was sick for three days. He slept a lot and kept the shade pulled down in his dark room. Barry had three whole days to think about how bad his life was.

On Friday, Barry's mother woke him up and said, "Come and eat your breakfast. You are well enough to go back to school."

Barry was in a grouchy mood. He whined, "Can't I please stay home from school just one more day?"

"No, Barry," replied his mother. She cleaned his fur with her tongue and fed him a special dog chow with meat chunks. She gave him a small loving nip on the back of his neck to hurry him out the door.

Barry shivered in the cool air.

"My life is so frustrating," Barry said with a sigh as he walked to school. "I have awful luck."

As Barry said that, a small light gray cloud showed up over his head, just like the clouds on a dark, overcast day.

Then Barry said, "*No one* likes me, and *nothing* I do is going to make that any better." As Barry said *that*, the small cloud grew darker. It was now a very dark gray cloud, like the clouds before a thunderstorm.

Finally Barry said, his eyes drooping, "I wish I had *never been born*. My parents would be better off without me." With these words, the cloud turned black, like the clouds that shut out the sun right before a tornado.

It was a sunny day outside, but the cloud over Barry's head blocked the sun completely.

With the black cloud over his head, Barry traveled in darkness.

The black cloud went everywhere with Barry. When Barry's mother invited him to play, he howled that he was tired and went to take a nap. Barry spent most of his time alone in his room. He was very tired (even when he got lots of sleep), and he wanted to sleep a lot.

When Barry's brother stuck his long nose in Barry's food dish, Barry didn't bark at him to chase him away.

Barry said, "Go ahead. I don't care if you eat my food. I'm not very hungry." His brother cocked his head in surprise and gobbled up all the food.

Barry didn't want to bother anyone with his problems. "My parents have problems of their own," he thought. "My life is a hopeless mess," he thought. "Why bother them?"

For Barry, it seemed forever since he had seen the sunshine.

Then one Saturday, Fred the Beagle came over to play. Fred barked, "Sorry for being nosy, but why don't you get rid of that black cloud?"

Barry gave a mournful howl, "I can't get rid of the black cloud. I have no control over it!"

Fred disagreed, "You're wrong. When you smile and say something positive, the cloud gets lighter. When you say something grouchy or negative, the cloud gets darker. If you change what you think and say, the cloud will probably go away."

Barry did not believe his friend, and he decided to prove him wrong.

First Barry said something hopeless: "I wish I had never been born!" The cloud turned black.

Then he complained about the weather: "I hate rainy days." The cloud turned a lighter gray.

Finally he said something positive: "Fred is such a nice friend!" The cloud turned fluffy and white. His friend was right!

"See?" asked Fred.

"I guess I do have control over the cloud," said Barry. While his friend Fred watched, Barry practiced saying things in a more positive way.

He changed, "No one likes me" to "Some kids don't like me, and others do." Instead of, "Things will never get better," he said, "I will do what I can." Each time Barry changed his words, the cloud changed color.

His friend Fred said, "You know Barry, you need to get out in the sun more. Fresh air and exercise will raise your energy. The less you do, the worse you feel." Then Fred barked, "Barry, I have to go home now to eat and practice chasing my tail. See you tomorrow at school."

Barry did what his friend Fred had suggested. He paid attention to what he said and got outside more. The fresh air and exercise helped his mood and two weeks later, the black cloud had nearly disappeared.

When his brother tried to gobble up Barry's food that night, Barry growled at him and chased him back to his own food dish. "Good," thought his brother, "Barry's back to his old self again!"

You might want to know how this story ends. Well, Barry's father got a new job and his mother howled less. Barry had some good days and some bad days, just like everyone else. After all, there is really no such thing as "happily ever after." Sometimes Barry's black cloud came back on bad days, but he no longer let it color his life the way it had before.

THE BOTTOM LINE: Do Something to Lighten Up!

Food for Thought Questions:

- How are you like Barry? _____

_____

- For you, what is a bad day? _____

_____

- What can you do to chase away your black cloud on a bad day?_____

_____

- Make a coping card for Barry. Teach him how to use his thoughts to change his feelings. Remind him how his thoughts, feelings, and behaviors are connected.

Story 13: Coping with Obsessive Compulsive Behaviors

Purpose(s) and Goal(s): ☒ Psychoeducation about obsessive compulsive symptoms after trauma. ☒ Treatment Intervention: relaxation and guided imagery, exposure and response- prevention.

Following abuse, an anxious child sometimes develops obsessive thinking and/or compulsive behaviors, such as touching things, counting things, handwashing, and fear of contamination. The story that follows provides an introduction to OCD and suggests a CBT intervention that may be used when practicing exposure and response prevention.

The Magic Stone[2]

Oliver Cornelius Danbury Frog, better known by his friends as OCD, had a serious problem. He was better known as OCD because no one wanted to say a long name like Oliver Cornelius Danbury, and it took him way too long to write it! OCD Frog was too exhausted to enjoy the swamp any more. The word exhausted, in case you did not know it, means that he was very tired all the time.

And why, you might ask, was OCD so exhausted? Well, first of all, OCD spent A LOT of time worrying that something bad might happen. For example, he was worried that a big bird might eat his mother, and he spent a lot of time watching the sky for birds.

OCD also spent A LOT of time every day hopping and croaking. His legs ached so much and his poor throat was sore, but he just couldn't stop. Oh, he knew that frogs were born to hop—but he HAD to hop 126 times every time he went out to hop, and he was getting very tired.

On top of that, OCD could not stop croaking. Yes, OCD knew that croaking was something all the frogs did at night in the swamp, but he HAD to croak 2,003 times in a very high voice. All the other frogs croaked in their deep "ribbet" tones, and there he was croaking and croaking and croaking like a soprano. In case you did not know it, a soprano is a singer who sings in a very high voice. OCD just could not stop.

OCD Frog had a secret. He KNEW deep inside that if he did NOT hop 126 times his mother would die. He also KNEW that by croaking 2,003 times, he was keeping the whole frog world safe and was preventing some horrible disaster. He wasn't quite sure what type of disaster. He just KNEW he had to keep croaking. Other frogs did not believe these things, but it did not stop OCD from hopping and croaking.

OCD had another serious, secret problem that was quite embarrassing. He was deathly afraid that the flies he ate were too dirty—he believed that the germs would make him sick. So OCD snuck away when he was ready to eat and washed off each and every fly ten times. He was losing weight too: you can imagine how long it took it took to wash all those flies! Other frogs laughed at OCD for doing this, but it did not stop him from washing flies.

A wise old neighborhood owl had been watching this poor frog from his perch high in the trees above the swamp. He could see that OCD needed his help. He decided that a little "magic" was in order.

So he swooped down to talk to OCD Frog and said, "My name is Hoot Owl. You don't know WHOOOO I am, but I am here to help you. I understand what a serious mission you think you have in life. You want to keep your mother safe, and you really care about our swamp world. I know you don't want to get sick on dirty flies."

He continued, "Unfortunately, YOU-WHOOOO can't keep bad things from happening just by hopping, croaking and washing flies. But you are afraid to stop doing these things just in case they are helping."

OCD Frog said, "Oh my goodness—that's it exactly!" He added, "You know, I feel absolutely MISERABLE! [In case you don't know it, "miserable" is when someone is very unhappy and frustrated, too.] I am exhausted, and I don't have any fun anymore. I don't WANT to keep doing these things, but I can't stop myself. What can I do?"

The young frog realized he had forgotten his manners and added, "Pleased to meet you, Hoot Owl. My name is OCD Frog."

Hoot Owl nodded his head back at the introduction. "Give me a minute," he said, "I need to think about what you might do to take your mind off all your worries." As he thought and thought about what OCD could do, Hoot Owl turned his head almost all the way around and scratched the back of his neck with his sharp beak.

He turned his feathery head back around and said, "You need something to focus on instead of your worries—something like a magic stone. You can pick one up over there by the stream. You might want to try that smooth brown one with the speckles on it or that pretty black and white one. Go pick one up, now, and then come back."

So OCD went over by the stream. "How do I know which one to pick?" he called back to Hoot Owl.

"It doesn't matter," said Hoot. "Whichever one appeals to you the most. The magic is inside you, after all. The stone just helps it work."

OCD picked up a particularly pretty smooth brown stone, and brought it back.

Hoot Owl said, "Now, touch the stone and say some magic words that calm you down and help you relax. You get to make up the magic words. Doing that will take your mind off your worries."

OCD Frog said, "What do I do after I say the magic words?"

Hoot Owl replied, "After you say the magic words, take a BIG breath in and out, to help the magic work. When you touch the stone and say these magic words, you will be able to hop, croak, and eat flies normally, like all the other frogs. You can touch the stone and everything will be OK. Try it and see."

The frog said, "How shall I touch it? Should I touch it 56 times? Should I use my tongue or my foot? Should I use both? Should I count while I touch and do the touches in just the right order?"

The owl smiled kindly and replied, "No, touch it only once. If you touch it more than once the magic won't work. You can touch it with your tongue OR foot. Not both. No counting! When you feel the urge to hop 126 times, touch the stone once and say the magic words. Then go check on your mother. When you feel the urge to croak 2,003 times, touch the stone once instead and say the magic words. Then go check on the frogs in the swamp. You can say the words out loud or inside your head. When you get the urge to wash flies, say the magic words. Then eat the flies."

Hoot Owl added, "Now I'm not saying this will be easy for you. It's no big deal if you mess up once in a while. Just keep trying. If you relax and focus on something other than your worries, you will get better a little at a time."

So OCD Frog picked up the stone Hoot Owl had pointed out, took it home, and kept it close to him at all times. About a week later, OCD saw a bird. He began to think that the bird would eat his mother and got very anxious! He almost started hopping 126 times, but instead he remembered what the owl had said. With hope, he touched the stone once, said his magic words (calm down—relax—breathe . . .), and took a BIG breath. His heart was pounding and he could hardly breathe! Soon he calmed down a little and went to check on his mother. She was fine! That night, he got the urge to wash a few flies, but the stone's magic helped and he ate the flies just as they were, fresh and delicious! Sure enough, he did not get sick.

OCD Frog did better from that day on. He continued to use his magic stone, and little by little he gained control over his worries. He knew deep inside that it was not the stone that helped him but his resolve to stop doing the things he had been doing; in any case, it was nice to have something to hold onto when he started to worry. Once in awhile, he worried, "What if this happened?" or "What if that happened?" But those times, and his anxiety, passed. OCD had more time to do the things he needed to do. He thanked Hoot Owl for his help. With all the time he saved, he had more time to play with the other frogs in the swamp. And you might be interested in knowing that OCD's mother lived a long and happy life!

THE BOTTOM LINE: A Little Worry Goes a Long Way.

Food for Thought Questions:

- How are you like OCD Frog?_____

- How do you act when you are worried? _____
  _____

- Do you have habits that are hard to stop? If so, what are they?
  _____
  _____

- What can OCD do to worry less?_____
  _____

- What can you do to worry less? _____
  _____

- Find a *smooth magic rock*. Remember, the magic is inside you. Hold the rock tight. Imagine your worry going from your head, down your arm, through your hand and into the rock. As the worry goes into the rock, you will feel the rock get warmer. *Keep the rock with you and use it every night at bedtime.*

Story 14: Containing Fear and Anxiety

Purpose(s) and Goal(s): ☒ Psychoeducation for children and adolescents about the need for psychological distance from the abuse. ☒ Treatment Intervention: to be used with children or adolescents who desire ways to *wrap up* anxiety that is interfering with school, sleep, or other functioning. The story can be used with guided imagery to provide the child psychological distance and decrease perceived helplessness.

After kids finish therapy for abuse, they feel better. But kids sometimes start thinking or dreaming about the abuse again at a future point in time. This story is a lot like the story *Little Butterfly's Wings and the New Cocoon* but for older kids. Kids need some tools to put the abuse out of their minds—it is important to get a good night's sleep and stop worrying.

Wrap It Up[3]

Sara Spider was perched in the middle of a large web, a frown on her face. As she frowned, you could see huge wrinkles on her somewhat-hairy brow. Her friend Torrence Tarantula, a large funnel-web spider, approached from the ground below and called up to her.

"Yoo-hoo," called Torrence. "Why are you looking so glum? It's a beautiful Saturday morning and the sun is shining."

"Go away and leave me alone," said Sara. I'm in a bad mood."

"OK," said Torrence, who wanted to respect Sara's wishes. "We all need our privacy. But before I go, is there anything I can do to help?"

"I don't know," replied Sara. "I guess I'll tell you what's bothering me. Last September, I went through a tough time. Do you remember the bad wind storm that came through Louisville and blew down all the trees and power lines?"

"Sure," said Torrence. "It was a terrible storm. The wind blew 70 miles per hour!"

Sara continued. "Well, during the storm my web, with all my children in it, blew away. I hid under a rock for months after the storm and was afraid to come back out."

"What did you do?" asked Torrence.

"I went to a spider counselor and talked about it," Sara replied. "I told my story, and the counselor told me that some things are outside my control. Bad things sometimes happen. The counselor helped me think about the good things in my life. I learned that I could rebuild my web. I did rebuild my web and even found some of my babies that blew away."

Sara was deep in thought. "The counseling definitely helped, and it's not as bad as it used to be. But I worry too much and can't sleep. Sometimes I still dream about the storm. And whenever the wind blows, I hide under a rock."

Torrence answered, "It takes time to get over something like that. But you don't want to carry the memories with you everywhere you go. And you need to reduce your stress. It can get in the way of healing."

"Yes," said Sara.

Torrence spoke again. "Maybe you have forgotten something."

"What have I forgotten?" she asked.

"Spider silk comes in handy. It is not only for wrapping up insects (to eat later) that you catch in your web." He smiled.

Sara was confused. "What do you mean?"

He replied, "You can wrap up your memories to keep them from coming back to bother you."

"Tell me more," said Sara.

Torrence went on, "After you talk about bad things, you can wrap them up. First, pretend to build a web in your mind. Then catch your bad memories or worries in it. After you catch them, you can wrap them up tightly like a cocoon, using your spider silk, and they won't bother you anymore."

Terrence added, "If you do this, you can even keep memories and worries out of your dreams. Each night before bed, wrap up things that might bother your sleep. After all, you are a worrier, Sara. You may need to work a little harder than most spiders to remind yourself not to worry."

Sara's face lit up. Her eyes brightened as she realized she might gain some control over the memories and thoughts that had taken over her mind.

Sara admitted, "Yes, I have always been a bit of a worrier. I obsess about many things. I'll have to try this."

That night when Sara went to bed, she imagined building a large web in her mind. She caught the memory of the wind storm in her web. She grinned as she saw it stick to the web. Sara realized she had it just where she wanted it—out of her mind and caught fast. She then imagined herself wrapping up the bad memory in a compact, white cocoon, so tight that nothing could get out. As she spun the thread and the cocoon took shape, Sara took a deep breath and relaxed.

By the time Sara finished wrapping the memory inside the cocoon, she was surprisingly tired. Sara fell asleep and that night, not one bad memory touched her dreams.

The next day, early in the morning, Sara called out for Torrence.

"Yoo-hoo! Torrence! Yoo-hoo!"

Torrence slowly crawled out of his funnel web on the ground and answered, while rubbing sleep out of his eyes, "Hello Sara. It's very early. How are you today?"

"Much better, Torrence," replied Sara. "I tried what you suggested and got a good night's sleep. From now on, if I obsess about something and can't get it out of my mind, I'll wrap it up. Thank you for reminding me that I have what I need to control the things that bother me."

THE BOTTOM LINE: Wrap It Up!

Food for Thought Questions:

- How are you like Sara the Spider? _____
  _____

- What thoughts and feelings about your past are hard to get rid of? _____
  _____
  _____

- What is one thing you want to wrap up and stop thinking about? _____
  _____
  _____

- Draw a large spider web. Write down the thing you worry or think about too much. Crumple up the piece of paper and stuff it inside a cardboard tube. Wrap the whole thing in Duct Tape. Put it on the web. If you want to, you can stomp on it before you put it on the web, to make sure it is gone.

Story 15: Self-Acceptance

Purpose(s) and Goal(s): ☒ Psychoeducation about changes in self-perception and low self-esteem. ☒ Treatment Intervention: to identify one's strengths, reduce self-dislike.

A little boy who came to see me weekly was a *worrier*. He had been having high levels of anxiety following repeated episodes of physical abuse by a family member. And on top of that, he was a perfectionist about his school performance and appearance. Many abused kids feel different than other kids, are self-critical, and believe no one likes them. This boy used the story that follows to identify his strengths and gain confidence.

The Furry Boa

Bobby the Boa Constrictor frowned. He had to start a new school that day, and he was really worried.

"No one will like me. I am the weirdest boa constrictor anyone has ever seen and everyone will make fun of me."

Bobby Boa *was* different from other boa constrictors. First, he was covered from head to toe in fur—he had been born that way. Instead of scales and smooth leathery skin, Bobby had thick, soft fur covering every surface of his body. It was a pretty odd sight; a snake slithering around wearing what looked like a fur coat!

Bobby had tried to shave his fur, but his parents said it would just grow back and to quit trying to change who he was.

"I'm so ugly," said Bobby. "I hate how I look!"

"You need to accept yourself as you are," they said. But who were they to talk? He was the only boa constrictor in his family to be born with fur, and when people saw him, they laughed. Bobby was pretty sensitive about being teased and avoided going out in public.

If that wasn't enough, Bobby had another problem. It was the *constrictor* part of his name. He didn't *like* to squeeze things, not even the next door neighbor's cat that was so annoying. Bobby didn't like to kill other animals and he was a vegetarian. He didn't eat meat. His parents said, "We love and accept you the way you are, son," but as you can imagine, Bobby got teased about that too by kids in his neighborhood.

Bobby wanted his mother to let him stay home the day he was supposed to start his new school, "I have a stomachache," he told his mother. "I ate too much popcorn and guacamole last night."

His mother knew that was not true—Bobby ate popcorn and guacamole every night, and it never made him sick.

So off Bobby went to his new school. The other kids stared at him. When he got to the classroom, the teacher said, "Please take off your coat, Bobby," and he had to explain, while everyone laughed, that it was not a coat. For the rest of the day, the kids teased Bobby, and he wished he could curl up under his desk and never come out.

Somehow he got through the day. As soon as school ended, Bobby headed for the park. He curled up in the sun on a park bench and was so tired that he fell asleep.

Bobby woke up to the sound of a kind voice and someone gently petting his fur. "What a beautiful fur boa," said the lady. "I wonder who left it here on the bench. It feels so cozy and warm. If they don't come back for it, I might just take it home with me."

Oh my goodness! Bobby opened one eye, just a little, and saw that he was no longer curled up on the bench. He was wrapped around a woman's shoulders! She was sitting on the bench next to where he had been curled up. She thought he was a *scarf*! A boa is a long, fancy scarf-like thing you wear about the neck or shoulders, made out of wool, cotton, fur, or feathers. The woman had seen his fur and assumed that he was an article of clothing.

Bobby peeked at the woman who was speaking but did not move. Bobby didn't want to frighten the woman, and as you know, most people would be scared speechless to have a snake of any type wrapped around their shoulders.

Bobby thought the woman was funny-looking. Her head was bald, she had no eyebrows, and there was no hair on her arms. She was shivering in the chilly air.

Bobby cleared his throat and said, "Ma'am, please don't be afraid, but I'm not a boa. I mean I *am* a boa, but I'm a boa constrictor snake, not a scarf."

The woman jumped, quite startled.

Bobby added quickly, "I won't hurt you. I'm a vegetarian and I don't like to constrict."

She was glad to hear that and said, "Well, there's a first time for everything. I am as bald as you are furry. I just started chemo for my cancer and walking tires me, so I sat down on this bench to catch my breath. I had no idea how chilly the air would be today."

"Sorry to hear about your cancer," said Bobby. He meant it. His grandmother had gone through cancer treatment the year before.

"Thank you," said the woman. "When I saw you on the bench I thought I would borrow you to warm my bare skin. You were just what I needed!"

She asked, "Would you mind warming my neck for a few minutes? I don't want to be a bother."

Barry was touched. The woman welcomed his fur to keep her warm.

"It's no bother," he said as he slithered up her arm, gently wrapped himself around her cold neck then dangled down her front.

"Thank you," she said as she petted his fur. "Having you around my neck is like a gentle hug! So many people avoid hugging me since I got cancer. I really needed a hug."

A few minutes later, they parted ways but agreed to meet again later that week. It was an *odd couple* sort of friendship that had started under unusual circumstances, but one they both hoped to continue.

Bobby thought, "I guess I am good for something. I never liked my fur, but it was just what that woman needed. And her kindness and acceptance was just what I needed after a hard day at school. Maybe I should try harder to accept myself as I am."

Life is a little like that. Lives are touched and needs are met, sometimes in the most unexpected ways.

THE BOTTOM LINE: Everyone Is Good for Something!

Food for Thought Questions:

- What do you least like about your appearance? _____

- Think about a time you got teased. How did you react? _____

- For the woman, what was special about Bobby? _____

- For Bobby, what was special about the woman? _____

- Describe a time you reached out to someone and made a new friend._____

Story 16: Unconditional Love

Purpose(s) and Goal(s): ☒ Psychoeducation for caregivers, children and teens about unconditional love. ☒ Treatment Intervention: to be used with caregivers, children or adolescents in family or individual therapy to discuss self-appraisal and not trying to change who you are.

Some caregivers have trouble loving and accepting children the way they are. The caregiver wants to change the child in terms of mood, sexual identity, religious belief, or behavior. The caregiver withholds love and affection when the child does not match the caregiver's expectations and the child becomes acutely aware of being "not good enough." Conditional love is damaging to a child's self-concept. It is one thing to disapprove of behavior, and it is another thing to reject or judge the child as *wrong or bad.*

The Bulldog's Dilemma

The chubby Bulldog looked pretty silly; in fact, you probably would have laughed to see him sitting there on the doggie bed. His normally coarse straight hair was curly, the result of a recent perm, and there was a pink bow stuck to the top of his head. He was dressed in a doggie tutu. He had a bulldog scowl on his face and he was slobbering all over himself. It was a ridiculous combination!

Brandon was attending his last class of doggie finishing school, where dogs go to learn manners, how to walk gracefully, and how to do cute tricks. Brandon Bulldog had *failed* the class. He was a bulldog among poodles, and no matter how hard he tried, he would never be as cute, graceful or mannerly as a poodle.

His owner came to pick him up, and the teacher said, "I'm sorry, but Brandon has failed the class. He did his best, but he is simply not cut out to be graceful or cute."

Brandon hung his head and got in his crate for the ride home.

Four years ago, his owner had come to the animal shelter. She asked for a poodle, but the shelter did not have any poodles. The shelter did have a bulldog named Brandon, however, whose owner had died, and Brandon wanted to be part of a loving family more than anything else in the world.

"I'll do whatever you want if you take me home," he said. "I'm not a poodle but I'll try my best to be good and obey. I'll sit at your feet, sleep by your side, take you on a walk every day, and play fetch in the yard."

"Well," said the lady, "I guess you can't help it that you're not a poodle. I really wanted a poodle, but I guess I'll settle for a bulldog."

With that, the lady took him home. Brandon tried hard to be a good dog. But the woman still dreamed of having a poodle. She fussed over Brandon, kept his hair curled, and dressed him in cute little outfits. She got upset when he drooled on the furniture. She frowned when Brandon slobbered his water all over the floor, but that is what bulldogs do, after all. And when he finished drinking he shook his jowls and water sprayed everywhere. It was a bulldog way of wiping his mouth. Brandon's owner got the idea of finishing school from a friend whose poodle had attended the classes. But Brandon had failed.

Brandon thought, "I am a finishing school failure. I try hard to be a good dog and please my owner, and if I could turn myself into a poodle I would. In her eyes, I am probably never going to be good enough." Brandon, his tail between his legs, was discouraged.

Two weeks later, Brandon and his owner went to the vet. In the waiting area was a woman with two bull-dogs. They were both slobbering all over the place and looked quite happy. Their owner was talking to them and smiling at them.

The other woman reached down to pet Brandon and exclaimed, "You poor thing! Such a beautiful bulldog and all dolled up like a silly poodle! Why on earth would anyone do that to you?"

She spoke to Brandon owner. "There is a bulldog club that you and your dog could join if you want to sign up. The dogs hang out and have a lot of fun."

Brandon owner said, "It might be fun for Brandon to play with other bulldogs. Why don't you give me the information?"

"OK," said the other woman. "But just one thing—he can't come looking like that. He needs to look like a bulldog, not like a silly poodle."

The owner said, "What's wrong with poodles?"

"There's nothing wrong with poodles," replied the other woman, "but bulldogs have such delightful character and personality. They are loyal, adorable and playful and try very hard to please their owners. Poodles are a little fussy and high strung; they need extra grooming and can be temperamental. In my mind, bulldogs are the *best type of dog.*"

"Hmmm," said the owner. "I hadn't looked at it that way, and Brandon *is* a good, loyal dog. I just always wanted a poodle."

Brandon heard the other woman talking and thought, "I *am* playful and loyal. I'm just not what my owner wanted or expected. But I was born a bulldog and I can't be anything else. I thought I had to change myself, but maybe it's my owner that needs a change of heart."

Hopefully Brandon's owner would come to accept him the way he was. After all, conditional love is almost worse than no love at all.

THE BOTTOM LINE: Accept and Affirm Who You Are.

Food for Thought Questions:

- How are you like Brandon? _____
  _____

- Who in your life gave you the idea that you are not good enough? _____
  _____

- Describe a time you changed something about yourself to please someone else. _____
  _____
  _____

- Make a list of things you don't like about yourself because you judge they are not "good enough."_____
  _____
  _____

- Make a list of things you really like about yourself, whether or not anyone else likes them. Share the list with a caregiver. _____
  _____
  _____

Notes

1 From *Family-Focused Trauma Intervention: Using Metaphor and Play with Victims of Abuse and Neglect*, by P. Pernicano, 2010, Lanham, MD: Jason Aronson. Reprinted and adapted with permission.
2 From *Metaphorical Stories for Child Therapy: Of Magic and Miracles*, by P. Pernicano, 2010, Lanham, MD: Jason Aronson. Reprinted and adapted with permission.
3 From *Family-Focused Trauma Intervention: Using Metaphor and Play with Victims of Abuse and Neglect*, by P. Pernicano, 2010, Lanham, MD: Jason Aronson. Reprinted and adapted with permission.

TRAUMA NARRATIVE WORK

Story 17: Pre-Verbal Trauma Narrative

Purpose(s) and Goal(s): ☒ Psychoeducation about how trauma leads to emotional and sensory arousal; educate caregivers about the lasting nature of pre-verbal trauma. ☒ Treatment Intervention: to reduce arousal and symptoms related to pre-verbal trauma (dreams, anxiety to cues, regression and helplessness, fearfulness). The story and interventions can be used with preschool and school-age children but also with older clients who have little memory of early trauma. The body can be calmed without cognitive awareness of what actually happened.

When abuse happens before you can talk, it makes it *very* hard to remember and talk about what happened to you. And sometimes you can't remember your abuse later; you might have pictures or dreams, but not the whole memory. You can develop fears of things without knowing why. You might have bad dreams and wonder if they are true. You might have funny feelings in your body or avoid people or places without knowing why. The Little Butterfly stories were written for a little girl that witnessed her mother's murder before she was old enough to talk.

Little Butterfly and the Bad Thing

Little Butterfly looked sad. Her head and wings hung down. Her colors had faded. Her eyes had no sparkle.

Do you want to know why she was so sad?

Little Butterfly had seen a *scary bad thing* happen to her mother. After that *bad thing,* her mother went away. Someone told Little Butterfly her mother would never come back. That is why Little Butterfly was so sad.

Little Butterfly sometimes dreamed about the *bad thing.* She could not remember the dreams after she woke up. Little Butterfly knew there were loud angry voices, and maybe even a gun and blood, but she was not sure.

Everyone thought Little Butterfly would get over the *bad thing* as time passed. But ignoring bad memories won't make them go away.

It helps to talk about a *bad thing.* But Little Butterfly did not have the words to do that. The *bad thing* happened before she could talk.

"Hi, Little Butterfly!"

It was Little Butterfly's best friend.

Her friend said, "Little Butterfly, you look sad. Come fly with me."

Little Butterfly said, "I can't fly with you," she said. "Remember, my wings don't work."

It was true. Little Butterfly had stopped using her wings after the *bad thing*. Now her wings were too weak to fly.

"Even if my wings worked, I'm too tired to fly," Little Butterfly said.

"Why are you so tired?" asked her friend.

Little Butterfly hung her head. "I have bad dreams about the *bad thing*. They wake me up at night, and then I'm tired and grumpy."

Little Butterfly's friend said, "It is hard to get a *bad thing* out of your dreams. Let's go to the Helper."

"Climb on my back," said her friend. Together, they flew to see the Helper.

The Helper's name was Samantha Spider. She was a friendly spider.

"How can I help you?" asked Samantha.

The friend asked, "Samantha, don't you have a special web where young children and little butterflies can stick their bad memories—the ones without words that give them bad dreams?"

"Why yes," said Samantha. She showed them a large purple web.

"Very young children and little butterflies don't have the words to talk about their memories. So we draw them. Then I wrap them up tight in spider silk. Once they are wrapped up, we stick them on the web."

The huge purple web had lots of bundles stuck on it, but there was room for more.

"I've never seen such a big web!" exclaimed the friend.

"Yes," said Samantha sadly. "Lots of little children and butterflies get hurt before they can talk. I needed a big web to hold their pain and sadness. And if this web ever gets full, I can make another."

"How does it help to stick *bad* memories on the web?" asked Little Butterfly.

Samantha replied, "It keeps them out of your dreams and you will sleep better at night."

"Do you want to try this?" Samantha asked Little Butterfly.

Little Butterfly agreed to try it.

Samantha and the friend helped Little Butterfly make a list of the scary things that came into her dreams. Of course, they did the writing, because Little Butterfly did not know how to read or write.

I'm not sure what your list would be, but here is Little Butterfly's:

Door pounding

Mother crying

Little Butterfly afraid

Torn wings

Man's loud voice and mean face

Gun

Mother hurt

Blood

Ambulance

They helped Little Butterfly draw pictures of the scary things from her dreams, one at a time. When she started shaking, her friend gently touched her shoulder.

Samantha said, "Take a deep breath. It's OK. We're here with you and you are safe."

Samantha spider wrapped each picture up tightly in spider silk. Little Butterfly stuck each bundle on the huge purple web. Little Butterfly sighed in relief when she was done.

"That's good," said Samantha. "Leave the *bad things* there."

Little Butterfly's friend flew her back to her Grandma's house. She was very tired from drawing and needed to take a nap. Drawing *bad things* can really tire you out! It is good to rest after you do this.

Little Butterfly fell into a deep sleep, without scary dreams.

It was a good start. When you are healing from a *bad thing* you do it one step at a time.

THE BOTTOM LINE: Wrap Up the *Bad Things*.

Food for Thought Questions:

- How are you like Little Butterfly? _____
  _____

- If you have bad dreams, what are they about? _____
  _____

- If you have flashbacks, list them here:_____
  _____

- Even though you don't remember it in your mind, how old do you think you were when you were first hurt or witnessed someone getting hurt? _____
  _____

- What memories do you want to stick on a big purple web? _____
  _____
  _____

- With your therapist, make a big purple web._____
  _____

Therapist Treatment Interventions for *The Bad Thing*

- See what the story elicits in the child or teen.
- Play Little Butterfly with puppets or sand tray.
- Use a dry erase board to write down the *bad things* from the child's dreams or memories. The child can talk and the therapist writes. Take a photo.
- Practice deep breathing while you and the child erase the list. Remind the child that dreams, and the memories on the list, seem very real but they can't hurt the child now.
- Take a relaxation break: blow bubbles for a few minutes and rock in rocking chair.
- Draw pictures of bad things from child's dreams, one at a time.
- Cut out magazine pictures that represent trauma.
- Stuff the pictures inside small toilet-paper tubes.
- Wrap up each tube in gauze or Duct Tape to make cocoon-like packages. Let the child stomp on them.
- Let the child stick each package on the purple web using the Velcro. Name each package. "No more X—it's all wrapped up."
- Draw or glue a big spider on the web to watch over it. Leave this web at the therapist's office.
- After all the packages are stuck on the web, ask the child to lie down on the floor and blow bubbles over the child's head. As the child pops each bubble, say, "No more X. All gone." Mention each thing the child put on the web. If the child's memories are not clear, use the words "bad thing."
- Remind the child that if bad things come into the child's dreams, he or she can tell the caregiver about them. They can draw them together and wrap them up. Then the caregiver can put them away until the next session.

Story 18: Sibling Trauma Narrative (Shared Abuse)

Purpose(s) and Goal(s): ☒ Psychoeducation for siblings about the impact of shared abuse. ☒ Treatment Intervention: to be used in individual, group, or family treatment with children and adolescents. This story is particularly helpful in TF-CBT and when doing a shared trauma narrative with siblings, to help them deal with their shared trauma. Helps prevent or address the conflict that can arise out of blaming behavior.

Sometimes abuse happens at a relative's or neighbor's home. Kids might even see brothers, sisters, or friends getting abused. Sometimes kids hear what is going on but are too afraid to tell someone. Later they might feel guilty or start blaming each other; they might even be mad at one another. They are trying to figure out why the abuse happened. This story suggests that if abused kids stick together, they can help each other get over it. This story helped two brothers *stick together* to talk about their abuse and stop fighting and blaming each other.

Stick Together[2]

The iguana brothers lay side by side in the hot sun. There were palm trees and a swimming pool. It was a beautiful place to rest—an oasis in the middle of the desert.

Iggy had a white bandage covering his right foot. Stubby had a white bandage covering his left foot. Both had cactus quills stuck in their backs. They were taking turns biting cactus spines out of each other's backs.

"Ouch!" cried Iggy. "Hey, that hurt!" complained Stubby.

They had survived a very tough time. As you got closer, you could hear them talking. Iggy said to Stubby, "I'll never forget that rattlesnake we came across two nights ago in the desert. He shook those rattles and struck before we could even move. I saw his mouth open, and I saw those huge fangs ready to strike. I knew I was a goner!"

Stubby said, "Yeah, I was sure he was going to get us, so I backed away as fast as I could. But you backed away at the same time, so we bumped into each other. I wish we had seen what was coming!"

"Yup," said Iggy. "What was coming was that huge cactus. After we bumped into each other, we both fell hard on top of it. That hurt like you-know-what!"

Stubby added, "It didn't hurt as much as the scorpions! Who would have known they would be taking a nap behind the cactus!"

For the next week, all the brothers could think about or talk about was their near-death experience in the desert. They dreamed about it every night. During the day, when either of them heard a noise like a rattle, they jumped in the air and yelled in fear.

Iggy and Stubby didn't feel safe. Even though there were no rattlesnakes or scorpions in the oasis, so they couldn't enjoy the peaceful surroundings.

The oasis had palm trees with coconuts, fruit trees with apricots, and cool water to drink. There was shade from the hot sun. There were other animals to hang out with, like camels and donkeys. Everyone else at the oasis was having a good old time, but not them. All Iggy and Stubby could do was scurry around and talk about rattlesnakes, the cactus, and scorpions. They took turns guarding the oasis, to be sure that no rattlesnakes or scorpions tried to enter.

One night when Iggy had a nightmare and couldn't sleep, he nudged Stubby awake. He said, "I keep thinking about *why* this bad luck happened to us and what we could have done to prevent it. There must be a reason." He slowly scratched his bony chin with one clawed foot.

"Actually, Stubby, I think it's your fault. If I hadn't been with you, I would have been fine that night. I just know it!"

Stubby replied, "No, you're wrong. My life was fine until that night in the desert. If you hadn't invited me to take a walk, it would still be fine. It's your fault I was walking in the desert!"

Iggy retorted, "You're the oldest—you're supposed to be on the lookout for danger and keep us safe!"

Stubby hollered back, "Well, if you had been looking closer, you might have seen the rattlesnake and warned us. Your eyesight is better than mine. So it's really your fault we fell on the cactus."

Iggy replied in a nasty voice, "If you hadn't been talking so much, I would have seen the cactus and moved away from it. Then we wouldn't be picking out cactus spines."

Stubby retorted in an angry voice, "Well, you might take a little of the blame yourself. When you landed on the cactus you startled me so much with your yell that I jumped up in the air. I came down right on top of that scorpion. It's your fault I got stung!"

By now, they were both scowling and shouting, and they turned away from each other with a "HMMPHH!".

There they were—two iguanas at a beautiful oasis—each one trying to blame the other for the troubles they had shared.

An older iguana had heard them arguing. He approached, then asked, "Do you mind if I make a comment?"

They said it was OK, but they were scowling at one another, and they didn't want to listen if it meant they had to quit fighting. The old iguana spoke, and ignored their scowling faces.

"As I see it, you were at the wrong place at the wrong time. No one is at fault. There wasn't anything either of you could have done to avoid the scorpions, snake, or cactus. Bad things happen to good people. Stuff happens."

"That can't be true," said the iguanas. "There has to be a reason for everything."

The older iguana replied, "What happened to you couldn't be helped, but how you get through it is up to you. I suggest you stick together. You are supposed to be playing on the same team—if you stick together, you can win. Hard times come and hard times go, but it takes an ally to beat the past. By the way, this oasis is a nice place to rest, relax and get over hard times if you can stop blaming each other."

He added, "If you want to blame anyone, blame the snake and the scorpion. They are mean and will strike out at anyone that gets too close."

Stubby and Iggy decided to stick together. They realized that it was not their fault they got hurt. It was true that the snake and the scorpion would attack anyone that got too close.

Stubby and Iggy also decided to advertise about the dangers in the desert. They joined protests against child abuse, made warning posters, and told their oasis friends about what had happened to them. They didn't want anyone else to get hurt. They wanted to keep the oasis safe.

"You know," said Iggy to Stubby one night as he lay by the cool oasis pool and sipped coconut milk. "I couldn't really enjoy the oasis until I got over what happened in the desert." There was a long pause as the brothers' eyes met.

"And stopped blaming you," Iggy added.

"Yah, bro" replied Stubby, giving Iggy a high five.

"Here's to teamwork," Stubby said.

"Cheers," said Iggy.

THE BOTTOM LINE: Stick Together!

Food for Thought Questions:

- What was your desert (scary place) and what dangers did you face there? _____
  _____
  _____

- What is your oasis (safe place)? _____
  _____

- What things or people do you need or want in your oasis to feel safe and happy?
  _____
  _____

- How can you keep the desert dangers outside the oasis? _____
  _____
  _____

- Pretend you are a transformer. There is always a before and after transformer. The before version is you as a victim in the desert. The after is you as a survivor in the oasis. Draw a picture of this transformation. Tell someone how you would transform to enjoy the oasis and get over the abuse. You can include helpers or objects because it is your story.

Notes

1 See Stories 4 (*Hidey Hole*) and 6 (*Bear of a Different Color*) for further examples.
2 From *Family-Focused Trauma Intervention: Using Metaphor and Play with Victims of Abuse and Neglect,* by P. Pernicano, 2010, Lanham, MD: Jason Aronson. Reprinted and adapted with permission.

CHAPTER 8

IN VIVO EXPOSURE

Story 19: Coping with Phobic Anxiety

Purpose(s) and Goal(s): ⊠ Psychoeducation for children and teens about the irrationality and time consuming process of using avoidance. ⊠ Treatment Intervention: to be used with children or adolescents who are phobic, fearful, or anxious following trauma intervention. The story can be used with guided imagery for *in vivo* exposure and practice in order to reduce avoidance.

Thoughts and feelings are very closely connected. Negative thoughts can lead to negative feelings, and negative feelings can cause you to *freak out*. It is important to face and conquer your fears. Action is the best thing to help you conquer your fears. The eagle in this story is afraid to fly, but in the end he conquers his fear. The story might give you some ideas of how to conquer your fears.

The Grounded Eagle[1]

You might wonder why a young, handsome eagle named Joe had just walked into a department store in Louisville, Kentucky and asked the stork-keeper to show him some size eight tennis shoes. The stork-keeper certainly wondered the same thing. In case you did not know it, a stork-keeper is a stork (type of bird) that sells things in a department store.

Joe the eagle had a white head and beautiful long wings full of shiny dark feathers. He had a nice, confident strut, and his feathers rippled as he walked.

"Excuse me," said the stork-keeper to the eagle, "I hope you don't mind my asking—but why is a nice, young eagle like you shopping for tennis shoes? Eagles don't need tennis shoes."

"Well," answered Joe, "I'm getting ready to walk to Tennessee, and I need some really good tennis shoes to protect my feet."

The stork-keeper asked, "You're going to WALK to Tennessee? That makes no sense at all! Everyone knows that eagles fly." He added, "I know it's none of my business, but is there something wrong with your wings?"

Joe looked a little sheepish (that means he was slightly embarrassed). He stared down at the floor and replied, "No, my wings are fine. I'm just afraid to fly. There are too many dangers. Walking will take a little longer, but at least I'll be safe."

The stork-keeper was surprised—he didn't know an eagle could be afraid of flying. After all, flying is an eagle's nature; his beautiful, strong wings can carry him very long distances. An eagle is born to fly!

The stork-keeper asked, "So what are you afraid of?"

Joe had a whole list of worries.

"I could fly into a tree in the fog or collide with an airplane. I could get struck by lightning or get caught in a thunderstorm. A hunter could shoot me or a tornado might blow me away. I could catch a cold up in the clouds and get pneumonia. A bigger eagle might attack me. I might fly in the wrong direction, get lost and end up in Pennsylvania instead of Tennessee!"

Joe opened his beak to continue, but the stork-keeper stopped him and said, "You're right. There are many dangers up in the sky."

Joe was surprised. Grownups usually tried to tell him everything would be OK or that he would be safe—they sort of lied to him, to try to make him feel better. It didn't really help, because Joe knew that there were dangers up in the skies. And it didn't help that the news on the radio and TV talked about so many bad things.

The stork-keeper continued, "Yes, there are dangers. But worrying *too much* keeps you from living your life."

The young eagle protested, "The world is dangerous, especially up in the sky!"

The stork-keeper replied, "There are dangers on the ground as well as in the sky—there are wild animals in the woods and humans driving cars on the roads. You can't avoid all danger."

Joe protested again. "All I can think about lately is getting sick or hurt while flying."

The stork-keeper replied, "No one wants to get sick or hurt. Yet eagles are born to fly. You need to get back in the sky as soon as possible. If you sit around worrying about all the things that could go wrong, you'll never get up there."

The stork-keeper scratched his head then asked, "Are there any good things about flying?"

Joe thought for a minute and replied, "There are some good things about flying. When I use my wings and soar, I feel free and strong. When I fly high, I can see for miles. I can see storms coming and take cover before they hit."

"Exactly," said the stork-keeper. "Those are all good things about flying."

Joe thought about what the stork-keeper had said. He knew he was born to fly. He didn't like walking, and it hurt his feet. It took too long to get places, and he couldn't see ahead to where he was going. He also was having trouble finding tennis shoes that fit an eagle's feet; for some reason, his claws kept getting in the way.

Joe thanked the stork-keeper for his help said, "OK, I'm not going to buy tennis shoes. I'm going to be brave and fly to Tennessee."

He asked the stork-keeper, "Would you come watch me get back in the sky?" Joe wanted some encouragement. He knew there was a chance he would "eagle-out" (that's eagle for "chicken out") right before he took off.

"Sure, Joe," said the stork-keeper, "I get off work at 4pm. I'd be happy to watch you take off."

"Good," said Joe. "Then I really think I can do it. I'll meet you at 4pm right behind the store. Thanks!"

At 4 o'clock, the stork-keeper and Joe met behind the store.

"Take a minute to relax," suggested the stork-keeper. "Close your eyes and pretend you are doing a perfect take-off."

Joe closed his eyes and imagined himself doing just that. In his imagination, he could see his big wings spreading and could feel the wind lifting him up into the blue sky. He could see it clearly, every step of his success. It was almost the real thing.

Then Joe opened his eyes and took a deep breath. The stork-keeper gave him a "thumbs up" (with his big claw, of course, since he didn't have a thumb). Joe leaped into the air and spread his beautiful wings. His wings were made to fly—they caught the air, and lifted him up. Joe looked both ways as he took off, so he didn't fly into anyone or anything. As Joe flew higher and higher, he felt strong and free. Joe was meant to fly, and Tennessee was just a short flight away.

THE BOTTOM LINE: Let Yourself Soar Like an Eagle!

Food for Thought Questions:

- How are you like Joe the Eagle? _____
_____
_____

- What three things are you most afraid of? Put these things in order of most afraid to least afraid._____
_____
_____

- Close your eyes and picture yourself doing something that you are afraid of. Do it from start to finish. If you get nervous, take a deep breath and keep going. After all, you are only imagining it, so it can't really hurt you.

- What did you see yourself doing? _____
_____

- How did you feel when you successfully did that thing? _____
_____

- Pick one thing that you are afraid of doing. Plan to do it this week. What did you pick and what is your plan?_____
_____
_____

- It helps to practice things that make us nervous. When will you practice? _____
_____

Note

1 From *Metaphorical Stories for Child Therapy: Of Magic and Miracles,* by P. Pernicano, 2010, Lanham, MD: Jason Aronson. Reprinted and adapted with permission.

CHAPTER 9

CONJOINT PARENT–CHILD WORK AND ATTACHMENT ISSUES

Story 20: Attachment Work for Pre-Verbal Trauma

Purpose(s) and Goal(s): ☒ Psychoeducation about how trauma leads to changes in child functioning; educate caregivers about the impact of pre-verbal trauma. ☒ Treatment Intervention: interpersonal activities for caregiver and child, to provide comfort during period of acute trauma. The story explains regression in the child and allows child to be *in charge of* the restorative process. The story and interventions can be used with preschool and school-age children but also with older clients that have little memory of early trauma.

Preschool children often regress behaviorally and emotionally in the face of trauma. A traumatic experience activates the attachment behavioral system and may lead to an increase in clingy, immature, or dependent behavior. By increasing proximity and responding to the child's need for comfort, a caregiver can help the child reduce fear and arousal.

The New Cocoon

I'm sure you remember Little Butterfly. She saw a very *bad thing* happen to her mother. Her friend took her to see a Helper, Samantha Spider, so she could stop dreaming about the *bad thing*.

Samantha Spider wrapped up some of Little Butterfly's *bad* memories. They stuck them on a big purple web. Little Butterfly stopped having so many bad dreams. But Little Butterfly's *wings still did not work*.

And that was not all. Little Butterfly wet her pants. She wanted to use her pacifier. She did not want to sleep by herself. She did not want to go to day care without her Grandma.

Little Butterfly's Grandma wanted to help her with her problems but did not know how. Grandma and Little Butterfly went back to see Samantha Spider.

"Samantha," said Grandma, "I love Little Butterfly. When she came to live with me I thought love and time would be enough. But love and time are not enough. The *bad thing* is bigger than both of us. Little Butterfly still can't use her wings. And she is having some other problems, too. Can you help her?"

Samantha replied, "Little Butterfly's wings are weak from not using them in a long time. If you give her special care, her wings will heal."

"What special care?" Grandma asked.

Samantha Spider said, "You wrap her in love. You spin a new cocoon around her and carry Little Butterfly until her wings are strong and healthy again."

She handed Grandma a baby sling.

"You can carry her in this, close to your heart. It is a little like starting her life over. She will tell you when she is strong enough to come out of the cocoon and use her wings."

"What about her other problems?" asked Grandma.

"She is full of fear," said Samantha. "If you carry her close to your heart, she will start to feel safe again. Then, those other problems will get better."

Samantha added, "You will need to talk to her while she is in the cocoon—tell her you love her and that she is safe. Talk about happy memories, sunshine, and flowers, and all the things you'll do together when she comes out of the cocoon."

Grandma spun a new green cocoon around Little Butterfly, using special silk made out of love. The cocoon let Little Butterfly breathe and there was sweet nectar inside.

"How does that feel?" she asked Little Butterfly.

"I feel safe and warm," replied Little Butterfly.

"Good," said Grandma.

Grandma put the cocoon in the sling. She carried Little Butterfly around night and day.

Grandma talked to Little Butterfly every day.

"I love you!" she said. "Do you have enough sweet nectar? Are you ready to come out and fly?"

Each day Little Butterfly said she was not quite ready. She liked being inside her new cocoon, close to Grandma's heart.

She felt her Grandma's love and it helped her heal from the *bad thing*.

Then one day, Little Butterfly answered, "Yes, I'm ready to break out of my cocoon. Don't help me—it will make my wings stronger to do it myself."

Little Butterfly worked her way out of the cocoon. She pushed and tugged with her head and wings—first a small hole, then a larger hole. It was hard work. Finally, Little Butterfly was out of the cocoon.

"Hurray," she shouted. "I did it!"

She was the same butterfly but different. Her eyes were clear; the fear was gone. Her brightly colored wings were strong.

"I'm proud of you Little Butterfly," said Grandma. "Now show me how you use your wings."

Little Butterfly spread her wings and began to fly. Grandma and Little Butterfly flew to tell Samantha the good news.

No one should go through such a *bad thing*. But when a *bad thing* happens, with time, love, a good friend, a kind Helper, and hard work, you can heal. Just like Little Butterfly.

THE BOTTOM LINE: Heal from the Inside Out.

Food for Thought Questions:

- Who can hold you when you feel small and alone?_____
  _____

- Why was it important for Little Butterfly to push her way out of the cocoon on her own, without help?_____
  _____

- How will you know when you are ready to come out of your cocoon?_____
  _____

- What can you do to make your wings stronger?_____
  _____
  _____

Therapist Treatment Interventions for *The New Cocoon*

- Look at nature pictures of real butterflies coming out of cocoons.
- Talk about how butterflies need to work their way out without help, so that they make their wings strong.
- Read and play out the story.
- Put play characters inside cocoons (wrapped fabric or wet toilet paper that later dries) and talk to them while they are inside.
- Ask the characters to tell you what they need to be stronger.
- Ask the characters what scares them and what helps them feel safe.
- Let the characters break out of their cocoons.
- Provide a sleeping bag or comforter to be used as the child's cocoon. Let the child climb inside. Do not roll the child in any sort of tight wrap, as this can cut off his or her breathing. (Alternatively, we have used sofa cushions.)
- While the child is inside his or her cocoon, engage in a back and forth attuned interplay that parallels the book:
  - Have child's caregiver remain close or hold the child.
  - Ask the child what he or she needs to make his/her wings stronger.
  - Ask the child what he or she is afraid of, and what the caregiver can do to help the child feel safe.
  - Ask child to describe what it feels like in the cocoon.
  - Coach caregiver to offer nourishment and comfort, asking the child if he or she is ready to come out.
- Practice the child breaking out of the cocoon when the child is ready.
- Encourage the caregiver to welcome the child if it does not happen spontaneously.
- Plan a bedtime ritual that allows the child to feel safe and nurtured.
- Allow child to create sleeping environment at home that feels as safe as the cocoon. Have a child-size sleeping bag available at home. Guided imagery may include the caregiver placing the cocoon somewhere protected before the child goes to sleep each night.
- With toddlers, make a sling (triangle piece of fabric) or use a front-carrier baby sling so that the caregiver can carry the child for a period of time each day. If the child is too big to carry, the caregiver can rest the child in his or her lap.
- Create a positive reward system at home for the child to celebrate expressing feelings directly and to reward behaviors that show increased autonomy.

Story 21: Living in Out of Home Care

Purpose(s) and Goal(s): ☒ Psychoeducation for children and teens about going into out of home care. ☒ Treatment Intervention: to be used with children, adolescents, and caregivers to address the reactions children have to being in out of home care.

Sometimes kids can't go back home. This story was written for a forty-something man who grew up in foster care and had never forgiven his mother. He expressed anger about it but underneath the anger was a great deal of sadness, hurt, and feelings of abandonment. When kids can't live with their family, they need to have a home away from home where they can feel loved and safe. Kids who can't go home might live in a foster home, live with relatives, or get adopted. It happens because a parent has problems and is not able to take good care of their child at that point in time. Kids often have strong feelings about this, which is normal. They can feel mad, scared, or hurt. They need adults to help them talk about those feelings.

The Good Enough Elf[1]

Once upon a time a young, green elf named Emma was all alone in the world and ready to have her baby. Her life had been very hard. Growing up, her mother told her over and over, "You are good for nothing." Of course it was not true. But like most children, Emma believed what her mother said.

One morning Emma woke up and knew it was "her time"—the baby was ready to be born. A few hours later Emma held her new baby in her arms and said, "I love you, little elf. I want you to have a better life than I did!"

Caring for a baby was not easy, and Emma was tired all the time. The baby cried a lot, as newborns often do. Once he cried all night. Nothing Emma did helped.

"I'm a bad mother," Emma thought. This was not true—Emma was being the best mom she could.

The next week, Emma's landlord came for the overdue rent. She had used the last of her money to buy formula and diapers for the baby, which was the right thing for a mother to do.

"GET OUT!" said the landlord. Emma and her son spent the night on the street.

Emma thought, "My son deserves a better life than the one I can give him."

Emma packed a small diaper bag and wrapped her baby in a warm blanket. She walked with her baby in her arms to a cozy-looking house on a tree-lined lane. A nice Troll family with six children lived there—they always seemed so happy. After checking to see that no one was watching her, Emma went up to the front door.

"My little love," she said, "I'm sure the Troll family will take good care of you."

She laid him down on the doorstep and knocked loudly, then hid behind a tree.

"What a darling baby elf!" she heard. Then, "Where did you come from? Let's go in out of the cold!"

The Troll picked up the baby, and the door closed. Emma, with tears in her eyes, walked away.

The Troll family took good care of the little green elf. He grew up strong and healthy, and the Trolls loved him. But one night they talked in worried, hushed voices about their bills and how crowded the house was. They thought the little green elf wasn't listening.

But the little elf *was* listening, and that night, while everyone was sleeping, he ran away. He didn't want to be a burden.

He didn't know where he should go. "I wonder if I will ever find somewhere to belong," he sighed.

What he really wanted more than anything in the world was to find his green elf mother and live with her again. He didn't remember his mother or why she had left him. There must have been a reason. He thought, "Maybe I cried too much or ate too much. Maybe I didn't sleep enough." Of course, it had not been his fault that Emma Elf gave him up.

"Maybe," he thought, "if I found my mother I would finally be happy. I would know who I am and where I belong."

The little elf didn't know his mother lived only 20 miles away. He also didn't know that she lived with a mean elf that hated children and drank too much elf-beer. Emma wondered what had happened to the baby she had given up so long ago. She had never forgotten him. She hoped he had a good life.

The little elf curled up to sleep under a huge pine tree. Finally morning came, and the sun started to rise, filling the sky with beautiful colors. The little elf shivered in the cold as he woke up. He was glad to see the light of day.

He was thinking about what to do next when he heard a voice. "Little elf! What are you doing alone in the woods?"

It was a big red elf, ahead on the path. The little elf knew he should not talk to strangers. But he was also not supposed to be alone in the woods. The little elf asked, "Who are you?"

The red elf called out, "Don't worry—I won't hurt you. I am on my way to work." Then he said with surprise, "Little elf, I know you! You look just like your mother Emma!"

"How did you know my mother?" asked the little elf.

The red elf replied. "I remember when you were born. Your mother loved you very much. But she was young and did not have enough money for food or rent. She cared for you the best she could. When her landlord kicked her out, she left you with the Trolls. I thought you still lived with them."

"I lived with the Trolls for a long time. But their house grew crowded and I didn't want to be a burden. Now, I have nowhere to live. All because my mother left me," said the little green elf in an angry voice.

"Yes," said the red elf, "she left you—with the hope of a better life."

The little green elf said, with a tear in his eye, "Sometimes I think I hate her, because she left me."

The red elf replied, "I understand why you might feel angry."

"Yes," said the elf. "I am Mad with a capital M."

"So you are Mad with a capital M," replied the red elf.

"I wonder," said red elf, "if you also might be a little hurt or sad?"

"Maybe a little hurt and sad," said the little green elf. "It is hard to grow up without your mother."

"Yes," said his older friend. "It is hard to grow up without your mother—it is a great loss."

"Well," said the green elf, "even if I am hurt and sad, I will never forgive her. She didn't love me."

"I think you're wrong about that," replied the red elf. "Your mother loved you enough to give you a better life." The little green elf thought about what the red elf had said.

He said, "So maybe my mother loved me after all. I always wondered why she left me. Maybe someday I will find a way to forgive her."

The red elf said, "You are too small to be out here alone. I bet you are hungry and tired. Why don't you come home with me? I can give you a good meal and a warm bed. And if you want to stay, you are welcome."

The little green elf asked, "Why can't you take me to my mother? You are nice enough, but I have always wanted to be back with my mother."

The red elf replied sadly, "Your mother is not in a good place right now. She still has a hard life. Maybe someday you will see her again, but right now, that's not possible."

The little elf asked, "Why are you offering me a home? Green elves and red elves have had trouble getting along for years! What will your neighbors think?"

The red elf replied, "Your mother didn't care if I was red or green. She was my friend. And you are welcome in my home."

The little green elf decided to stay with the red elf, and they grew to care for one another. He sometimes dreamed of his mother and wished he could see her. Since that wasn't possible, living with the red elf was the next best thing.

THE BOTTOM LINE: Sometimes Loving Means Letting Go.

Food for Thought Questions:

- How are you like the Elf?_____

- What does it mean for someone to feel like a burden?_____
_____

- Most children have good and bad mixed feelings about their parents. After all, nobody is perfect. How does this apply to you?_____
_____

- Who could you turn to for love and support if your parent was going through a hard time and could not care for you?_____

Note

1 From *Family-Focused Trauma Intervention: Using Metaphor and Play with Victims of Abuse and Neglect,* by P. Pernicano, 2010, Lanham, MD: Jason Aronson. Reprinted and adapted with permission.

CHAPTER 10

ENSURING FUTURE SAFETY AND WELLBEING

Story 22: High-Risk Behaviors

Purpose(s) and Goal(s): ☒ Psychoeducation about risk-taking, self-destructive behaviors, weighing risks and benefits, controlling impulses. ☒ Treatment Intervention: self-control to reduce engaging in high-risk behaviors.

Some abused children and teens engage in high-risk behaviors such as fire setting, hurting animals, drug use (to numb or alter feelings), promiscuous sexual behavior, sexual behavior with a younger child, pornography, cutting (self-injury), or suicidal gestures. It can be very difficult for these young people to inhibit their urges and cravings. The story that follows can help kids start to talk about their compulsively driven or addictive behaviors.

The Moth and the Flame

The little moth scrunched up his face and said with a frown, "I *can't* wait. I have to do it. I have never seen anything so beautiful. I have to touch it—now. I can't stop myself. I have tried and tried to resist it. But I can't. If I can't touch it, I think I will go mad!"

He was speaking of the flame. The flame was inside a Coleman Lantern (propane lantern used for camping) on the patio table; it had the most intense, white light you had ever seen. There were two small lit mantles in the center. The light was hypnotic. It lured the small moth: it was calling out to him.

"Come, touch, you will find ultimate pleasure!"

Everyone had told the moth that touching the hot white light would destroy him. At that moment, he didn't care. He was drawn to the light, and willing to annihilate himself in order to find that ultimate pleasure.

As the moth watched the light glow in the dark night, his pulse raced. His heart pounded, his mouth watered, and he craved just one touch. He was sure that it would be worth it.

The moth flew from the porch railing and headed toward the light.

Just at that moment, another young moth reached the light.

"SPTPTTTTTT!" went the moth as it merged with the flame. Black charred wings fell to the bottom of the lantern. The moth had been burnt to a crisp.

The other young moth, watching, stopped his flight.

He was no longer sure that touching the light would be such a good thing. The heat he craved was a heat that destroyed. It was true, what they told him. In touching the light, he would destroy himself.

He would wait, for now. As hard as it was to resist the light, he did not want to self-destruct.

"I can wait," he said. "I want so badly to touch the light, but I can resist it. I can fly in a different direction. I may never find another thing that pulls me toward it with so much power and attraction, but it is not worth it if I destroy myself in the process."

He took his eyes off the light and flew sadly in the other direction. The risks were too great: one moment of pleasure was not worth total self-destruction.

THE BOTTOM LINE: A Moment of Pleasure is Sometimes Not Worth the Risk.

Food for Thought Questions:

- How are you like the moth that resisted the flame? _____
  _____

- How are you like the moth that gave in to the flame? _____
  _____

- Why should you weigh the risks and benefits of your possible choices? _____
  _____
  _____

- What do you want to do that is self-destructive? What draws you to that behavior or thing?___
  _____
  _____

- What are two good reasons why you should not do the self-destructive thing? _____
  _____

- When you are tempted to do the self-destructive thing, what are two other things you can do instead?_____
  _____

Story 23: Safety around Perpetrators

Purpose(s) and Goal(s): ☒ Psychoeducation for caregivers, children and adolescents about the need to identify risks and come up with a safety plan. ☒ Treatment Intervention: to be used in safety planning with children or adolescents and their caregivers when the environment or neighborhood presents ongoing risks.

Kids should not have to keep themselves safe. They need others, usually adults, to help them figure out what is safe and what is not safe. Young kids should be supervised at all times; adults should not assume that a neighbor, friend, or relative is safe to be around kids.

The Hungry Alligator and the Mean Snake[1]

"I'm in a bad mood," said the alligator to the snake.

"Me, too!" said the snake. "Let's go find someone to eat."

"Yeah," said the alligator. "I feel like eating someone. And if I don't find anyone good to eat, I'm going to bite someone with my big, sharp teeth."

"Yessss!" hissed the snake. "I'd love to strike someone with my big fangs."

The alligator and snake were in snappy, mean, sourpuss moods. The snake had almost been turned into a snakeskin purse the week before, and the alligator had almost become someone's expensive shoes. They had escaped in the nick of time.

The alligator and snake were very hungry. There was not much food to be had in the Florida swamp where they lived. Florida is a crowded place, full of alligators, snakes, and older retired people.

A group of friends walking through the swamp heard, "HSSSSSSS!" Slithering their way was a mean-looking green snake with a huge mouth and two big fangs sticking out of his mouth like a pair of buckteeth. With him was a nasty-looking bumpy-snouted, long-tailed alligator.

"Hello, neighborsssssssss," hissed the snake with a sly smile, when he was about 20 feet away.

Kanga Kangaroo called out to Madeleine Monkey and Mike Manatee, "I can't fit both of you inside my pouch. Quick, get behind me!"

Kanga and Madeleine lived at a nearby zoo, and their friend Mike lived in a small cove in Smyrna Beach. Kanga had a baby kangaroo in her pouch, which was why she had no room for Madeleine or Mike!

"Hello," said Kanga bravely to the snake and the alligator. "Don't come any closer," she said.

"Lunch," said the snake to the alligator in a quiet sneaky voice.

"Oh, goodie," said the alligator in a whisper, licking his chops as he moved closer.

"No," said Kanga. "Please move back. It's not nice to eat your neighbors."

"Oh, we're not going to eat you. We want to be friends. What would it hurt to hang out on this sunny afternoon? We promise to be nice. We promise not to hurt you."

Kanga didn't believe the alligator. Everyone knows that alligators have trouble keeping their promises. She had been smart to put her friends behind her and to ask the alligator and snake to move back. You can't let an alligator or a snake get too close. It is their nature to strike, even if they act nice, smile, and pretend to be your friend.

You would be very foolish indeed to let an alligator or snake give you a hug or kiss. If you let a boa constrictor curl up around you, he might squeeze the life out of you before you even realized what was happening. If you let an alligator give you a backrub, he could take a bite out of you from behind and you would never see it coming. And you would be even more foolish to accept an invitation to go swimming with them or to meet them for dinner. Probably, you would *be* the dinner if you accepted *that* invitation.

Kanga wanted her and her friends to be safe. She knew she had to think fast.

Kanga whispered to Mike and Madeleine, "They haven't eaten in a long time. They are going to eat *us* if we don't do something! Let's take them to the zoo—they can find some food there."

Kanga told the alligator and snake, "We would like you to be our guests for lunch at the zoo."

As I said before, snake and alligator were very hungry.

"OK," said snake and alligator. "We'll go with you to the zoo. But if we don't like the food there, we'll eat your friend the manatee."

That was a horrible thought. Manatees are large, gentle animals that move slowly. Mike had no protection against the hungry alligator and mean snake.

Madeleine, Mike, and Kanga led the way to the zoo. Luckily, it was the end of the day, and the zoo snack bars had lots of leftover food. Kanga and Madeleine dumped a big pile of food inside a large empty cage. There were five hamburgers, eight slushies, and three bags of popcorn. There were six hotdogs, three chicken nuggets, two ice cream bars, and seven snow cones.

"Here is your food," called out Kanga. "Come into the cage. This is the eating area for guests. You can eat to your hearts' content."

When the alligator and snake saw the food, they forgot everything else—they went into the cage and began eating.

Karla and Madeleine backed out of the cage and quickly locked the gate so no one could come in or out.

"Why did you lock the gate?" asked the alligator.

"We need to be safe," said Kanga. "You have big teeth and are stronger than we are; we can't defend ourselves. With you in our swamp, we won't be safe. Sooner or later you will get hungry again, and you might eat us."

The alligator and snake were very angry. "You tricked us!"

Kanga replied, "It is what it is. At least this way, you get to eat and we get to be safe."

The alligator and snake gave Kanga mean looks.

"You'll be sorry!" said the snake. "Alligators and snakes don't like being double-crossed!"

"You don't have to like it," said Kanga. "But you brought it on by your own actions."

The alligator and snake finished all the food in no time.

"We're still hungry!" shouted the snake and alligator.

Madeleine and Kanga used a sling-shot to fling more food into the cage. They did not want to get too close. They threw in ten bags of salted peanuts, two servings of nachos with peppers, ten cheeseburgers, and five ice cream cones.

The not-quite-as-hungry alligator and snake gobbled it all down. As the last cheeseburger and ice cream cone disappeared, you could hear two loud burps.

You may find this story helpful the next time you come across a hungry alligator or a mean snake. First, do whatever you need to do to stay safe. Then put them somewhere like a cage or zoo if you decide to feed them. But if they ask you to join them for dinner, you should politely decline. Alligators and snakes make very bad hosts—and you don't want to become the dinner!

THE BOTTOM LINE: Do What You Need to Do to Stay Safe!

Food for Thought Questions:

- Why should you not trust the alligator? _____
  _____
  _____

- Can alligators change? _____ If yes, what would it take for the alligator in this story to change? _____
  _____

- What would you need to do to be safe near an alligator? _____
  _____

- Has an *alligator-type* person ever persuaded you to trust him? _____

- What happened? _____
  _____

- Create a safety plan for being around an *alligator-type* person. _____
  _____
  _____

Story 24: Grooming Behavior

Purpose(s) and Goal(s): ☒ Psychoeducation for caregivers and children about grooming behavior in adults and unsafe situations in the community. ☒ Treatment Intervention: to be used with children or adolescents who were solicited to participate in child pornographic activities or other game-like abuse. Exploited children sometimes believe that they gave consent and cooperated in the activity and that it was their fault the abuse occurred. This story shows clearly the adult responsibility for exploitation and the harm that can result.

A young teen in foster care had been photographed by neighbors without her clothes. They plied her with drugs and alcohol, and the party-like atmosphere was hard to resist. This exploitation left her feeling ashamed and vulnerable. Caregivers need to be aware of children's whereabouts in the community and supervise them closely, especially after they have been abused. This story is about grooming behavior and exploiting children.

Party Games

Jordan Giraffe had been invited to his first birthday party, and he was very excited!

Casey Crocodile was celebrating his 12th birthday and had invited all the animals from his African village: Lion, Monkey, Crocodile, Gorilla, Snake, and Elephant. Jordan's mother said he could go as long as one of the other animals looked after him.

Jordan's mother was a little nervous that the Crocodiles were having the party at their house down by the river. She did not really trust that family. They had big teeth and sometimes ate other animals. But she thought, "I might as well let Jordan go. There will be many other animals there, and there is safety in numbers."

"Mom," asked Jordan, "What do the animals do at a birthday party?"

He wanted to know what to expect, of course.

His mom answered, "Jordan, a birthday party is fun. They have food like pizza, birthday cake, and ice cream. There will be African music with flutes and drums. The animals will dance and play games."

"That sounds like fun," said Jordan.

The day of the party, Elly picked Jordan up and told his mother she would watch over him and keep him safe. Together they walked down to the river. Jordan's birthday present for Casey was a long back-scratcher, since everyone knows crocodiles have trouble scratching their own backs.

Soon they arrived at the party, and it was just as Jordan's mother had described. There was music playing and lots of food for everyone. Mrs. Croc was in the water at the river's shoreline, and Mr. Croc was setting up the games.

Jordan stayed close to Elly. He did not like the looks of Casey's parents. They had big long snouts and huge sharp teeth. And he did not like the river. As you may know, Giraffes hardly ever go in deep water—their long necks make it very hard for them to swim.

Casey's father came over to the children and said, "Let's start the games. The first game is pin the tail on the monkey."

This was a new game for the animals. No one knew how to play it.

Mr. Crocodile said, "You wear a blindfold, I turn you around; then you take the monkey tail and try to pin it on that monkey over there on the tree. As you can see, that monkey does not have a tail. The animal that pins the tail closest to where it belongs wins a prize."

Mr. Croc pointed to what looked like a large furry, fake monkey hanging on a tree at the river's edge.

"Here is the monkey tail," said Mr. Croc as he held out a long furry thing hanging from an African dart. "Who wants to go first?" he asked.

"Don't hold back," he said when no one offered to go first. "This game is really fun!"

The animals didn't know what to say. It looked like Mr. Croc was holding a *real* monkey tail. But surely it wasn't real? After all, this was a game.

"Where did you get that?" asked Elly Elephant. "It looks real."

"It *is* real," said Mr. Croc. "It is part of my animal tail collection. When an animal has an unfortunate accident in the river, I try to save the tail. This tail belonged to a poor, unfortunate monkey that drowned. Don't be scared—it can't hurt you."

"I guess I can go first," said Jordan. To be honest, he wasn't sure he wanted to play the game at all. It didn't seem like much fun. But he didn't want to act like a baby in front of the other animals. They all knew it was his first birthday party, and he didn't want anyone to make fun of him.

Jordan took the monkey tail in his mouth, since all four of his legs were on the ground.

Freddy Frog, an African poison dart frog, called out, "Jordan, be careful of that dart. Mr. Croc put some of my poison on it the last time he went hunting."

It was true. The dart holding the monkey tail was an African poison dart.

"Thank you for warning me, Freddy," said Jordan. Then he asked Mr. Croc, "Are you sure this game is safe?"

"Don't be a baby," said Mr. Croc. "The poison on this dart is long gone. This game is harmless fun."

Jordan agreed to play. He did not think that Mr. Croc had any reason to lie to him. Mr. Croc put a blindfold on Jordan and spun him around. Then he moved him in the direction of the tree.

Jordan reached the tree, felt the furry monkey with his nose, and stuck the tail where he thought it should go.

"OK, Jordan," said Mr. Croc. "You can take off the blindfold and see where you stuck the tail."

Jordan saw that he had stuck the tail on the monkey's paw. He felt a little sick to his stomach. Not because the tail was on the paw—but because the thing hanging on the tree was a *real* monkey skin.

"Mr. Croc," said Jordan. "That's a real monkey skin. I don't want to play this game anymore."

Mr. Croc frowned. "Duh! Yes, it's a real monkey skin. This is Africa. Animals die every day. Why waste a perfectly good monkey skin? I went to a lot of trouble to make sure you would all have a good time. If you are going to ruin the party, you can go home to your mother."

Jordan didn't know what to think. But he did not want to ruin the party or go home yet.

He said, "Mr. Croc, I don't want to leave the party. Do you have another game we can play?"

The other animals gathered around Jordan. They were as shocked as Jordan by the turn of events but no one spoke up. They all agreed it was time to play a different game.

Mr. Croc had set up 12 logs in a circle.

"Have a seat," he said. "This is the best game of all."

"There are 12 seats—but there are 13 animals," said Ella.

"Yes," said Mr. Croc. "This game is called musical logs. There are only enough logs for 12 animals. I start the music, and we all dance and move around. When the music stops, you sit down on the nearest log. The one animal that does not get a log has to jump in the river. We take out one log each time we play. We keep playing until only one animal has a log. Everyone else will be in the river."

And so they started the game. The music played, a wild sound with drums and flutes. Everyone danced and sang along. Then the music stopped. The animals scrambled to get a log to sit on. The first one out was Mike Monkey. Into the river he went with a splash. Everyone laughed. Mr. Croc took out one log and started the music again.

Everyone was cheering and dancing and having a great time. Suddenly, Mike Monkey cried out.

"She's trying to eat me!" he cried. "Help! Help!"

It was true. While everyone was distracted by the game on shore, Mrs. Croc had swum up in the water behind Mike Monkey. You could hardly see her in the river. Only her eyeballs and the top of her tail were showing. As they watched, her big mouth opened. Soon Mike Monkey would be a *goner*.

"STOP!" shouted George Gorilla. Elly Elephant lumbered into the river and stood between Mrs. Croc and Mike. Jordan followed. Leon Lion pounced off the riverbank and landed on top of Mrs. Croc. For a moment, she was startled and took her eyes off Mike Monkey.

"Quick!" shouted Jordan to Mike. "Jump on my back and I'll carry you to safety." Mike Monkey jumped faster than you could blink an eye and Jordan carried him piggyback to shore.

"You should be ashamed of yourself!" Elly Elephant said to Mr. and Mrs. Croc. "This was no game. This was a sneaky no-good crocodile trick to get monkey meat for your dinner! And to think you would do such a thing to a group of innocent children! We are leaving and we will not be back."

Elly walked Jordan home and they told Jordan's mother about what had happened. She was outraged. "It is just as I thought—never trust a Croc family with big sharp teeth and narrow beady eyes!"

Then she gave Jordan a big hug and said, "It is awful to have someone trick you like that. It must have been very scary!"

Jordan said, "Yes. I hope I don't have bad dreams tonight about monkeys and crocodiles. And I don't ever want to go to another birthday party!"

His mother replied, "If you have a bad dream, I'll stay with you until you get back to sleep. But most birthday parties are fun, and true friends will never eat you."

That was true. A true friend will never eat you. And Jordan realized something else. If a game does not seem fun, the best thing you can do is leave quickly and find somewhere else to play.

THE BOTTOM LINE: Never Play Games with a Crocodile!

Food for Thought Questions:

- Name someone that would stick by you in a tricky situation: _____

- How are you like Jordan? _____

- If you were acting this story out, who would play Mr. and Mrs. Croc? _____
_____

- How can you tell when someone is trying to trick you? Give an example. _____
_____

- Why did Mr. Croc *really* invite the animals to the party? _____
_____

Story 25: Cross-Generational Blind Spots

Purpose(s) and Goal(s): ☒ Psychoeducation for caregivers and children about cross-generational trauma and risk. ☒ Treatment Intervention: to be used with children or adolescents and their caregivers when the caregiver experienced trauma at the hands of the same person who abused the child. The story is also helpful when a caregiver does not recognize that he or she is exposing children to risk by allowing them to be around a family member.

Grandma's Alligator is a helpful story to read with a family when the therapist suspects someone in the extended family may be exposing vulnerable children to dangerous family members or situations.

Grandma's Alligator

The Ostrich family had gone to Grandma's house for dinner. And unless Grandma made a tough decision, it would be the last dinner they had together at her house. They all really liked going to Grandma's house, except for the *pet alligator*. Grandma didn't seem to realize what a problem the alligator had become.

"What alligator?" you might ask.

Well, as far back as the family could remember, Grandma had a pet alligator that had free run of the house. She got it when it was a baby, just six inches long and as cute as it could be. It slept with her and played with the grandkids in the swimming pool out on the screened patio when they were little. But each year it got a little bigger and its teeth got a little sharper. Until now, no one really objected to having the alligator in the house. They had ignored it for the most part and tried to stay out of its path. Now, it was too big to ignore—a full-grown alligator.

Having an adult alligator around can be a bit dangerous; after all, an alligator with free run of the house can cause problems—it chews on furniture, it whips its tail around and knocks knick-knacks off the coffee table, and it costs a lot to feed it. And oh, yes, it eats the pets. Every time Grandma got a new dog or cat, the alligator would eat it when no one was looking.

The kids weren't able to really relax at Grandma's house. They had to keep their eyes open and watch out for the alligator. They never knew when it might try to eat their dog or bite one of the children. And they didn't want it to eat Grandma when they weren't there to protect her!

Sometimes the alligator still wanted to sleep with Grandma or one of the grandkids that was spending the night, but don't worry, Grandma made it sleep out on the screened patio. No one wanted to sleep with the alligator; and Grandma put a belt around its snout at night while they were sleeping, just in case.

The truth was that no one really wanted to have a full-grown alligator loose in Grandma's house.

The family decided that they had to tell Grandma how they felt about the alligator. Grandma was so used to having the alligator around that she didn't see the danger.

As the Ostrich family ate dinner together, Ozzie Ostrich pulled out a photo album. "Look Grandma," he said. "I put together a picture album of your pet alligator."

Ozzie had gone through all the family photos and found quite a few of the alligator, from when it was very little until now, when it was full grown.

Grandma smiled at Ozzie and took the album. She started thumbing through the pages and smiled.

"Ah, there he is the first day I brought him home from the Everglades. Cute little guy, isn't he? He had hardly any teeth then. Look how much he grew that first year! Oh look, there he is a little older—on a leash at the golf course. He was getting bigger and tried to eat a baby in a stroller; it's a good thing he was on that leash."

She paused at the next picture and looked sad. "That picture is right before the alligator ate our little dog and gave your Grandpa a heart attack. I really miss your Grandpa and my little dog! The alligator stayed on the leash after that."

"Grandma," said Ozzie, "Look at *this* picture. The alligator is not on a leash and I doubt a leash could even hold him."

It was a recent picture of the alligator off the leash in Grandma's living room. He was sitting in front of Grandma and you could see that he was six feet long. Grandma was only five feet three inches tall, so the alligator was bigger than her!

"Look how big he is!" said Grandma. "I have to admit that this picture makes him look mean and scary. But I know he won't hurt me. I sometimes do let him off the leash when I'm here alone with him—he knows I love and trust him."

"Love and trust have nothing to do with it Grandma," said Ozzie. "He isn't safe. I know you still see him as your cute little pet, but he is big, strong, and dangerous now. It is hard for you to see him as he really is. He should not be allowed to be around children, pets or you. We want you to take him to the zoo to live or back to the Everglades."

Ozzie put his head down and looked sad. "And if you don't take him to a safe place like the zoo or the Everglades, then Mom says we can't come visit you anymore. We aren't safe around the alligator."

Their mother was a good mother. She knew that her children should not be around a dangerous, full-grown alligator. Even though Grandma loved him, he could not be trusted around children—or pets, for that matter. When you love someone or something, it can be hard to see danger, even if it is right there before your very eyes. Grandma would have to make a choice to protect her grandchildren and keep them safe.

THE BOTTOM LINE: Sometimes It Is Hard to See What Is Right Before Your Very Eyes.

Food for Thought Questions:

- Why didn't Grandma see the danger? _____
  _____

- Why did Ozzie speak up? _____
  _____

- How can you tell when a harmless situation becomes dangerous? _____
  _____

- How do you tell someone you don't feel safe when that person acts like things are OK? _____
  _____
  _____

- How are you and your family like Ozzie and his family?_____
  _____

- What can a child do when a grownup ignores safety? _____
  _____

- Describe a time you did not speak up even though you felt unsafe. _____
  _____

- Who could you talk to if you felt unsafe? _____

Note

1 From *Family-Focused Trauma Intervention: Using Metaphor and Play with Victims of Abuse and Neglect*, by P. Pernicano, 2010, Lanham, MD: Jason Aronson. Reprinted and adapted with permission.

PART III

THERAPY STORIES TO USE WITH ADOLESCENTS

CHAPTER 11

PSYCHOEDUCATION

Story 26: Fight and Flight

Purpose(s) and Goal(s): ☒ Psychoeducation for caregivers, children, and teens about the concept of radical acceptance. ☒ Treatment Intervention: to be used with caregivers, children, or adolescents who are reacting to abuse through avoidance or angry defensiveness. The story personifies the abuse as a monster and allows the client to name what it is he or she is struggling with. The story is best used early in trauma work.

The story that follows is about a monster. The monster is another word for the abuse you went through—you might even call it the *abuse monster*. In the story, the wizard learns how to face his monster. *Radical acceptance* is a term that means facing and accepting what you can't change. It does not mean that you agree with what happened, but that you face it and let it go instead of fighting it or running away from it

The Monster Within[1]

The Master, a wise old wizard, spoke to the young wizard, "We all have monsters within us. Some are small and easy to ignore but others are strong, sneaky, and mean. They are born and grow strong from the hard times of our lives. Be mindful of the lies they will tell you, as they will try to convince you to let them out; if you let them out before you are ready, they will overpower and destroy you with blame, sadness, anger, and guilt. Never doubt their power to hurt. And never try to deal with your monsters alone. In time and with help, you will learn to cope with your monsters."

The young wizard loved learning spells and potions and he studied hard for his exams. He had started wizard training when he was five years old. He enjoyed wizard classes and attended faithfully.

Then there came a period of hard times for the young wizard and his family. Everyone goes through hard times, as you know, but these were very bad hard times—so awful that they were nearly unspeakable.

"Let us out," his monsters said from within. "We can help you get over your hard times. We can teach you many things: how to get revenge, how to hurt those that hurt you, and how to hide your true feelings. We know you better than anyone else. Don't listen to that old Master! He can't possibly understand what you have gone through! Why should you fear us? We are part of you!"

The Master noticed that the young wizard's attitude had changed as a result of the hard times. He was more irritable and withdrawn, and he stopped going to class. The Master was concerned that the monsters within might be lying to the young wizard and offered his help.

"Don't listen to him!" said the monsters. "You need to handle this on your own. It is the only way you will get over your hard times."

The young wizard replied that he was "fine" and declined the Master's help.

The monsters' voices grew louder inside his head. They called him a coward and told him he was weak. The young wizard did not like the way the monsters talked to him and mocked him. He wanted to put them in their place, but instead he tried to tune them out.

The monster voices grew louder—they kept daring him to let them out. They blamed him for his family's hard times.

"That old wizard doesn't know what he's talking about. If you let us out, we can give you great power. Your hard times will be over."

The young wizard had trouble ignoring their constant chatter. He was tempted by the talk of great power and started to question what he had been taught.

Then one day a friend came over to study magic with the young wizard.

The young wizard turned to a page in the magic book that was way beyond his training.

The title was, "Facing Your Monsters."

His friend warned, "You aren't old enough to face your monsters. And I'm not old enough to help you. Remember their power to hurt."

The monsters said, "Who is he to give you advice? You don't need any more advice! Go ahead. This is your chance. Show him what you can do."

Before he could change his mind, the young wizard drew his wand and started reading the words of the spell. He twisted his wand down and to the left.

An ugly, smelly, pimply-faced monster flew out of the tip of the young wizard's wand. It towered over the boy! People watched in horror as it snorted in his face. Yellow-green globs of mucus splattered on those close by.

The monster grinned and shouted, "Free at last!" The Monster sneered at the young wizard and said with disdain, "Foolish boy to ignore your Master's advice! You have used magic far beyond your ability. I will bring darkness to you and your kingdom."

The villagers of course screamed and ran off in all directions. A cold, stiff wind had crawled inside their bones. The time of peace as they had known it had passed.

"What is going on?" asked the Master as he stepped out of a low hanging cloud.

The young wizard hung his head. How many times had his teacher warned him?

The young wizard begged the Master to help him, saying, "Surely you can fix this?" You could hear the fear in his voice.

"No," said the Master, sadly. "Only you can fix this. The Monster is part of you. Until you figure out what you *must* do, darkness will follow you." With that he disappeared.

The young wizard did what anyone his age would do—he escaped. He ran for miles through the mountains and valleys, from one village to the next.

It was futile to run, which means it was no use. Wherever the young wizard went, the monster followed. "I am part of you!" he shouted. "You cannot escape me!"

It was true. As the Monster pursued the young wizard, dark clouds followed them and the monster's fiery breath destroyed everything in his path. The Monster grabbed villagers with his long spiked claws and tossed them like puppets into the sky.

"This is my fault!" cried the young wizard. He felt great guilt and shame.

The young wizard decided to lure the Monster away so that no one else would get hurt. He found a place to hide in a cave, deep in the hills. He knew that he could not hide for long, because the Monster would follow. As he waited for the Monster, he thought about what the Master had said.

"What is it I *must* do?" he asked.

An idea came to him.

"The Monster is part of me. I can't escape him and I can't hide from him. So I will destroy him, even if I die in the process. That is surely what I *must* do."

"Come fight me, Monster," shouted the young wizard as he left the cave.

The Monster was there, waiting for him.

The wizard's hands shook in fear as he drew his wand. It is a brave and terrifying thing to face your death before you are old and gray.

"Rrrrrrrrrrrrrrrrrr!" bellowed the Monster. It moved toward him. "I've been waiting for you!"

"Prepare to die!" declared the wizard. "You have brought terror to the entire kingdom. I will destroy you if it is the last thing I do!"

The wizard moved toward the Monster, ready to fight.

The Monster laughed, "You foolish boy! I am part of you. You can't destroy me."

"But I will try!" answered the boy who moved closer to the Monster.

Just then, the voice of the Master spoke clearly in his head.

"The Monster is part of you. You cannot hide from him and you cannot destroy him. Think. You know what you *must* do."

In that moment, the young wizard knew what he *must* do. He dropped his wand, opened his arms wide and rushed forward to meet the Monster. He howled loudly with all the fear, grief, remorse, and pain inside him. Their eyes met. Then the wizard wrapped his arms around the Monster in a fierce embrace.

Poof! went a puff of smoke as the monster disappeared back inside the wizard.

The Monster was gone, and darkness passed from the valley.

"Well done," said the Master as he stepped out of a low-lying cloud. "You learned the truth—something I could not teach you. We cannot hide from our monsters and we cannot kill them. They are part of us. You could only be whole again by facing and embracing your Monster."

I wish I could say the young wizard never again made mistakes . . . but I can't. At least his mistakes from that day on were small ones, however, with results no worse than turning a crystal ball into rubber and making deodorant that smelled like poop.

There are times in our lives when we come face to face with the monsters within us. But it is amazing what we find within ourselves when we face and embrace them with courage and hope.

THE BOTTOM LINE: Face and Embrace Your Monsters!

Food for Thought Questions:

- How is your abuse (or memories of your abuse) like the monster in this story? _____
  _____
  _____
  _____
  _____

- On a separate piece of paper, draw a picture of your abuse monster as if it were real.

- What do you do when you are scared by thoughts or memories of your abuse? _____
  _____
  _____
  _____

- How do you hide from your abuse (for example, refuse to talk about it or act like it doesn't bother you)? _____
  _____
  _____
  _____

- How do you fight to protect yourself so you won't get hurt again?_____
  _____
  _____
  _____

- There is a term called *radical acceptance.* It means that you totally accept (embrace) what happened to you and you understand you can't change it. Even though the abuse was wrong, you vow to learn from it and stop fighting it or running from it.

- What does it mean to "face and embrace" your abuse monster? _____
  _____
  _____

Note

1 From *Outsmarting the Riptide of Domestic Violence: Metaphor and Mindfulness for Change,* by P. Pernicano, 2011, Lanham, MD: Jason Aronson. Reprinted and adapted with permission.

CHAPTER 12

AFFECT IDENTIFICATION AND EXPRESSION

Story 27: Showing Your True Feelings

Purpose(s) and Goal(s): ☒ Psychoeducation for caregivers, children, and teens about emotional expression. ☒ Treatment Intervention: to be used with caregivers, children, or adolescents in family or individual therapy to discuss emotional expression and non-verbal congruence with emotion.

Children that have been abused often include masks, armor, and clown faces in their Rorschach responses; the urge to self-protect and *cover up* genuine affect is strong. One day an adolescent male victim of sexual abuse arrived for his first session. What stood out was the large *silly grin* pasted on the boy's face as he described powerful anger and his inability to get close to anyone. His facial expression resembled the Joker in the *Batman* movies and was non-synchronous with his words. I remembered Patricia Crittenden pointing out at a workshop that those that show all their teeth when smiling may have thinly disguised anger or fear. After all, the *don't come any closer* snarl of a cornered dog is a sign of fearful aggressiveness, and right before the attack his mouth is drawn up in a caricature grin. The story that follows addresses the smiling mask and the anger, fear and sadness that lie beneath.

The Mixed-Up Clown

"I'm mad and mean, and you better not come any closer!" shouted the clown, as everyone laughed.

"I'm sad and lonely, and need a hug," tried the clown as everyone continued to laugh.

The clown could not get anyone to take him seriously. He said to the lion tamer, "Why won't anyone pay attention to me?"

The lion tamer replied, "It might have something to do with that big red grin painted on your face. You are always smiling. So no one believes you when you express other feelings. They think you are joking."

"But I really am mad and mean, and sad and lonely," said the clown. "I have to wear clown makeup for my job."

"That's true," said the lion tamer. "But no one said that you have to put on the *same face* every day."

"What do you mean?" asked the clown.

The lion tamer answered, "You *could* put on your makeup to match your mood. That way you would show people your true feelings. Your face would match what you feel on the inside. There are lots of faces to choose from, each with a different emotion."

"You mean *change my clown face*?" he asked.

"Precisely," said the lion tamer. "The clown face is like a mask. It doesn't always match what you are really feeling. But if you choose to, you can match your face to your true feelings. It's up to you."

"I have used this smiling face for so long that I don't know how to change it," the clown said. "How do I change it?"

"Well," said the lion tamer, "You change the features. You can raise or lower the eyebrows, you draw the mouth up or down, and you can darken or lighten the eyes. You can vary the colors.

"And you could start by taking off your makeup," suggested the lion tamer.

"Take it off?" asked the clown.

"Yes, you could clean off your clown makeup—wipe your face clean. Then go look in a mirror and make different faces to see how your real face looks as your real feelings change."

The clown went home and tried the mirror thing; he felt a little naked without the clown makeup, but he was amazed at how his facial expression changed with his feelings. The next day for work, he painted his clown face as a sad one—mouth downturned and eyes drooping. When he reported for work, he said, "I'm sad and lonely and need a hug!" No one laughed. In fact, they looked sympathetic, said, "Aww, you poor clown," and gave him a hug.

The clown had not realized that he could control the response he got from others, and that he could change his makeup to show his true feelings. Now he could choose his own clown face and vary his expression, one day at a time.

THE BOTTOM LINE: Show Your True Feelings!

Food for Thought Questions:

- Discuss a time others thought you were joking but you were telling the truth. _____
  _____

- How are you like the clown in terms of hiding your feelings? _____
  _____

- What emotion is hardest for you to show? Practice it in the mirror. _____
  _____

- How good is your caregiver at *reading* your true feelings? _____
  _____

- Who in your life is able to read your true feelings? _____

Story 28: Blaming Others

Purpose(s) and Goal(s): ☒ Psychoeducation for children, teens, and families about *dumping* moods on others and distress tolerance. ☒ Treatment Intervention: to be used with children, adolescents, and caregivers to address mood dysregulation and family members acting out to get attention at the expense of others. The story encourages distress tolerance, and the metaphor allows family members to process the ways in which they deal with conflict and enable them to take responsibility for being more assertive.

Kids need to learn coping skills for self-control. You don't want to be *over-controlled,* which is sort of like being a *grownup* when you are still a kid. If you are *over-controlled* you might act like a robot and have trouble expressing your feelings. Your life is too boring when you are *over-controlled.* But you also don't want to be *under-controlled,* which means you are wild or hyper and so emotional that you do things without thinking. You need to be able to tolerate distress (strong negative feelings) and not take it out on others.

Poop in the Barnyard[1]

It was a cloudy, rainy day in the barnyard, and the animals did not sound happy.

Samantha Sheep was baaing for her breakfast. Watch Dog was barking to play a game of fetch. Barn Cat was meowing for someone to pet her. Milk Cow was mooing for someone to milk her. Wagon Horse was snorting and stomping his hooves in the barnyard dirt waiting for someone to groom him. Usually by now the girl had come to take care of their needs.

The girl was sitting on the barnyard fence in the rain, smirking at the animals and swinging her feet, her hair and clothing soaking wet. "So there!" she said to the animals in a nasty voice.

The girl's mother called out from the front porch of the house. "Did you finish your chores?" The girl had been sent to the barnyard to do her chores: feed Samantha Sheep, play fetch with Watch Dog, pet Barn Cat, milk the Milk Cow, and groom Wagon Horse.

The girl hated rainy days and she hated her chores. Dark, cloudy, rainy days made her sulk and pout. And when she pouted, she did not want to listen to her mother or to anyone else, for that matter. So, she sat on the fence in the rain and ignored her mother.

The mother grabbed an umbrella and headed toward the barnyard. When the girl saw her mother, she wiped the smirk off her face.

The mother saw something very strange. Each animal had brown stuff on his or her face. She didn't know what it was, but she knew something was up. "What have you done to the animals?" she asked her daughter.

The girl said, in a very grouchy voice, "I stepped in poop on my way to do the chores—sheep poop, cat poop, horse poop, and cow poop. The animals pooped all over the barnyard and my new tennis shoes are ruined!"

Her mother frowned. "That's what animals do. And they poop even more when they get upset for not being milked, fed, or groomed. But what have you done to them? There is brown stuff on their faces."

The girl avoided answering her mother's question; she had taken her bad mood out on the animals and she knew she would be in trouble.

The girl said, "I woke up in a bad mood today, then the poop in the barnyard made my mood even worse. It smelled awful. It looked nasty. And there were flies all over it."

"Yes," said her mother, "Poop smells. And it looks nasty. And flies get all over it. But what did you do to the animals."

The girl looked down and said, "I gave it back to them—flung their poop in their faces. I rubbed Barn Cat's face in it, too. My new tennis shoes are ruined and it's their fault! They deserved it."

There was a long silence.

The girl had been right: she was in trouble.

Her mother said, "I understand you were in a bad mood. But the animals depend on us to take care of them. You can't fling poop at poor, defenseless animals. The next time you feel like flinging poop, do the opposite."

"What do you mean?" asked the girl.

The mother replied, "When you have mad feelings, instead of doing what you feel like doing, do the opposite. When you feel like using your hands to hit or throw poop, use them for something that is the total opposite. Doing the opposite will help you calm down."

"Tell me more," said the girl.

Her mother said, "Brush the animals, gently. Or pet the goat. Or feed the animals treats. Do something with your hands that would be done with kindness instead of meanness."

Without saying a word, the girl grabbed the hose and started washing off the animals' faces. Her mother was right. Using her hands to do something nice took the madness out of her heart.

Poop may be dark and nasty and smell bad, but it is part of life on a farm. When you find poop in a barn-yard, you clean it up—you don't throw it in anyone's face!

THE BOTTOM LINE: Flinging Poop Makes Matters Worse!

Food for Thought Questions:

- Dumping your feelings on someone is a lot like flinging poop. Give an example of a time you "flung poop" (dumped your strong feelings) in someone's face. Say what happened and how you were feeling._____

_____

- How did the other person respond? _____

_____

- What did you do afterward?_____

_____

- What could you do (the opposite) instead of flinging poop? _____

_____

- Describe a time when someone flung poop in your face (dumped their feelings on you). _____

_____

_____

- How did you feel when someone flung poop in your face (dumped their feelings on you)?____

_____

- What do you wish the person had done instead? _____

_____

- Make a coping card for the girl to use the next time she is in a very bad mood and feels like taking it out on others.

Story 29: Mood Regulation and Self-Control

Purpose(s) and Goal(s): ☒ Psychoeducation about mood regulation, connection between past trauma and current intense moods, features of Borderline Personality Disorder (BPD), anger management. ☒ Treatment Intervention: for anger control with a focus on reducing blame and increasing distress tolerance. The story can be used within a mindfulness or DBT treatment approach. It could be used in individual or group treatment with adolescents or adults; also, if a child's caregiver is very intense, the child will respond to this story with a better understanding that he or she is not to blame for the parent's anger.

A feral cat is *wild*. It has not been petted, loved, consistently fed, or attended to. It is hard to *tame* a feral cat once it is used to living in the wild. Some kids are like that. They get used to abuse or neglect, and they don't know how to accept kindness and stability. This story was written for an angry teenage girl who had been abused most of her life. She didn't feel loved or lovable. She had a bad temper and took it out on other people. She cursed and threatened people when she got upset. She even dumped her anger on people that were kind to her. When you don't feel loved, it can make you angry and make it hard to get along with others. It is important to learn appropriate ways (through mindfulness, relaxation, guided imagery, or DBT) to cope with anger and not dump it on other people.

The Feral Cat[2]

"YOWL, YOWL, YOWL!!" cried Freda Black Cat at the top of her lungs. "I'm going to leave and never come back!" she hissed.

Gaga Gray Cat, the target of her anger, was crouched on the other side of the room.

Freda was standing in the kitchen by her empty food dish. Her cat bed was soaking wet.

"I know what you did, Gaga," growled Freda. Her fur was raised and her ears were twitching. Freda's tail whipped back and forth.

Gaga Gray talked to Freda as she moved slowly toward her.

"Freda, calm down a minute and let me expl . . ."

Freda spit at Gaga and drew her sharp claws.

"You heard what I said!" she yowled. "No more lies!"

"Just let me expl . . ."

Freda swiped at Gaga with her clawed paw and hissed, "Yessssss, you want to explain. Well, not thisssss time, you two-timing pussssy cat. I hate you!"

Freda swished her tail and leaped across the room. Then she squatted on Gaga's soft bed, and peed all over it.

Freda shrieked, "Take that! See how you like it!" as she raced out of the room and down the hall.

Gaga gave up. She could not reason with Freda at times like this.

You probably wonder why Freda was so upset. Well, Freda was someone that got upset very easily. Freda's anger had one setting—*high!*

Freda came from a long line of feral cats. In case you don't know what a feral cat is, I'll tell you, because it is important to the rest of the story.

A feral cat grows up in the wild and is not tame. That is because no one took care of it or loved it when it was little. A feral cat is often hungry and fights to survive. It doesn't trust others and won't let anyone come too close.

Freda's mother (also a feral cat) had said, "I didn't ask for all these kids. I didn't ask for such a hard life. Freda, never trust anyone. It's a dog-eat-cat world!"

That's how Freda grew up—cold and hungry in the sewers. But when she was two years old, a child found her on the streets. The child felt sorry for her and took her home.

Freda didn't trust anyone to love her or keep her. She never purred and she had a very bad temper. She often started cat fights with Gaga

"I'll get them before they get me," she thought.

Gaga had always believed kindness could fix everything. She hoped it would cure Freda's meanness. But Gaga was wrong. Freda's bad temper did not improve. Sometimes she got so mad that she scratched her own face! And when she got maddest of all she started saying, "If you won't do what I want, maybe I'll kill myself."

"Freda needs to learn to control her temper," thought Gaga. "She would have a hissy fit if other cats treated her the way she treats them."

Freda calmed back down after her temper tantrum and acted as if nothing had happened. She went into the bedroom where Gaga was resting. Freda jumped up on the bed and began licking her fur.

"Freda?" asked Gaga in a cautious voice. "Can I explain something now?"

"It won't do any good," said Freda. "But go ahead."

Gaga stated calmly, "I didn't eat your food. And I didn't pee on your bed."

"I don't believe you," said Freda. "If you didn't, then who did?"

"It was the dog," said Gaga, "You know how he hates us cats. I saw him gobble down all the food in your bowl. Then he went over to your bed and lifted his leg. I had nothing to do with it."

Freda thought, "Oops—I did it again. I accused Gaga of something she didn't do."

But she said, "Gaga, I can't control my anger—that's the way I am. You can take it or leave it. I'm not going to change for anyone."

Freda added, "You know how it is with us feral cats. We get mad. But don't worry, I'm over it now. Sorry about that." Freda swished her long tail and closed her eyes. She didn't sound or look very sorry.

"Freda," said Gaga. "It's not OK." She said this carefully. She didn't want Freda to get upset again.

Freda opened her eyes in surprise. "What do you mean, 'It's not OK?' "

Gaga replied, "I know you grew up as a feral cat, but that doesn't give you the right to be so mean. You should not take your anger out on others. You would have a hissy fit if other cats treated you the way you treat them."

There, it was said.

Freda almost yowled and scratched Gaga. But she held back. What Gaga said was true. Freda would never let others treat her the way she treated them.

"What do you expect *me* to do?" Freda asked (her snotty attitude showing). "I can't control my anger."

"It's not 'can't', Freda," said Gaga. "It's 'don't or 'won't'. You don't control your anger but you *can* learn to control it."

Freda said, "When I'm mad, I *have to* let it out, right then."

"You could sit on it," said Gaga.

"Sit on it?" asked Freda.

"Yes," replied Gaga. "Sit on it. Wait, take some time, and don't react. Think before you spit. Let your fur go down a bit. All the things they teach in Cat-O-Lick School to help you calm down. Feelings come and go. You can learn to control your anger."

"I've never been to school," said Freda.

"Well, it's never too late," suggested Gaga. "And it's a purr-fect time for you to start."

To make a long story short, the Girl enrolled Freda in Cat-O-Lick school.

Freda's classes were called weird things like Being Mindful, Think before You Yowl, Anger Control, Meditation, and Stress Management, better known as Paws Before Claws. In only two weeks, Freda learned to keep her claws to herself. She and Gaga started to get along better. One of her homework assignments was to let the girl come a little closer each day.

It was Saturday after the second week of class. Freda and Gaga were curled up on the bed in the girl's room.

"What is that funny noise?" the Girl asked as she walked in.

It was Freda. She had learned to purr.

"Oh my goodness, it's *you*, Freda. You're purring!"

The girl smiled and moved closer to Freda. "That's a good girl," she said. Freda watched her with one watchful eye as if ready to pounce. "Take it easy," went the girl.

The girl slowly reached out her hand and started to pet Freda. Instead of yowling and bolting, Freda let the girl continue. Freda didn't really trust her completely yet, but the gentle hand woke up something in her that had been asleep for a very long time.

By the way, it is true that you can't tame a feral cat, but if a feral cat really wants to, it can tame itself.

THE BOTTOM LINE: Tame Your Temper!

Food for Thought Questions:

- How do you behave like Freda toward others? _____
_____

- Name someone in your life that behaved or behaves like Freda? _____
_____

- Give an example of a time you took your feelings out on someone else and a time someone else took his or her feelings out on you. _____

- What advice do you have for Freda to help her calm down?
_____
_____

- What or who helps you calm down when you are upset?_____

- Pretend you are Freda's anger-school teacher. Come up with a school lesson plan to teach Freda to stay calm, change her thinking, and stop taking her anger out on other people. Make a coping card for her to use when she starts to get angry.

- Pretend you are teaching Freda a lesson on using absolutes ("always", "never", "no one", "can't"). When she talks back or uses an absolute, help her come up with a good response that is based on facts.

Notes

1 From *Outsmarting the Riptide of Domestic Violence: Metaphor and Mindfulness for Change*, by P. Pernicano, 2011, Lanham, MD: Jason Aronson. Reprinted and adapted with permission.
2 From *Outsmarting the Riptide of Domestic Violence: Metaphor and Mindfulness for Change*, by P. Pernicano, 2011, Lanham, MD: Jason Aronson. Reprinted and adapted with permission.

CHAPTER 13

COGNITIVE COPING

Story 30: Cognitive Processing

Purpose(s) and Goal(s): ☒ Psychoeducation for caregivers, children, and teens about taking time to *simmer* thoughts and feelings in order to allow time for processing. ☒ Treatment Intervention: to be used with caregivers, children, or adolescents in family or individual therapy to discuss self-appraisal and not trying to change who they are.

Some people respond without taking time to think and process, and end up, blurting out thoughts and feelings. Responding without thinking can offend and alienate those around you. The story that follows has a cooking metaphor about turning down the heat on spaghetti and simmering the sauce for good flavor. It suggests that an individual takes time to process intense thoughts and feelings before sharing them with someone else.

Let It Simmer

"Are you hungry?" asked the man as he carried a big bowl of spaghetti sauce and a platter of spaghetti to the kitchen table.

"That was fast," said his partner. "And I didn't even smell it cooking."

"I used the recipe you gave me," said the man, "for the home-cooked spaghetti."

"But that recipe takes hours," replied the partner.

"Well, I put in all the ingredients the recipe called for, and I'm hungry. Let's sit down to eat," the man said.

The man put a pile of partially cooked spaghetti noodles on his partner's plate.

"Why are the noodles only half-cooked?" asked his partner.

"The pot kept boiling over and made a big mess on the stove. So I finally just turned it off," he replied.

"Half-cooked spaghetti is not worth eating," replied the partner. "When you cook spaghetti, as soon as the water starts to boil, you have to turn down the heat. That way, the water stays hot and the spaghetti continues to cook until it is ready to eat."

The man added a big scoop of sauce on top of the spaghetti.

The partner picked up his fork, took a big bite and spit out a chunk of still-raw onion as well as a piece of undercooked sausage and some raw tomato.

"This sauce tastes awful!" exclaimed the partner.

The man admitted, "Yeah, it doesn't taste anything like when you make it."

The partner asked, "So you said you put in all the ingredients—then what?"

"I was in a hurry," said the man, "so I skipped the 'simmer for two hours' part for the sauce. I dumped everything in the pot and cooked it for ten minutes. And, as you already know, I took out the spaghetti a little early."

His partner said, "You have to simmer spaghetti sauce. Simmering gives the sauce time to blend. All the flavors and spices mix in. You can't rush a good sauce. If you hurry it, you ruin the sauce. No one can swallow a sauce full of raw onion and uncooked sausage! And no one can digest undercooked spaghetti."

"I hate to wait," said the man. He admitted, "You know, I do that in life too, not just in my cooking."

"Yes, I know," said his partner. "You are sometimes in a hurry to share your thoughts and feelings. You interrupt others and take over the conversation when you think you have something important to say. When you are in a hurry—with your feelings, your decisions, or your spaghetti sauce—the result is never as good. Some things need plenty of time to simmer if you want a good outcome."

THE BOTTOM LINE: Some Things Need to Simmer: Don't Rush the Sauce!

Food for Thought Questions:

- Describe a time you were in a hurry and rushed something that needed time to simmer (a relationship, feelings or thoughts you wanted to express, a school project, studying for a test, etc.).

  _____

  _____

- There is a thing called *distress tolerance*. You learn to tolerate distress when you have strong feelings—you *sit on those feelings, examine them and connect them* before you express them. That way you don't let them overpower you.

  When did you let your feelings overwhelm you? _____

  _____

  When did you let your feelings simmer so that you could figure them out and express them later?

  _____

- When you let things simmer, you don't *react*. You take time and *choose* what you will say or do. Describe a time you were angry and lashed out at someone. _____

  _____

- Pretend your anger is in a big pot, blended in with other feelings like hurt, sadness, rejection, embarrassment, etc. Draw the pot and the feelings inside. Let your feelings *simmer* and talk about what triggered them.

Story 31: Vigilance

Purpose(s) and Goal(s): ☒ Psychoeducation about vigilance and the startle response. ☒ Treatment Intervention: to be used with adults and teens to reduce hyper-vigilance and paranoia following abuse. The therapist can use this story within stress inoculation, EMDR, TF-CBT or CPT. The story line leads to the development of coping suggestions. The story will allow the client to identify those things in the environment that continue to trigger fear. After reading the story, the therapist can teach stress management, mindfulness, or relaxation to use as a competing response. The story can precede *in vivo* exposure.

Once you are really safe, it is good to learn how to cope, stay calm, and enjoy life. This story was written for a mother who had been abused in childhood and as an adult. She did not trust anyone. She believed that no matter how good things were, something bad was going to happen and she was always on the lookout. She said, "I'm looking for land mines." It took a long time for her to trust others and be less vigilant, but this story helped her understand her reactions to trauma triggers even though she no longer lived in an unsafe environment. After reading this story, you can talk to your therapist about your own land mines and how to stop responding with fear.

Looking for Land Mines in Disneyland[1]

The little girl had just arrived at Disneyland and she could not believe her eyes. No, it was not Cinderella, walking toward the castle. And it was not Goofy and Donald Duck, doing a little dance for the children.

She was staring at a soldier in full combat uniform and body armor. The soldier was tapping his foot on each stone of the path in front of him; moving forward one step at a time. He was frowning in deep concentration.

The little girl ran over to the soldier and tugged on his sleeve.

"Excuse me!" she said. "What are you are doing?"

The soldier had not noticed the little girl. When he felt the tug on his sleeve, he was startled. In an instant, he was ready to fight.

The little girl backed away. "Hey!" she said. "I'm not the enemy. Please tell me what you're doing."

The soldier replied, "Sorry about that. I'm looking for land mines!"

"In Disneyland?" asked the girl.

"AB-SO-LUTE-LY!" declared the soldier. "You don't ever want to miss a land mine—even in Disneyland. I know. I was deployed overseas last year. Every time I turned around someone was stepping on a land mine. I stepped on one myself and barely survived. Others were not so lucky."

"There are no land mines in Disneyland," the little girl said to the soldier.

"You never know," he said. "And it's better to be safe than sorry."

The girl was silent. She didn't know what to say. The soldier was missing out on the fun of Disneyland because he did not feel safe.

The girl suggested, "I wonder if you could take off the body armor and go on a few rides with me. It might help you calm down. The war was dangerous and bad things happened there. But *that was then, and this is now*. There are no land mines in Disneyland—you are safe here."

"Well, OK, I guess I can take off the body armor. The sun is very hot."

The soldier took off the body armor and walked with the girl to the Dumbo ride, but he continued to tap his foot on the stone path. Just in case . . .

Just then, a large Mickey Mouse came up to them, holding out his white-gloved hand.

The soldier commanded, "Take cover!" as he knocked the girl to the ground and crouched to protect her.

He shouted, "Stop right there, Mouse! Take off those gloves and show me your hands!"

Poor Mickey . . . He was so scared by the soldier's loud voice that he started to shake and almost wet his pants. The little children near him began to cry.

"What's going on?" Mickey squeaked in a high voice.

"I just know there's a hand grenade hidden in those huge white gloves!" said the soldier.

"I only wanted to shake your hand and thank you for serving our country," squeaked Mickey.

Mickey tossed both white gloves on the ground and showed his hands, nothing in either of them.

"Sorry," muttered the soldier. "When I was in the war, a hidden hand grenade almost blew me up. I didn't want to take any chances."

The little girl answered, "Well, you're not in the war anymore. You're in Disneyland and you're scaring the children. That was then and this is now. There aren't any land mines or hand grenades in Disneyland. No one here is your enemy. It's time for you to use your brain to cope with your fears."

Together, the soldier and the little girl made a coping card. It had all kinds of coping skills the soldier could use in Disneyland to relax and stop looking for land mines. Then the soldier went on the Dumbo ride with the little girl. He felt a little nervous without his armor but kept reminding himself that he was safe (one of his coping skills). He told himself that if all those little kids were on the Dumbo ride, there was probably no danger. Next, they rode, "It's a Small World After All"—it was cute, but the singing of the cheerful, little dolls got on his nerves by the end of the boat ride. At least the singing distracted him from worrying about land mines (another coping skill).

When it was time for the park to close, the soldier thanked the girl for spending the day with him. He had bought a Mickey Mouse T-shirt to wear over his uniform and seemed more relaxed than earlier in the day.

As the soldier walked out of the exit, he turned around one last time and said to the girl, "It's hard to break old habits, but I'm going to try. I'm going to come back tomorrow with my coping card and practice my coping skills. Thanks for helping me. It is time for me to stop looking for land mines in Disneyland. And probably even time to stop looking for land mines everywhere else I go. I will have to practice and work hard, but I have two more days left on my three-day pass, and I want to enjoy my Disneyland experience."

There is a time to protect yourself but when danger has passed, it is time to relax.

THE BOTTOM LINE: You can Stop Looking for Land Mines when the War Is Over!

Food for Thought Questions:

- How are you like the soldier in Disneyland (looking for or expecting danger)? _____
  _____

- What are your land mines (bad memories you keep thinking or worrying about)?_____
  _____

- Has danger passed in your life? Are you able to relax? Why or why not? _____
  _____
  _____

- How is your life now different from when you were abused? _____
  _____

- What can you say or do to relax when there is no danger?_____
  _____

- Make a coping card that says what you plan to do when you get scared. _____
  _____
  _____

- Think of a time when you were relaxed and happy? What was different? _____
  _____

- Close your eyes and remember that feeling of being happy and relaxed. Really feel it. The next time you get stressed, imagine this happy time, feel it in your body, and let yourself relax.

Story 32: Coping with an Eating Disorder

Purpose(s) and Goal(s): ☒ Psychoeducation about eating disorders and self-criticism. ☒ Treatment Intervention: to be used in individual therapy to address negative self-talk with an eating disordered client. The story provides a good example of a CBT exercise for part-self confrontation.

Children who have been abused sometimes develop eating-related problems such as anorexia or bulimia. The cognitive component of these disorders is powerful and can lead to self-destructive behaviors that are quite habit-forming. The negative, critical voice in a child's head may be a parent, a perpetrator, or other voice from the past. It is important that the child learns how to talk back to his or her twin in the mirror.

The Twin in the Mirror[2]

Once upon a time, a girl and her parents lived together in *The House of Rules*. There were rules about how to eat, what to say, and how to behave posted in every room of the house. Each rule started with the words, "You should . . ." or "You should not . . ." The rules taught everyone how to "Should Upon" themselves. The girl's parents had also been raised in *The House of Rules,* so they taught their daughter to follow the rules without question.

One rule was, "If someone asks, 'How are you?' say, 'I'm fine' even if you aren't." Another rule was, "If you can't say something nice, don't say anything at all." A third rule was, "Don't worry—act happy." And a very important rule was, "Our love is all you need." So the girl and her parents said only "nice" things to one another and lived "happily" in their *House of Rules*.

The girl was smart and talented. She tried hard to be a *good girl* and to please her parents, because she hoped that someday, if she followed all the rules, she might become *perfect*. But the girl worried in secret about many things, so as to not bother her parents. She worried about her grades when she got a B, because she wanted to have straight As. She worried that she didn't have enough friends. She worried about growing up and illness. She worried about natural disasters and all the bad things she heard in the news. She worried about her parents. She worried she would upset her parents if she told them about her worries . . . So she kept them to herself.

I will tell you that the girl and her family had gone through some very hard times. Really bad things had happened, and no one really wanted to talk about them. Her parents told her it was all *in the past* and acted as if nothing had happened—they said she should *move on*. The girl didn't know how to do that.

One morning, the girl stood in front of her bedroom mirror to check her hair before leaving for school. She suddenly heard a loud, critical voice. "What are *you* looking at? You don't need to stare, you know!"

Where was that voice coming from? "Don't just stand there looking stupid!" continued the voice. "Don't look so surprised; I'm right in front of you!" The girl could hardly believe her eyes and ears—her identical twin was talking to her from within the mirror! The twin spoke again. "Cat got your tongue? No wonder you don't have many friends."

The twin was so rude! The girl did not like how the twin was talking and started to leave the room. The twin saw her leaving and shouted in a bossy voice, "You come back here and listen to me; I'm not finished!" The girl slowly walked back to the mirror and peered in at her twin. The twin said, "That's better. You know what you need to do to REALLY be happy?"

Now that caught the girl's attention—she would love to REALLY be happy. "No," said the girl, "What do I need to do to REALLY be happy?"

The twin replied, "You need to lose some weight. When you lose some weight, you won't look fat anymore, and then you will be happy. Take a look in the mirror and see for yourself."

The girl took a good look in the mirror and realized that her twin was right. Her body had started to change recently, and there were soft curves in places that used to be lean and firm.

The girl looked back in the mirror and said to her twin, "I could stand to lose a little weight. I'll give it a try."

The girl's twin acted like a drill sergeant. She made her do 100 sit-ups and jog around the block five times. The girl skipped meals, which everyone knows is bad for your health. She weighed herself every day, sometimes twice a day, and listened to her twin in the mirror. The twin's voice was always in her head, and she was very critical.

"You're still too fat," said the twin.

The girl got thinner and thinner, but she still wasn't REALLY happy. Her parents did not notice at first that she was losing weight. When they finally noticed, they took her to the family doctor, because they thought her weight loss was about eating and nutrition. They watched her closely at home, restricted her freedom, and kept track of what she ate.

The girl continued to lose weight. The family doctor suggested that the parents take their daughter to a wise helper, and they made the appointment.

The girl went to see the helper and answered lots of questions. The helper seemed very interested in the girl's thoughts and feelings and wanted to hear about the family's hard times. The helper talked to the girl's parents, too, and encouraged the parents to share their thoughts and feelings, to let the daughter be in charge of her eating, and to give her privacy at home.

The girl and the helper met a few times, and the girl continued to talk about her family, her worries and the twin in the mirror.

The helper said, "If you want to get better and be happy, the first thing you have to do is talk back to the twin in the mirror and stop believing everything she says."

"Why would I want to do that?" asked the girl.

The helper replied, "The twin lies and blinds you to how you really look."

The girl said, "That can't be true—she would never lie to me. She is my best friend."

The helper disagreed, "She does not act like much of a friend. A friend is on *your* side and sees the *best* in you. The twin is much too critical."

The helper suggested ways the girl might talk back to the twin in the mirror. "Stick up for yourself. Tell her the facts when she lies. Don't let her boss you. If you keep listening to her, you will not get better. You are giving her the power to destroy you."

There was a long silence as the girl thought about what the helper said. She had been losing weight for many months, and her twin still told her she was too fat.

She said, "I guess I don't have to listen to everything she says. I'll try talking back to her and see what she does."

Later that day, the girl went into her room, stood in front of the mirror, looked her twin in the eye and said calmly but firmly, "I don't think you have been acting like much of a friend!"

The twin replied, in a bossy tone of voice, "I'm the only friend you have!"

The girl declared, "Then maybe I need some new friends—friends that will like me the way I am. You are much too critical!"

The twin looked mad when the girl said that; she pouted and refused to talk to the girl any more that day.

Over the next few weeks, the girl continued to talk back to her twin. It got easier each time. When the twin said, "You're too fat," she replied, "I am not too fat. In fact, based on height and weight tables, I am probably too thin." When the twin said, "You will be REALLY happy if you lose weight," the girl replied, "Losing weight won't make me REALLY happy. I have lost a lot of weight, and I am still unhappy." And when the twin said, "I am stronger than you, and I will win this battle," the girl was able to say, "I am stronger than you think and I will not let you destroy me."

The girl was proud about standing up for herself. One morning, she said to the twin, "I'm not going to let you—or my weight—control my life any more." You may be surprised to hear that when the twin ordered her to weigh herself every day, she put away the scale. That made the twin really mad, and she pouted for a whole week!

The girl continued to meet with her helper, and during one of their talks the helper said, "You are doing a great job talking back to your twin. Now it's time for you and your parents to have some new rules and for you to tell them about your worries."

"New rules?" the girl asked.

"Yes," said the helper. "The old ones weren't working. It's time to try something new."

The helper met with the girl and her parents the very next week. The helper said to the parents, "I know you love your daughter." They nodded their heads; it was true. "And I think you want your daughter to grow up healthy and happy." Again they nodded their heads. Lastly, "I think you value honesty and want your daughter to be truthful with you." For a third time, the parents nodded.

The helper explained, "I want to suggest some new rules, so you can show your love in a new way." Here are the rules the therapist shared with the family:

1   No one is perfect—strive to be ordinary.
2   Do not *should upon* yourself.
3   Celebrate small successes.
4   Success is not about eating or weight.
5   Nothing is too bad to talk about.
6   Love yourself first.
7   Change takes time.
8   The only person you can change is yourself.
9   Live one day at a time.

The mother said, "Of course no one is perfect. But what do these new rules have to do with our daughter getting better? All she needs to do is eat and gain weight."

The helper said, "Your daughter does need to eat and gain weight. But as rule number four says, success is not about eating and weight. Your daughter needs to love herself, talk about her past and worry less. She needs to learn how to grow up. And she needs you to love her as she is, listen to her thoughts and feelings, and help her get over what happened in the family."

The girl agreed, "I think the helper is right. I need to love myself and worry less. And I need you to listen to me and love me as I am."

"You know we love you," said her parents.

The girl replied, "You love who you think I am or who you want me to be. I'm not even sure who I am yet, but I'm figuring that out."

The girl had realized that getting healthy was not about eating or food; it was about learning to love herself, worrying less, and being free to grow up.

So the girl and her parents went home and tried the new rules. It was a little like learning to ride a two-wheeler bicycle. You know, you get on the bike and feel a quite unsteady and wobbly. You fall now and then, but you pick yourself back up and try again. And while you're on that bike, your parents are running along beside you, one hand on the seat, cheering you on and letting go every once in awhile until you finally get your balance. The girl's parents eventually learned to let go and the girl "got her balance." She reminded herself that one day at a time, she was finally getting better.

Then one day, her helper said, "It's probably time to get rid of that old mirror. You need a new mirror that reflects who you really are." The girl thought about it and agreed.

The girl went home and took down the old mirror, in spite of loud protests from the mean twin. She put it out in the trash. At the thrift store the next day, the girl found a new mirror. It was sitting in a dusty corner of the store, as if it were waiting for her. It was a pretty mirror with soft, built-in lights. She bought it, took it home, and hung it in her room. The gentle light brightened up her room. As she stood in front of it, she heard a voice, "Hello there! Thanks for bringing me home."

What? As the girl looked in the mirror, there was that twin again. Or was it? This twin looked just like the other twin, but she was smiling, and her eyes were friendly and bright. Her voice was soft and kind. No, this was someone new.

The twin said with a smile, "No, I'm not her. I'm here to cheer you on, not criticize you. I'll tell you the truth, sometimes things that you don't want to hear. I'll let you see yourself as you really are."

The girl realized that this new twin would be a real friend and help her change her view of herself. After all, happiness comes from how we interpret what happens in our lives. The girl came to understand that the past, the good and the bad, is always with us. It is what it is.

THE BOTTOM LINE: See (and Accept) Yourself As You Really Are.

Food for Thought Questions:

- How are you like the girl in the story? _____
  _____

- How is your family like the girl's family? _____
  _____

- What worries of yours are hard to talk about? _____
  _____

- If you are self-harming, what is your goal? _____
  _____
  _____

- Whose voice is in your mirror? (Sometimes it is a voice you know or message from the past.)___
  _____
  _____

- How has your past made you stronger or given you new coping skills? _____
  _____

Story 33: Choices in Dating Relationships

Purpose(s) and Goal(s): ☒ Psychoeducation for teens and caregivers about characteristics to look for in partners. ☒ Treatment Intervention: to be used with adolescents or caregivers who "miss" warning signs in partners or repeatedly select partners that pull them down. This metaphor can refer to substance abusing, dependent, untrustworthy, unfaithful, or abusive partners.

This is a humorous story about someone that uses poor judgment in selecting partners. The main character dates eggs, and each egg she chooses has a *visible crack* that is missed or overlooked. The story is helpful when working with a client that has not yet developed a *template* for a healthy relationship.

No More Rotten Eggs[3]

Carla Chicken's mother stood at the door of her daughter's bedroom.

It was noon on a cold Saturday morning. Carla was getting ready to take her shower, and her headphones, now hanging around her neck, were blaring out music from her iPod.

"Do you have a minute?" asked her Mom.

"Uh-oh," thought Carla. "Here we go again! What have I done now? Did I sleep too late? Did I forget to put my dishes in the sink? Did I wake them up when I came in at 2am?"

Carla hated living at home. She had dropped out of school and could not yet afford to live on her own. It seemed like her mother was always prying into her business.

"OK," said Carla.

Carla's mother came into her bedroom and wrinkled up her nose.

"What is that smell?" she asked.

"What smell," asked Carla.

"That rotten egg smell. It's so nasty it makes me want to puke," said her mother with a trace of sarcasm.

"Oh," said Carla, "*that* smell! Well, that smell probably came from Eddie Egg."

Carla was dating Eddie Egg, the 12th egg Carla had dated in the last year—an even dozen.

She had dated Humpty Dumpty Egg before Eddie, but he had fallen off a wall two weeks ago. All the king's horses and men could not put him together again, so Carla had moved on.

You might remember the nursery rhyme about Humpty Dumpty. Let me clue you in on something the nursery rhyme didn't tell you. When Humpty Dumpty fell off the wall and broke into pieces, he smelled awful. He was rotten inside: on the outside he was so cute in his little shirt and tie, but on the inside he was just one more smelly, rotten egg.

"Who is Eddie Egg?" asked Carla's mother.

"He's the guy I'm dating, Mom. You know, ever since Humpty Dumpty fell off the wall."

Carla's mother was worried that her daughter was dating a new egg so soon after breaking up with Humpty Dumpty. She had noticed the hairline crack on Humpty's underside and had tried to tell Carla, but her daughter wouldn't listen to her.

And she had tried to tell Carla about the ten eggs before him—they had been cracked and rotten as well. She knew that Carla was a grownup now and she should stay out of her business, but her daughter had terrible taste in eggs.

Her mother had told Carla, "I wish you would stop dating rotten eggs. At least you could check the eggs in the carton before you bring one home. It's easy for an egg to get cracked after it leaves the nest."

"Leave me alone, Mom" said Carla. "Who I date is my business."

"I worry about you, Carla," said her mother. "And I wish you would be more careful. An egg might look OK at first glance, but you have to look for cracks. A nice, farm-fresh egg has no cracks and it doesn't smell. A smelly egg is rotten inside."

"Mom," said Carla. "Eddie is not cracked or rotten. He came here right from work and didn't have time to clean up. He usually smells fine."

"Carla," said her mother. "If you check Eddie out, I bet you'll find a crack."

"Not Eddie," said Carla. "I know I dated some rotten eggs before, but now I know what to look for. Eddie is not like the ten eggs before him. There's no way he is cracked. He's very sweet. He dresses really well, takes me to the clubs, and has good taste in music."

"It's easy for an egg to hide his cracks in the dark lights at the clubs," said her mother. "Bad eggs use sweet talk to make you think they are nicer than they really are."

"I know, Mom," replied Carla with a grin as she gave her mother a hug. "It's nice that you worry about me, but I'm a big girl now."

"Well," said her mother, "I just don't want to have to say, 'I told you so.' "

After her mom left the room, Carla went and took her shower, got dressed, and called Eddie on her cell phone. They planned to go the club again that night.

Carla wasn't blind to what her mother had said. So she invited Eddie over to meet her mother before they went to the club. She knew that she picked a lot of rotten eggs, and she wanted to prove her mother wrong.

"Why do you want me to meet your mother?" asked Eddie. He did not look very happy.

"My mom wants to meet you," said Carla. She didn't want to tell Eddie it was *her* idea.

Eddie arrived that evening and rang the doorbell. Carla answered the door and called out, "Mom, Eddie is here. Come meet him so we can leave for the club."

"I wonder what's going on," thought Carla's mother.

Carla turned on the bright lights of the front hallway and invited Eddie inside.

Eddie stepped inside and Carla sent her mother a look that said, "See if you can find a crack in this fine young egg."

Carla's mother stepped up close to Eddie to introduce herself.

"Hello, Eddie. I'm Carla's mother. How are you?"

Eddie did not answer. He grunted, looked at the floor, and said, "Come on, Carla. Let's go to the club."

As Eddie turned around to go back out the door, Carla's mother sniffed the air and looked pointedly at her daughter. Then Carla sniffed the air. She caught a whiff of something rotten.

Carla's mother pointed down at Eddie's bottom half and said, "Carla, isn't that a crack?"

"Why yes, Mom. I see what you mean," said Carla. She crossed her arms and looked Eddie straight in the eye.

"Eddie," said Carla. "Are you a rotten egg?"

Eddie's face suddenly grew mean. "What's it to you?" he snarled. "Nosy B!" he said to Carla's mother. "I'm out of here!"

Eddies stalked out the door and closed it in Carla's face.

Carla knew *eggs*-actly what her mother was thinking. "You were right, Mom," she said. Her mother replied, "Better to find out now than later . . ."

Carla had now picked a dozen bad eggs, so she decided to take a class called, *Picking out Good Eggs.* During the weeks ahead, Carla learned lots of helpful hints like: "before you date an egg, look it over in bright light"; "take an egg home to meet your family"; "don't date an egg who uses air freshener every five minutes"; "pick an egg that likes to talk with you"; and "look for an egg who has left the nest."

You won't be surprised to hear that Carla was eventually hired by the *Courier Journal* Features department to write a column called *Carla's Guide for Picking a Good Egg.* She hoped that others might learn from her experiences. As everyone knows, rotten eggs are worth a dime a dozen, and Carla was worth a lot more than that!

THE BOTTOM LINE: No More Rotten Eggs!

Food for Thought Questions:

- How are you like Carla? _____
  _____

- What are your blind spots in picking partners? _____
  _____
  _____

- List some of your rotten eggs and what fooled you about them: _____
  _____
  _____
  _____

Carla's Guide for Picking a Good Egg

Family: Has he left the nest? How does he treat his family? Does he want me to meet his family and friends? Does he ask about my family? Does he want to meet my friends?

Employment: Does he have a job? How many jobs has he had? How long does he keep them?

Education: Did he finish his education or is he working on it?

Lifestyle and Values: Does he drink or do drugs? Does he sell drugs? Does he have a criminal record? Is he honest with me? Did he cheat in a past relationship? (If yes, he may cheat again on me) Does he run out of money and ask to borrow from me? Does he encourage me to make friends and spend time with them?

Attitude: Does he blame other people for his problems? Is it always "hard luck" or "not fair"? Does he think he's always right? Does he make a lot of excuses? Can he say, "I'm sorry?" Does he keep score about money and who does what? Is he kind and generous? Is he controlling? Is he judgmental?

Interest in Partner: Does he like to spend time with me? Does he ask what I want to do? Does he give me equal time with his friends? Does he usually come to me only for sex? Does he ask about my feelings? Does he like to talk to me? Does he talk only about himself or does he show interest in me?

Trust: Does he trust me? Is he suspicious? Does he try to control or check up on me, even in a "friendly" way? Does he ever, even once, check my computer, phone, or the mileage on my car?

Emotional: Does he have a mean streak? Does he have a good sense of humor? Does he share his feelings? Does he have mood swings? Does he blame me for his moods? Has he ever shoved me when he's angry? Does he mistreat children? Does he avoid conflict (walk away, refuse to talk, give me the silent treatment)?

Notes

1 From *Outsmarting the Riptide of Domestic Violence: Metaphor and Mindfulness for Change*, by P. Pernicano, 2011, Lanham, MD: Jason Aronson. Reprinted and adapted with permission.
2 From *Metaphorical Stories for Child Therapy: Of Magic and Miracles*, by P. Pernicano, 2010, Lanham, MD: Jason Aronson. Reprinted and adapted with permission.
3 From *Outsmarting the Riptide of Domestic Violence: Metaphor and Mindfulness for Change*, by P. Pernicano, 2011, Lanham, MD: Jason Aronson. Reprinted and adapted with permission.

TRAUMA NARRATIVE

Story 34: Feeling Broken or Damaged

Purpose(s) and Goal(s): ☒ Psychoeducation about PTSD and impact of trauma, the feeling of being damaged, the hope for healing, the importance of going to treatment and talking about the trauma. ☒ Treatment Intervention: for adolescents and adults in early-stage PTSD treatment or prior to beginning Cognitive Processing Therapy (CPT), Prolonged Exposure (PE), or TF-CBT. This is an excellent story to read to the client during relaxation or mild trance state. The client will use the story material to re-experience his or her trauma and feel the potential for healing. The imagery of the glass bowl can then be used to depict the client's own abuse.

This story, like *Bear of a Different Color*, introduces the trauma narrative process. A hurricane is a strong trauma metaphor, and it was my trip to a glass studio that provided the metaphor for healing. The story has become a favorite with therapists and clients, as it elicits a strong right-brain response to the imagery of brokenness and the transformative healing process. I was most touched to hear of a client who wept during the story, saying that the story triggered her feelings of brokenness ("damaged goods"); then provided the sensation of healing. For her, this story instilled hope and was a meaningful, spiritual experience—it represented the relinquishing of control and the possibility of becoming a new creation.

The Cracked Glass Bowl[2]

The hurricane was finally over. The blue skies over the ocean were filled with fluffy clouds, the shining sun reflecting down on the waters.

A small, cracked, green glass bowl bobbed up and down in the ocean. She looked around at the devastation and said, "It's a wonder I survived the storm!" There were uprooted trees and debris scattered as far as the eye could see.

It *was* a wonder that the glass bowl had survived the storm. The storm had hit the coast with powerful winds and blinding rain. The green glass bowl had been lifted off the ground: Green in the midst of black, she was flung into the disorienting darkness, out of control, at the mercy of the storm's destruction. It had been a terrifying experience. The last thing she remembered was being hit on the head by a flying object.

"How are you feeling?" The green glass bowl opened her eyes at the sound of the voice. She found herself resting inside a slightly larger blue bowl. Blue bowl was one of her best friends.

"I feel a little disoriented," she said. Then the green glass bowl saw her reflection in the water and cried out with dismay. "The storm has changed me. I am so damaged and broken that I will never again be the same."

It was true that the storm had changed her. She had a hundred small cracks on her surface and two long, deep cracks that went all the way through, with straw and dirt embedded in them. There were deep gouges and large chips missing on her edges.

That night, she went home with her friend. Without his support, she would have fallen into a hundred little pieces.

The next day, her friend asked, "When do you want to start the healing process?"

"Healing process?" asked the cracked green glass bowl.

"Yes, the fire," her friend replied. "Damaged glass bowls go through the glassmaker's fire to be healed."

"I don't think so," said the green bowl. "I have heard about the hot, searing fire that heals. Others say it is a very painful process! The glassmaker makes you *talk about* the hurricane. There is no guarantee, and when you come out, you are different through and through."

"That's true," said blue bowl. "But the artist is very skilled. He talks to you about the hurricane so that you can stop thinking and dreaming about it. He is patient and works *with* you as you endure the heat of the fire."

The green bowl argued, "I have heard that glass sometimes shatters in the fire."

"Not many are destroyed by the fire," replied the blue bowl. "Most are healed and come out new and different. You have to weigh the risks against the benefits."

The green bowl declined the fire. "I'd rather not go through that. Many did not survive the storm. Maybe surviving is enough. I want to put the hurricane behind me and would rather not think or talk about it."

"Survival alone is never enough," said the blue bowl. "You will remain fragile for the rest of your life."

Life went on. The green bowl could not forget what she had experienced during the hurricane—the smell of the ocean, the overpowering wind, the dark sky, the screams of injured people, fearful children crying for their parents, and flying objects. She felt grouchy, did not sleep well at night, and had bad dreams about the hurricane. She startled easily and got nervous at the slightest sign of wind or rain. It was as if the storm had penetrated deep within her soul.

Green bowl soon realized that if she didn't try the fire, she would never get over the trauma of the storm.

So one morning green bowl said to her friend, "OK, I'm ready."

"Ready for what?" asked the blue bowl.

"I'm ready for the fire," she said. "That is, if you will take me to the glassmaker."

"No problem," said her friend, smiling.

Later that day at the glassworks, the artist explained the process.

He said, "First you will tell me what you want to look like at the end: tall and thin, off-centered, perfectly balanced, short and broad, whatever. I can add colors to the green if you want a change in your hue or I can mix swirls or sparkles in with the green. Then I'll put you in the oven—you will feel your glass soften and melt. As that happens, the cracks will blend together and disappear. At that point you will be malleable, which means I can shape you. As I work with you, I will ask you to tell me what you experienced in the hurricane. It will help me understand your feelings of brokenness. And it will help you get over the trauma. While we talk about the hurricane, I'll use these tongs to pick out the pieces of grass and dirt."

"How will you know when you are finished?" asked the green bowl.

"*You* tell *me* when we are finished. When you are satisfied with the result, I take you out of the fire and let you cool. After cooling, your glass will be smooth—no cracks, no chips, and no gouges. You will be a new creation. All that will be left is your memories of the storm."

"A new creation . . .," said the green bowl. "I can hardly imagine myself as anything but a damaged bowl full of cracks."

The green bowl told the glassmaker what she wanted to look like and he suggested some colors to enhance her appearance.

Then the glassworks artist gently put the green bowl into the oven. He talked with her about the hurricane and green bowl shared what she remembered. The red-hot fire and painful memories brought tears to her eyes. It was nearly unbearable, and she cried out. But then she felt her outsides and insides start to soften. It was the strangest feeling as her cracks disappeared! She relinquished control, endured the searing heat, and allowed the healing process to take over. She let her thoughts and feelings flow while all that she had ever been merged into one great lump of molten glass.

At that point the glassmaker removed her from the oven, added colors she had selected and shaped her with special tools into the form she had described. As she cooled a little, he put her back in the fire to soften the glass once again. The searing heat did not bother her as much this time. The green bowl emptied her mind of worries, and relaxed, fully centered. She trusted the artist to re-shape her and felt safe in his hands. In and out of the oven she went—it was a long process and her very essence was being changed.

As he took her out of the oven for the last time, the glassmaker reassured her. "Don't worry if you seem a bit off color at first. As you cool, your true colors will come out and you will be very beautiful."

It was true. After only a few minutes, the now cooled lavender-bluish-green bowl was a work of art, a re-creation. She had chosen a simple form, with smooth flowing lines, swirls and blends of color. She was a bold statement and well-balanced. One small bubble of her original green color remained unblended, a reminder of her former self.

"Thank you," she said to the artist, with tears in her eyes. "I would not have believed that such change was possible."

"Thank *you* for telling me your story," replied the artist. "I know how hard it was to do that."

The lavender-bluish-green bowl met her friend in the waiting room.

"I was going to ask you what took so long," he said as he stared. "But it is obvious. I am not sure I would have known you without that one small green bubble. Your essence is the same, but you are entirely different."

"Yes," said the bowl. "I am more different than I believed possible. The heat of the oven was very painful, but the fire—and telling my story—provided what I needed to become a new creation."

Perhaps this story will be a reminder that healing, although painful, is worth the effort. For it is not enough to survive the storm, battered and cracked. When you are ready, take a leap of faith like the green bowl and become a new creation; after all, with science and art combined, plus a little hope and faith, almost anything is possible.

The Bottom Line: The Whole *Is* Greater . . .

Food for Thought Questions:

- How are you like the cracked glass bowl? _____
  _____
  _____

- What events or relationships caused your cracks and gouges?_____
  _____
  _____
  _____

- Why did the bowl think that surviving was "enough"? _____
  _____

- The bowl is afraid to go through the fire. Say something to encourage her. _____
  _____

- Was it worth it for her to go through the fire?_____
  _____

- If you went *through the fire* what would you need to talk about to heal? _____
  _____

On a separate piece of paper draw two bowls. First, draw yourself as a cracked glass bowl. Use any color or colors you wish. Draw in the cracks and gouges—each crack stands for something that hurt your body, mind, or feelings. Put some dirt or grass in any cracks that still hold lots of pain. Write on each crack the age at which you were hurt and what or who it was that hurt you. The second drawing is you as a *newly created* bowl after going through the fire, healed without cracks. Again, use any colors you wish. How are the two bowls different?

Story 35: Defensive Protection

Purpose(s) and Goal(s): ☒ Psychoeducation for teens or adults about *wearing* defensive *armor* in response to negative life events. ☒ Treatment Intervention: therapists can use this story to help clients identify events that led to defensive, protective behaviors. They can then engage in CBT intervention to identify the clients' own defensive behaviors, such as avoidance or social isolation, and the thought patterns that sustain those behaviors. Additionally, therapists can help clients "experiment" with new behaviors and challenge relational patterns using "facts."

Some trauma victims wear "armor" around their hearts and develop defensive or protective strategies (cognitive and/or behavioral) that outlast the trauma, restrict functioning, and prevent healthy interpersonal relationships. What worked at the time of the trauma is no longer adaptive. This story depicts the layers of protection that result from overuse of non-adaptive coping strategies.

Polly's Plight[3]

A girl and her mother were waiting to order their food at McDonald's and trying not to stare at the person in front of them. You could not tell whether it was a man or a woman. He or she was covered from head to toe in a suit of armor, except for two dark eyes peering out of the opening over the face. The person saw the girl trying not to stare and asked, "What's your name?"

The girl answered, "My name is Becky, what's yours?"

The person answered, "My name is Polly."

Then the little girl asked, "Isn't it awfully warm in there?"

Polly replied, "Yes, but I'm used to it. I have worn this armor since I was a child."

The girl wanted to ask some more questions, like "Why do you wear it? What do you look like under the armor?"

The girl's mother saw her daughter's curiosity and said, "Please leave Polly alone and let her order her food."

Polly said, with a smile in her voice. "It's OK. I don't mind answering your daughter's questions. Would you like to join me for lunch?"

So they all got their food and sat down to eat together.

Becky asked Polly why she was wearing armor.

Polly replied, "I wear it for protection."

The little girl asked, "Protection from what?"

Polly answered, "I don't really know anymore. I used to need it. But nothing bad has happened in a long time."

"Would you like to take it off to eat?" asked Becky.

"I guess I could take it off," said Polly.

So they all pulled and tugged on pieces of armor until a huge pile of metal was lying on the floor.

Oh my goodness!" exclaimed the girl as she stared at Polly in surprise. "Look what Polly's wearing under the armor!"

Polly looked like a human cocoon, with layers and layers of fabric, tape and other things wrapped around her. The outside layer, now that the armor was gone, was Velcro. It, of course, was very rough and prickly.

Becky said, "Polly, you are wearing Velcro and many other layers under the armor."

Polly explained, "When I was about your age, something bad happened to me, and I wanted to cover up. I remember the first layer—it was a furry coat—it made me feel safe at a bad time in my life. After that, whenever anything bad happened to me, I added a new layer."

Polly added, "The layers are good protection. If I fall down, I bounce back up. I can't scrape my elbows or knees. If someone hits me, I can't feel it."

Becky asked, " "What are some of your other layers?"

Polly replied, "Let me think a minute so I get them in the right order . . ."

Then she began,

"Layer #1 is a furry coat."

"Layer #2 is a black leather jacket."

"Layer #3 is a "heavy-duty" tin-foil mummy wrap."

"Layer #4 is Duct Tape."

"Layer #5 is a hand-stitched quilt."

"Layer #6 is a down jacket."

"Layer #7 is an insulated black diver's suit."

"Layer #8 is a lamb's wool cape."

"Layer #9 is a sandpaper poncho."

She said, "I'm not sure about layers 10 and 11."

Polly added, "And as you can see, the top layer now, #12, is Velcro, prickly side out. Layer #13 was my suit of armor. I added the armor when someone poked me with a barbeque skewer. I figured nothing could get through a suit of armor."

Becky commented, "If nothing bad has happened in a long time, I don't really see why you stay all covered up. With all those layers for protection, you can't *feel anything*—not the sun on your skin or the rain on your face. No one can give you a hug, and it must be very hard to ride a bicycle or go swimming."

Polly admitted, "I miss hugs, and I wish I could feel rain and sunshine on my face. But my layers keep me safe."

The little girl asked, "Can't you take a few off? You probably don't need all of them. Just because you needed them before doesn't mean you need them now."

Polly wrinkled up her forehead, deep in thought, and said, "Well, I guess I could take off the Velcro and a few other layers."

Polly lifted her arms up over her head, and they helped her take off the Velcro. As the last strip of Velcro came off, they saw Layer #11, a layer of soft red flannel, underneath.

"This is a real adventure," said Polly. "I forgot there was a soft flannel layer underneath the Velcro."

Then they peeled off the flannel and saw layer #10, which turned out to be clingy cellophane. When they got down to layer #9, the sandpaper poncho, Polly said she had to go.

"That's enough for one day," she announced. They exchanged emails and Facebook information and went their separate ways.

Later that day, Polly sent Becky an email. "I'm meeting some friends tomorrow at Pernicano's Pizza, 5pm, and you are welcome to join us." The girl and her mother agreed.

They next day they met at Pernicano's, where Polly introduced them to a group of her friends. The waitress who took their order tried not to stare at the sight of Polly in the sandpaper poncho.

"A large double cheese–triple pepperoni and a pitcher of root beer," they said.

"This is my *coming out party*," announced Polly. "While we wait for the pizza, I would like you to help me take off the other layers."

So while they waited for their pizza, Becky, her mother, and Polly's friends helped Polly peel off the layers. Off they came, one by one! Polly kept saying things like, "Ooh, that one's ugly!" or "Duct Tape is hard to peel off in a restaurant!"

Polly began to look less round and a little more human. Soon you could see a sweet smile, rosy cheeks, and dark eyes.

"You're very attractive," said Becky. "But you hid it well."

"Until now, it didn't seem to matter," said Polly.

When they got to the furry coat, the last layer, Polly paused. She looked serious and sad. "I don't know if I can take this one off. It brings back bad memories."

Becky replied, "It's OK—you don't need it anymore. You don't need to hide *any* part of you."

Polly realized that the bad times had not changed *who* she was; they had just changed how she saw herself. And so Polly unbuttoned the furry coat, took it off, and dropped it to the floor.

"Now we can finally see who you really are," said the little girl.

Just then, the waitress brought their pizza. She put it down and sliced it with a metal wheel. "There's something different about you," she said to Polly as she tried to figure out what had changed.

"I can't figure it out," she said, "but whatever it is, it is a good change!"

Polly and Becky shared a smile, because they agreed with the waitress. There was a visible change in Polly, and it was a very good one, indeed.

THE BOTTOM LINE: Peel Off One Layer at a Time!

Food for Thought Questions:

- How are you like Polly? _____

  _____

- At what age did you put on your first layer?_____

- How many layers have you added since that first layer? _____

  _____

- List events in your life that resulted in new layers of protection and what those layers would be made of. _____

  _____

  _____

  _____

- How do your layers help and how do they hurt?_____

  _____

- Who can help you take off layers?_____

- Draw a picture of yourself with all your layers of protection and a second picture of you after taking off the layers.

Story 36: Dissociation and Part-Self Work

Purpose(s) and Goal(s): ☒ Psychoeducation about dissociation, regressed states of functioning, and flashbacks. ☒ Treatment Intervention: with individual adolescent or adult clients displaying dissociative symptoms. The story portrays the dissociative process and is applicable for addressing intrusive memories or regressed states. It is helpful when considering the possibility of dissociative identity disorder. When a client reports memory loss, regresses, or loses time, this story helps the client consider the impact of trauma at different ages.

This story is about a young teen who used dissociation to cope when she was very little. It was her way of surviving really awful things that happened to her. She felt shattered and broken. During treatment, she started to have traumatic memories about the past and this story helped her talk about her trauma as it emerged.

A Safe Place to Call Home[4]

The girl liked reading the books from *A Series of Unfortunate Events*. She could relate to the children in those stories. As far back as she could remember she had lived with mean people. She really wanted a safe place to call home!

When she was little, she lived with her parents. She didn't remember very much about that time. Her parents had lots of problems and they weren't very nice to children.

On her eighth birthday, she went to live with her Grandma. Grandma would have made a good Disney villain. A villain is the person in the movie that does bad things and you hope they will lose and suffer in the end. Take your pick . . .

- The cruel one in *101 Dalmatians*. Cruella, as you know, killed puppies for their spotted fur.
- The sneaky one in *Sleeping Beauty* who made the princess prick her finger and go into a deep sleep.
- The lazy stepmother in *Cinderella* who made her work while her own daughters lived in luxury.
- The jealous queen in *Snow White*, who tricked her into eating a poisoned apple.

The girl's Grandma pretended to be nice but when no one was looking she turned into a mean, selfish, wicked witch. Grandma had done *unspeakable* things to her.

After Grandma, the girl lived in foster homes. One by one, they gave up on her.

The girl finally decided to move into her own house. It was a small house with little rooms, and most of the rooms were locked. She didn't have a key to open the locked doors so the girl lived only in the rooms that were open to her.

The girl heard noises at night coming from the locked rooms and it gave her the creeps. She did not sleep well and she did not feel safe. Sometimes she thought she was crazy, but she wasn't crazy at all.

One night, a voice woke her from a deep sleep.

"You stupid girl!" shouted a teenage voice.

The girl got out of bed and tiptoed down the hall to the locked door where the voice was coming from. She knocked, and waited.

"Go ahead, Stupid," said an angry voice. "Open the door and let me out."

"I don't have the key," said the girl. "And you sound too mean. I don't want to let you out."

"You would be mean, too, if you had been through what I've been through."

"I'm not letting you out," said the girl. "And I'm going back to bed."

The girl ran back to her bedroom, saying, "There's no such thing as ghosts . . ."

She locked her door, got in bed, and went back to sleep.

A few hours later, the girl woke again from a deep sleep. She heard a younger voice coming from one of the other locked rooms.

"Let me out—I'll be good, I promise. I don't mean to be bad. Here, I'll cut a switch and you can whoop me. Please don't leave me alone in here."

The girl was not as scared this time. She unlocked her bedroom door and went down the hall to the locked door where she heard the young voice. She knocked and said, "Who is in there? What is wrong?"

"You know me," said a young voice. "Please let me out."

The girl said, "I don't know you," and then "I can't let you out. I don't have the key. But I can talk to you through the door. You sound too young to be awake this late."

"I'm ten years old," the voice replied. "I have trouble sleeping. I get scared at night."

"What are you scared of?" asked the, girl.

"I'm not ready to tell you," the young voice answered. "But maybe I will when I'm ready."

The girl went back to her bedroom and locked the door. She went to sleep after telling herself 100 times that she was not losing her mind.

When it was almost morning, a very young voice woke her from the deepest sleep yet. The voice was crying in fear and pain.

"Please make it stop! I'm sorry I wet my pants! I promise to be good!"

The girl ran down the hall to the room where the young child was crying.

She knocked and called through the door, "Please don't cry. I won't let anyone hurt you. No one is here but you and me. This is a safe place."

The child's voice cried out, "I don't feel safe behind a locked door in a dark room. Please let me out!"

"I'm so sorry," said the girl sadly. "I don't have a key to this room." She did not want to leave the scared child alone in a dark, locked room.

The girl said, "Let's talk through the door. Sit with your back against it. I am right here on the other side. I will stay here as long as you need me, until you can get back to sleep. And I promise I won't let anyone hurt you."

The child cried for awhile and the girl comforted her. The girl sang her a lullaby and told her stories with happy endings. She said, "Pretend I'm wrapping my arms around you and go back to sleep. I'll be here when you wake up in the morning." The little girl settled down, and they both went to sleep.

When the girl woke up the next morning, she knew what she had to do.

First, she needed to find a way to unlock and open all the doors. She wanted to talk to the children behind the locked doors. It sounded like their lives had been just as bad as hers.

She also needed to make some changes in her house—it needed a total makeover.

The girl went back to the first locked room. The mean-voiced person behind the first door told the girl where to find the master key that could open all the doors in the house. "I'm sorry I was such a bitch last night. I don't trust anyone and don't want to get hurt. I use a mean voice to scare people off."

The girl found the master key and unlocked the doors one by one. It took quite a long time! There were hugs and tears and rejoicing at the doors of the house finally being opened.

The girl said, "I want to sit down and talk with each of you, but first this house needs a lot of work. We need a safe place to call home."

You would never believe what that house was like after the makeover. They installed a good alarm system so that the house was safe from intruders. They built a large open room at the center of the house. The kitchen had a long table, big enough to seat ten. There was a pretty garden out back. There were also safe bedrooms with comfortable beds and room monitors. No more small, closed locked rooms.

After the makeover, the girl, the teenager, the ten-year-old, and the very young child sat down at the table together to talk.

"I want to hear your stories," said the Girl, "I'm a good listener, and we have all the time in the world. Also, I would like to tell you what I went through growing up."

They had many memories to share, and even though you might think it would be hard for them to talk to one another, it was not. It was as if they had known each other a *very* long time.

THE BOTTOM LINE: Find a Safe Place to Call Home.

Food for Thought Questions:

- How are you like the girl in this story? _____

  _____

- If it was your voice behind one of the doors, how old would you be, and what would you be saying?_____

- What would you talk about if you joined the others at the long table _____

  _____

- Draw a picture of a house with locked rooms. Draw yourself inside one of the rooms, the age you are now. List five strengths or things you like about yourself. Inside three of the other rooms, draw yourself at three younger ages, times when bad things happened to you. Write what happened to you at those ages. Imagine unlocking the doors one by one and talking about what happened to you at those ages.

Story 37: Self-Integration

Purpose(s) and Goal(s): ☒ Psychoeducation for children and teens about self-acceptance. ☒ Treatment Intervention: to be used with children or adolescents who have trouble accepting aspects of their past. The story addresses shame, embarrassment, and avoidance.

Kids sometimes feel disgust, embarrassment, or shame when thinking about things from the past. They may tell lies, brag about themselves (embellishing the truth), or cover up things about their families so that others will accept them. This story will help kids accept themselves as they are—the good with the *bad*.

The Unraveled Tapestry[5]

Donna was laying on her purple and green comforter in her purple and green bedroom, staring at the bright purple walls, deep in thought.

As Donna stared at her walls and listened to music, her eyes were drawn to a woven tapestry.

Donna said, "I have had that ugly thing hanging on my wall since the day I was born."

The tapestry was not really ugly, but it was interesting; it was full of threads and materials of all types, textures, and colors. You might have heard the saying, "The whole is greater than the sum of its parts." Well, the tapestry was like that. Each separate thread was not much to look at, but together the threads were a work of art.

Some of the tapestry threads were rough and some were smooth. There were threads of silk, rope, plastic cord, pot holder loops, and strips of cloth, and even pieces of clean, white baby diapers. There were woven threads of black wire, and pink yarn, and computer power supply cords. There were shiny brocade fabrics and red corduroy as well as blue denim and sheer curtains.

Donna liked the brocade and corduroy, but she *hated* some of the other threads. The tapestry was self-weaving—like something out of a Harry Potter book. The first thread appeared the day Donna was born, and every time something important happened, another thread was woven in. That meant that some of the threads were from important good times and some from bad times.

"I know," thought Donna, "I can take out some of the threads. No one will ever notice." Donna decided to take out all the threads she did not like, the ones that bothered her or reminded her of bad times in her life.

The first thread Donna pulled out was one made of gauze bandage. It had been woven the day she got stitches in her forehead after falling on the playground. She didn't want to remember that day! Then she took out the thread from the dress she wore the Christmas her parents got divorced. She also decided to remove the shoelace from her first grade tennis shoe; one day at school, Jimmy had teased her about those tennis shoes and made her cry.

So Donna unwove the tapestry, one *bad* thread at a time, until there was a pile of unwanted threads sitting on the floor of her bedroom. She hung what was left of the tapestry back on her bedroom wall and hid the *other* threads way in the back of her bedroom closet.

Now, there were big gaps in the tapestry. The bedroom wall showed through the gaps. The loose threads of the tapestry slumped and stuck out from the wall. But Donna didn't care. She had finally gotten rid of the pieces she didn't like.

A couple of days later, while Donna was daydreaming in her bedroom, she heard a knock on her door.

"Who is it?" Donna called out.

"It's me," said her best friend Jane. "Can I come in?"

"Sure," said Donna.

Jane entered the room with a smile, but when she saw the tapestry her eyes opened wide with surprise.

"What happened to THAT?" asked Jane.

Donna said, "I didn't think you would notice."

Her friend looked her straight in the eye. Donna looked away, avoiding her friend's eyes.

"Come on, Donna. What did you do to the tapestry? Pieces of it are missing."

"Oh," said Donna. "I fixed it. I took out the parts I didn't like and put them away. I want to forget about those parts."

Jane disagreed. "I always thought it was beautiful just the way it was. It isn't whole without the other threads. All those threads are part of you."

"Well, I kept the best parts, the good parts," said Donna.

Jane replied, "It was all good. Now it has unraveled and is falling apart."

"I don't want the bad parts in there," argued Donna.

"Life is good and bad," said Jane. "You need both kinds of threads to hold the tapestry together. You might not have noticed, but without the darker threads, the brighter threads lose contrast and are not as beautiful. The bad threads are tough but they make the tapestry stronger."

Her friend went home, and Donna stared carefully at the tapestry on her wall. She had not noticed it before, but the bright pretty threads still on the tapestry all looked the same. They were made of light, thin materials without much depth. They were drooping and unraveling without the darker threads to hold them in place. The threads hidden in her closet had more texture and interesting stories to tell.

Donna had a sudden "aha." "I can re-weave my tapestry!"

Donna went to her closet and pulled out the pile of tangled, darker, textured threads. She wove them in using a pattern of her own creation. When she finished, the tapestry had a whole new look. Donna hung the tapestry back on her wall.

Donna thought, "The new tapestry is somehow better than the original one. I don't know how that happened. I used the same old threads—all I did was re-weave them."

It was true. The dark, coarse threads contrasted with the brighter colors and the new tapestry was a thing of beauty, whole and complete.

THE BOTTOM LINE: Every Thread Counts!

Food for Thought Questions:

- Draw a sagging tapestry, with many threads missing. Now, on a separate piece of paper, draw the threads you took out of the tapestry. They should be many textures and colors. Label each thread with something bad that happened to you in the past.

- With the help of your therapist and caregiver, create and weave a tapestry. First make the tapestry threads. Draw them on a piece of paper, write on each one what it stands for, and then cut them out—some will be good things in your life memories and some bad. You can make them different widths, colors, and textures. You can glue stuff on the threads if you like. Your caregiver and you can each label some of the threads. Remind your caregiver to make some threads about happy memories and some about things the caregiver has trouble talking about. You do the same. In a therapy session, glue a square "frame" on a piece of cardboard, just gluing the ends. Then glue some up and down threads on the frame, connecting each end to the frame. Last, weave in the good and bad threads, one at a time, in and out across the up and down threads. Take turns with your caregiver. Talk about each thread as you weave it into the tapestry. When you finish, label the tapestry. See how beautiful it is. As you look at it, remember that each part of it is part of you—and none of it is "bad". Now it is whole.

- Which three threads were hardest for you to talk about? _____
  _____
  _____

- Which three threads were easiest to talk about? _____
  _____

- What does it mean to say, "The whole is greater than the parts?" _____
  _____
  _____

Notes

1 See also Story 5 (*Bear of a Different Color*) and Story 18 (*Stick Together*) for further examples.

2 From *Outsmarting the Riptide of Domestic Violence: Metaphor and Mindfulness for Change*, by P. Pernicano, 2011, Lanham, MD: Jason Aronson. Reprinted and adapted with permission.

3 From *Family-Focused Trauma Intervention: Using Metaphor and Play with Victims of Abuse and Neglect*, by P. Pernicano, 2010, Lanham, MD: Jason Aronson. Reprinted and adapted with permission.

4 From *Outsmarting the Riptide of Domestic Violence: Metaphor and Mindfulness for Change*, by P. Pernicano, 2011, Lanham, MD: Jason Aronson. Reprinted and adapted with permission.

5 From *Metaphorical Stories for Child Therapy: Of Magic and Miracles*, by P. Pernicano, 2010, Lanham, MD: Jason Aronson. Reprinted and adapted with permission.

CHAPTER 15

CONJOINT PARENT–CHILD WORK AND ATTACHMENT ISSUES

Story 38: Coping with Heartbreak

Purpose(s) and Goal(s): ☒ Psychoeducation about feelings and thoughts associated with loss and abandonment. ☒ Treatment Intervention: to be used with adolescents in family or individual therapy for emotional identification and expression. This work allows teens to deal with adult rejection and explore ways to be safely emotionally vulnerable.

When someone you love hurts you, it can break your heart. A girl in a group home was sarcastic, rude, and mean to other people. When asked why, she said she had a plastic heart. Her real heart had been sent on vacation because it had been "broken" by her mother. The story allowed her to discuss ways her mother's behavior had hurt her. One night the therapist overheard her reading the story to her mother over the phone, to help her mother understand what she was feeling. The story helped her come to grips with her mother's rejection and be able to accept kindness from other adults.

The Girl with the Plastic Heart[1]

Dedicated to P

A girl and her friend walked down the sidewalk one bright, sunny day. As an older woman walked toward them, the girl smirked at her friend. It was as if to say, "Watch what I'm going to do!"

She bumped the woman hard enough to knock her off balance. The girl kept walking.

The girl's friend helped the woman up and explained, "Don't mind her. She knocks *everyone* off balance."

"And why is that?" asked the woman.

The friend replied, "It's because she has a plastic heart."

"A plastic heart?" the woman asked.

"Yes," replied the girl's friend. "Her real heart is on vacation."

"What do you mean?" the woman asked.

The friend answered, "Her real heart got broken over and over by those she loved—especially by her mother. It needed a rest and time to heal. So she replaced it with a plastic heart."

"Why a plastic heart?" asked the women.

"A plastic heart can't feel," said the friend.

The woman looked concerned. "When you send your heart on vacation, it gets lazy. Let's go talk to your friend!"

The woman and the girl's friend ran to catch up with the girl with the plastic heart.

"*Why* is that old woman with you?" the girl asked her friend.

The friend replied, "I told her about your plastic heart."

"My plastic heart is none of her business," said the girl.

The woman spoke directly to the girl. "Hearts on vacation grow lazy and selfish. Your real heart is probably telling others that you are a heartless person for sending it away."

The girl frowned. "I need to go find out if that is true!"

The girl led them to the resort where her real heart was staying. The woman had been right. The heart was sitting by a pool, flabby and lazy. It was wearing glittery sunglasses and sipping a fruity drink.

"Where have you been and what do you want?" the real heart asked the girl.

The girl said, "Your vacation is over. I'm taking you home with me."

"You don't need *me*," said the heart. "You have that cheap plastic model. And I don't know if I *want* to come back."

Then the heart took a really cheap shot. "You're no better than those that broke *your* heart. You sent me away and forgot about me!"

"I'm not like the people that broke my heart," said the girl. "I'm loving and dependable, and I keep my promises."

She added, "I sent you on vacation to heal. You have healed just fine. Let's go pack your bags."

The real heart knew it did not have a choice. It was time to go home. Off they went to pack.

The woman handed the girl a soft scarf when she returned with the heart.

"Here," said the woman, "You can use it as a heart-warmer. It protects your real heart from being broken."

The girl gently wrapped her real heart in the heart warmer. She removed the plastic heart and replaced it with the real thing.

"There," she said. "That's better."

The real heart whispered something to the girl that no one else could hear.

"I almost forgot," the girl said to the woman. "Thanks for the heart-warmer. I'm sorry I was so hard-hearted earlier!"

"That's OK," said the woman. "I understand."

The woman said goodbye to the girl and her friend.

Later, the girl wondered what had happened to the plastic heart. The girl would never know it, but the woman really did understand.

The girl's plastic heart was sitting on a shelf in the old woman's house—right next to a second plastic heart and a photo of the woman's real heart sipping a drink at a vacation resort.

THE BOTTOM LINE: Don't Set Your Heart Aside.

Food for Thought Questions:

- Have you ever been hard-hearted? Describe. _____

  _____

- Who said or did something to break your heart?_____

  _____

- Name three things that help mend a broken heart. _____

  _____

- Draw the outline of a large heart. This is your heart. Next, draw cracks inside the heart. On the cracks, write things people did or said that broke it. Take the heart to an adult you trust. Ask that adult to glue BAND-AIDs on the broken heart. Tell the adult things that would help mend your broken heart. The adult will write those things on the BAND-AIDs.

- Cut out another heart that is big enough to hold lots of love. Make a list of people you care about or who seem to care about you. Hint: Think about people who listen to you, are nice to you, and treat you well. Then cut out small paper hearts and label them with the names of people on your list (or use candy hearts). Glue or paste them inside the larger heart. See how much love it can hold. If you have a real mom, a stepmom, and a foster mom, they can all go in your heart if you want them there. When you start to think that no one loves you, look at the hearts and remind yourself that you are loved.

- Then make a second list of people you are not ready to let inside your heart. Write down what those people need to do or say for you to be ready to bring them inside. Cut out small hearts and write those names on the hearts. Store them somewhere. During therapy—if and when you are ready—add those hearts to the others. You do not have to do this unless you have a true change of heart toward the person.

Note

1 From *Family-Focused Trauma Intervention: Using Metaphor and Play with Victims of Abuse and Neglect*, by P. Pernicano, 2010, Lanham, MD: Jason Aronson. Reprinted and adapted with permission.

CHAPTER 16

ENHANCING FUTURE SAFETY AND WELLBEING

Story 39: Moving in a New Direction

Purpose(s) and Goal(s): ☒ Psychoeducation about the change process and why some efforts to change are not successful. ☒ Treatment Intervention: to be used with children, adolescents, or adults to discuss goal-setting and self-defeating efforts to change. The story illustrates how to evaluate the risks and benefits of moving in a new direction.

To be successful, you have to work hard, use the right tools, be in the right place, and set goals that you can achieve. No amount of blind hope, effort, or motivation will lead to success when the goal is totally outside your control. Change sometimes requires making a move, either in the tools you are using or the way in which you are using them. I consider this my "Serenity Prayer" story. You have to change what you can (with courage), accept what you can't change, and know the difference. You can stay in the same place and continue to use the same unsuccessful tools or you can move in a new direction and seek realistic change.

Gold in the Desert[1]

Once upon a time, a girl was walking in the desert, just down the road from her house. Have you ever seen a desert? A desert is dry, bare, and flat as far as the eye can see.

The hot sun glared down from high in the sky that day. Everything was dusty, and fine grains of sand kept getting into the girl's shoes. The heat made waves in the hazy air, and off in the distance you could see the faint outline of a range of tall, snow-topped mountains. No one lived near the girl—her house was "out in the middle of nowhere" according to her friends.

As the girl walked, she drank from her water bottle and put some more sunscreen on her face and arms. Then suddenly the girl heard a loud voice: "Oh, CRAP!" The voice came from a tall man who was kneeling in the sand a few feet in front of her. Sweat was pouring down his red face as he scooped up some sand and sifted through it with a flat pan. The pan had very tiny holes in it and sand poured through them.

As the girl watched, the man threw down his sifter and said, again, very loudly, "Oh, CRAP!" The girl giggled. Everyone knew that "CRAP" was a bad word and not a nice thing to say. "I must be doing something wrong," said the red-faced man.

The girl was very curious and could not figure out what the man was doing. "Excuse me, Mister," the girl said as she approached, "What are you trying to do?"

"That's obvious," he said. "I'm searching for gold. I've sifted sand all day and haven't found *any* gold. I'm starting to get very upset. I've always been told that if you believe in yourself and work hard, you will be successful."

The girl said, "I can see you are upset, but everyone knows you sift for gold in a stream or mine gold up in the mountains. There is no water here, and the mountains are miles away."

Then the man said, "I feel like a failure, because I haven't found any gold. I must be doing something wrong."

The girl replied, trying to not hurt his feelings, "Mister, you're not doing anything wrong. You're looking for gold in the wrong place. There is no gold here: Never has been, never will be. You might find gold up in the mountains. You're using the right tools—you're just looking in the wrong place."

"Tell me more," said the man.

"You could use that pan to sift through the sand in a stream up near the mountains," the girl answered. "If you want to find gold, you need to leave the desert."

"I was afraid of that," he replied. "I've always lived in the desert and don't really want to go anywhere else. I don't like to travel, and I'm very comfortable in the desert. I want to stay in the desert *and* find gold. What if I try my hardest, pray night and day, and use my very best sifting technique?"

The girl said, "Even if you try your hardest, pray night and day, and use your very best sifting technique, you won't succeed. Sifting for gold in the desert is like trying to squeeze water out of a rock."

"You can't squeeze water out of a rock!" the man said.

The girl smiled playfully and handed him a small, hard, dry desert rock. "Go ahead and try," she said. "Squeeze it really hard." Just for fun, he gave the rock a squeeze. Of course, nothing came out of the rock.

She said, "Squeeze a little harder." So the man squeezed with all his might, but no water came out.

The girl teased, "Maybe you're not doing it right. Maybe you need to twist it or sit on it or rub it—surely if you keep trying, you will squeeze some water out of that rock?"

The man replied, "No, I can't squeeze water out of this rock."

"And why is that?" the girl asked.

He stated, "Because there is no water in it."

"Exactly," said the girl, "and there is no gold in that sand. Go to where the gold is if you want to find the gold."

The man realized that the girl was very wise for her young years. He could stay where he was (and quit hoping to find gold) or move on to a new place where gold was plentiful. It was his choice to make.

THE BOTTOM LINE: Go for the Gold!

Food for Thought Questions:

- What is your gold? _____
  _____

- Where might you need to go to find your gold?_____
  _____

- What do you need to change to move in a new direction?_____
  _____
  _____

- What old behavior is hardest for you to give up and why? _____
  _____
  _____
  _____

Story 40: Escaping Family Patterns

Purpose(s) and Goal(s): ⊠ Psychoeducation for children and teens about making different choices than parents, especially in the area of substance abuse. ⊠ Treatment Intervention: to be used in family or individual treatment with children, adolescents, and caregivers to address parental habitual behaviors, such as substance abuse, that impact children.

Kids who are abused sometimes really want their parents to change and try really hard to get their parents to make that happen, but that's unlikely if the parent is not ready to change. This can happen when the parent has a problem with drugs or pills, alcohol, or mental illness, or if he or she dates the wrong people. These things make it hard for an adult to care for children. The adult's problem might make him self-centered and blind to what he is doing. If your parent has a substance abuse problem or mental illness, you can't change that and it's not your fault. It is not bad to hope that your parent will change, but your parent has to decide whether or not to make that leap. It is OK for you to accept that your parent is not ready to change and to find other people and supports to help you. Whether or not your parent decides to take a new path, it is OK to have a life of your own.

Swimming in the Swamp[2]

Laura Labrador loved to swim. Every morning before school, she went to swim in the smelly, muddy water of the swamp. The cattails made her sneeze, and the lily pads tangled around her feet. The water at the swamp was very stinky, because the waste-water plant dumped waste there. Waste water, by the way, is what goes down your sink and your toilet.

People who walked near the swamp held their noses and said, "Phew! What a terrible smell!"

Laura kind of liked the smell. Her parents had taught her to swim at the swamp when she was very young. Everyone in her family swam there and they all smelled like swamp water. They had never known any other life.

Laura knew that people in town talked about her and her family. "Those smelly swamp dogs," people whispered. "They should go live somewhere else."

After Laura took her swim each morning, she shook herself off, rolled around in the dirt, and jogged to school.

No one else at Laura's school swam in the swamp. When the other dogs saw her coming, they groaned. "Here comes stinky Laura!" Laura tried not to let their teasing bother her, but it did—it hurt her feelings.

One afternoon, Laura took a different path on her way home from school. The path stopped at a wooden dock, and there was a clear blue lake under the dock. Laura went out on the dock, from where she could see little minnows swimming around in the water.

"Sniff, sniff," Laura went, trying to smell the water. "This water doesn't smell! What kind of swamp is this?"

"Hey, girl," she heard. "Where did you come from?" A person was rowing a boat up to the dock. The person climbed up on the dock and tied off his boat. He reached into his pocket for a yellow tennis ball, and tossed it into the water. Without thinking, Laura leaped from the dock into the water.

"Splash!" went Laura.

Brrr! How strange! The water was icy cold and it tasted delicious. There was no smell. No cattails. No lily pads. Just nice fresh water.

Laura swam out, grabbed the ball in her mouth and paddled back to shore. She shook off and dropped the ball at the man's feet.

"Good girl," said the man. Laura wiggled as she waited for another toss.

Toss–Splash! Toss–Splash!

Laura and her new friend played until the sun started to set; then she said goodbye and headed home to her family.

As Laura went in the front door of her house, she noticed something she had not noticed before. It was the swamp smell.

Laura's mother saw her come in the door and said, "What happened to you? You're later than usual."

Laura said, "I took a new path and went swimming."

Her mother said, "Where did you swim? You smell funny. And what happened to your fur? How did it get so clean?"

Laura replied, "I got clean in the new swimming place. I've never seen water like that: it's blue, clear and full of little fish! It smells nice and tastes good. You should come with me, Mom. You could get clean, too."

Her mother answered in a stern voice. "Laura, the swamp water is good enough for me and was good enough for the Labs before me. I'm warning you—stay away from that new swimming place."

Laura's mother didn't want her daughter getting funny ideas about swimming in a new place.

Laura disobeyed her mother. She knew her mother wouldn't like it, but she swam every day at the new place. She liked being clean and playing ball with the person who owned the rowboat. She tried to get her mother to go with her, but her mother made a lot of excuses.

"I'm too tired," she would say. Or, "I like my life the way it is." Laura's mother even tried to pull her back into the life of the swamp. "Come on, Laura," she said one morning. "We never spend time together any more, and I hardly ever see you. Let's go swim in the swamp."

"OK, Mom," she barked. "Let's go swim together."

They raced each other down the path, chasing tails. When they got to the swamp, Laura's mother dove into the murky black waters, and Laura followed. The water clung to her fur and the smell made Laura gag. The swamp gas made her dizzy and it was hard to breathe.

"Isn't this fun, Laura?" asked her mother. "Isn't this better than swimming alone in the lake?"

"Mom," said Laura, as she climbed out of the swamp and shook off. "I don't like the swamp anymore. I like being clean. I guess I'd rather swim in the lake than swim in the swamp."

Her mother replied, in a not-so-nice voice. "You're no fun. What kind of a Labrador are you? You think you're too good for the rest of us! Someday you'll be sorry!"

Laura felt sad to hear her mother talk like that. She ran to the lake with tears in her eyes and took a quick swim to clean off the swamp muck. As she walked to school, Laura reminded herself, "My mom doesn't mean to hurt my feelings. I know she loves me. She just doesn't like change."

It was true—Laura's mother loved her. She was just afraid of Laura's new and different kind of life.

Laura loved her family and wished she could convince them to swim in the clean water of the lake, but the swamp water was all they had ever known. But even though she could not change her family, Laura knew she had the right to *change herself*. She could swim in the lake *and* love her family the way they were.

THE BOTTOM LINE: You Can Choose Your Own Swimming Hole!

Food for Thought Questions:

- How are you like Laura?_____

  _____

  _____

- How are you like Laura's mother? _____

  _____

- What is your family's swamp? _____

  _____

- Why did Laura's mother want to keep swimming in the swamp? _____

  _____

  _____

- Parents who use drugs or alcohol are a little like Laura's mother. Why do you think parents who use drugs and alcohol don't want to stop or get treatment so they can change?_____

  _____

  _____

  _____

  _____

Notes

1 From *Metaphorical Stories for Child Therapy: Of Magic and Miracles*, by P. Pernicano, 2010, Lanham, MD: Jason Aronson. Reprinted and adapted with permission.
2 From *Outsmarting the Riptide of Domestic Violence: Metaphor and Mindfulness for Change*, by P. Pernicano, 2011, Lanham, MD: Jason Aronson. Reprinted and adapted with permission.

PART IV

THERAPY STORIES TO USE WITH CAREGIVERS

CHAPTER 17

ADULT ISSUES AND BLIND SPOTS

Story 41: Co-Dependency

Purpose(s) and Goal(s): ☒ Psychoeducation for caregivers about co-dependency. ☒ Treatment Intervention: to be used with caregivers to weigh the risks and benefits of staying in an unhealthy relationship. The story is an excellent lead-in to relationship issues where one partner is being taken advantage of by the other. This story is powerful in a women's group with victims of intimate partner violence to help the participants discuss caretaking behavior and co-dependency.

The women's group needed a jumpstart to get them talking about the ways in which they allowed themselves to be victimized and taken advantage of by their partners. It is an eye-opening story with enough "gross factor" to elicit humor and insight.

Don't Let the Leeches Suck You Dry

A woman had been swimming all afternoon in the muddy lake. As she came out of the water, her friend gasped.

"What are those nasty things all over you?" asked her friend.

"They are leeches," said the woman. "But calm down, they won't hurt me."

"Leeches?" asked her friend. "Don't they suck your blood?"

"Yes," said the woman calmly, "They are blood suckers, but they can't help it: it's their nature."

The woman started to towel off and put on her clothes.

"You need to get them off you before you dress," said her friend.

"No," the woman replied. "They're fine. They want to be with me everywhere I go. I told them I would be there for them. And they need my blood to survive. In fact one said that if I didn't help him he would die."

"But you are covered in them!" her friend protested. "They will suck you dry."

"Nonsense," said the woman. "Losing a little blood won't hurt me—I have plenty. I like to be needed, and I need to be loved. I could never forgive myself if one of them died because I refused to help."

Her friend grew quiet. She thought the woman was making a big mistake but the woman would have to learn that for herself.

The woman woke up the next morning looking a little pale. Then she noticed that the leeches were nice and fat with her blood. She felt a little light-headed from the blood loss, but she headed back to the lake to swim.

An hour later, the woman came out of the lake. There were even more leeches on her than before. They covered almost every inch of her body. The first group of leeches had sent word to the other leeches in the lake. The word was that if they stuck to the woman, they would have a free home and never go hungry: she was the kind of woman who would never turn them away.

You might wonder why the woman let a bunch of leeches take advantage of her like that. "What did they do *for her*?" you might ask. Well, they provided a little company and they made her feel needed. What more does a woman want?

The next morning the woman's skin was white as a ghost. The leeches were plump and healthy, filled with the woman's nourishing blood. She felt tired and listless.

"Where did all my energy go?" she wondered. She could hardly walk and didn't feel like going swimming.

Her friend, who looked worried, said, "I heard the leeches talking last night. They called you an *easy target* and they were laughing at how gullible you are. Please don't let the leeches suck you dry!"

The woman didn't want to believe her friend. She stayed in bed all day because she was so tired. Later that afternoon, as she woke up from a long nap she heard the leeches talking. She kept her eyes closed and listened.

"Why should I work for blood? She'll give me all I want!"

"Just give her a sob story and she'll take care of you forever."

"She needs to feel needed. In her book, there's always room for one more."

"This meal ticket will never say no."

"A place to sleep and three square meals a day. What more could I ask for?"

The woman felt hurt and angry hearing them talk. She realized she had been giving a lot more than she had been getting: the blood-sucking leeches cared only about themselves. Her friend had been right.

The woman told the leeches it was time for them to move on and called her friend to come help her remove the leeches from her body. Leeches can be very stubborn about moving on.

When the woman's friend arrived, she resisted the urge to say, "I told you so."

"Come on," her friend said. "Let's go down to the lake and cut these suckers loose." As the two headed for the door, they passed a full-length mirror.

"Just a minute," the woman said as she stared at her reflection. She saw what the leeches had done to her. The leeches were nasty looking against her pale skin and she had a tired look in her eyes.

"Yuck!" she said. "What an awful sight! The leeches sucked me dry, and I let them do it!"

"It's OK," said her friend. "You couldn't see it until you were ready. But now that you see it, you can do something about it."

Together, they walked down to the lake. The woman and her friend picked the leeches off one by one then threw them back in the lake.

For the woman, it was a new beginning. Of course, she needed some time to get strong and healthy again. She vowed, "The next time someone makes me a bunch of promises, I'll make sure he has a blood supply of his own."

The Red Cross collects blood from donors every day, and they give it to people who need it, such as those who have been in car accidents. But not even the Red Cross will share lifeblood with a bloodthirsty leech. Why should you?

The Bottom Line: Don't Let the Leeches Suck You Dry!

Food for Thought Questions:

- How are you like the woman in this story? _____
  _____

- Name your leeches: _____
  _____

- Have you ever been a leech with someone else? If so, describe. _____
  _____

Story 42: Relational Control

Purpose(s) and Goal(s): ☒ Psychoeducation for caregivers about the nature of relational control and emotional abuse. ☒ Treatment Intervention: to be used with caregivers in group or individual therapy to discuss the control strategies in intimate partner violence and emotional abuse.

Intimate partner violence often begins with signs of coercive control and/or emotional abuse. The story that follows compares IPV to a dance and shows the ways in which a woman might be pressured to change her behavior to please her partner.

The Dance

The woman waited eagerly for her partner to arrive for their dance lesson. Each week they learned a new dance, and this week they would learn the salsa. The woman loved the sensuous, lively style, and she was dressed in a beautiful and colorful salsa costume

The woman's heart dropped as she saw her partner enter the dance studio wearing a tight black leotard and ballet slippers.

Before she could utter a word, her partner said, with a critical frown, "You are dressed all wrong for ballet. How could you forget what to wear?"

"The teacher said we were dancing the salsa this week," the woman replied.

"You're wrong," he accused. "And this is not the first time you have messed up."

The woman wanted to please her partner. But lately, it was becoming more difficult. Her partner told her what to wear and then blamed her for wearing the wrong thing. She learned her dance steps to follow her partner's lead, but he would change the steps in the middle of the dance or tell her she had learned the wrong dance. These things seemed to be happening a lot lately.

"Come dance with me," ordered the partner. The woman did her best, but it was hopeless. Salsa and ballet just don't mix.

Her partner turned away with a scowl.

"Go change," he said. "Put on your ballet leotard and then come back out."

The woman didn't really want to change. She wanted to learn the salsa, and the others in the class were in their salsa costumes.

Everyone stared at the woman, even the instructor, as she headed to the dressing room to change. The woman felt embarrassed and humiliated.

A few minutes later, the woman headed back to the dance floor wearing her leotard and ballet slippers.

Her partner was standing there with a smirk on his face. He had on his sexy tango costume, dark and forbidding. He smirked at her in her ballet garb.

"What are you doing now?" he asked. "Didn't I tell you to put on your tango costume?"

"No," she replied. "You said ballet."

"You're wrong," he said. "But it can't be helped. Come dance with me."

Once again, it was hopeless. The steps and music of the tango and ballet are too different.

"This is your last chance," the man said to the woman. "Go put on your tango costume. Maybe this time you can get it right."

By now the woman was more than a little confused. She didn't want to start an argument, so she went into the dressing room and changed into her flashy tango costume.

As the woman came back out of the dressing room, she was aghast. Her partner was now in a formal ballroom dancing outfit.

"I don't know what's wrong with you," he said. "I'm ready to dance the waltz."

The dance instructor had been watching while the man confused and embarrassed his partner. She approached the couple.

She said to the man, "This dance is not all about you. Dance requires give and take. It is both a skill and an art. To dance well, you need to trust each other and show off your partner's talents. You risk losing your partner if you try to control the dance."

She turned to the woman with a smile. "You prepare well for your dance lessons, but it is hard to dance when your partner keeps you off balance. Good dance requires give and take. You might consider dancing alone or finding a dance partner that is a better *fit*."

The woman replied, "I guess I am trying too hard to please my partner. I can find a new dance partner or dance alone if this keeps up. After all, it may take two to tango, and I love the tango, but a solo tap or ballet is always a good alternative! "

THE BOTTOM LINE: Learn to Give and Take or Find a New Dance!

Food for Thought Questions:

- How is an abusive relationship like a dance? _____
  _____

- How are you like the woman in the story? _____
  _____

- What advice do you have for the woman in the story? _____
  _____

Story 43: The Cycle of Violence

Purpose(s) and Goal(s): ☒ Psychoeducation for caregivers and teens about the cycle of violence. ☒ Treatment Intervention: to be used with caregivers or adolescents who are involved in abusive relationships or ones that seem at risk of becoming abusive. The story is appropriate for therapy (individual or group), or as part of the curriculum for an IPV women's support group, in order to discuss patterns and triggers of violent behavior.

This story depicts the thinking and attitudes in abusive partners and their victims, as well as the cycle of violence. It shows the somewhat elusive nature of violence and how suddenly it can arise. Those that read the story will clearly see some of the core schemas that must be addressed in both partners in order to eliminate violence in intimate relationships.

Chip Away[1]

"Now, Stella," he said. "Don't be like that. Let's kiss and make up and go to bed." The speaker was Sidney Satyr and he was Stella Statue's boyfriend. In case you did not know it, a satyr is half-man, half-goat. You could smell the half-goat part of Sidney. He worked at a nearby farm grazing on grass and came home each night smelling of sweat and goat manure. Stella was a beautiful Italian statue carved out of white marble. Her lines were graceful and everywhere she went, people admired her. Many of Stella's friends wondered what she saw in Sidney—it was probably that handsome goatee, his endearing charm, and the wild, unpredictable side of him. Stella thought he was so sexy and manly.

"No," she said. "I won't kiss and make up until you say you're sorry for yelling and threatening me."

"You know I didn't mean it, Stella. I would never use the chisel on you. My temper got the best of me, and I couldn't stop myself. And why should I apologize? You know I have a baaaaad temper. When you called me a 'lazy goat' I saw red. I would never lay a hand on you."

It was true that Stella had called Sidney a "lazy goat." She had found his dirty underwear and a whole bunch of dirty dishes and leftover food in the bedroom. She told him he should pick up after himself. Sidney got all red in the face, pulled a chisel and mallet (for chipping ice when he wanted a cold drink) out of the drawer of his bedside table and threatened to chip her with it.

"OK, Sidney, let's just forget about it and go to bed." Stella had decided to let it drop. She hated to make waves, and Sidney had a terrible temper.

"Goodnight," she said, as she gave Sidney a kiss. He stroked one of Stella's white marble breasts and wrapped his arms around her.

Sidney was glad Stella didn't make him apologize. He thought, "She really needs to keep her mouth shut. She knows it makes me mad when she nags me about my dirty clothes and dishes. All that griping really gets on my nerves."

About a week later, Sidney came home from work and found a note from Stella. It said, "Sidney, I'm going to the health club with Sue and then we'll get something to eat. I'll be home by eight; there's some lettuce and other greens in the refrigerator for your dinner."

Sidney thought, "I shouldn't have to eat alone. My girlfriend should be here when I get home from work, not hanging out with that bitch Sue. "

Sidney didn't like Sue. She was one of those feminists and put a lot of crazy ideas in Stella's head. Sidney drove to the health club, found Stella and said, "I came to pick you up. Let's go home and eat."

"I left you a note, Sidney," said Stella. "And I'm not ready to leave. I told you where I was and when I would be home. Sue and I planned a ladies' night out. So I'll see you at home later."

Sidney raised his voice and started to get really angry, so the health club manager asked him to leave. Sidney grew even angrier as he drove home alone. "Stella didn't listen to me, and she disrespected me—how dare she embarrass me in public like that?"

It was Sidney's bowling night, so he went to the lanes, had a few beers, and enjoyed the company of his teammates. When he returned home, Stella was still out with Sue. Sidney paced, ranted and raved while he drank a few more beers. He got the chisel and mallet from the bedroom. "Just to show her who's boss," he said.

As soon as Stella returned home at 9.30, she said, "Sorry I'm a little late. We had to wait awhile for a table before we could eat."

Sidney took the mallet and pounded it into his hand.

He shouted, "'Where the hell have you've been?"

Stella stepped back, wary of Sidney's anger. She could tell he had been drinking. She was tired and didn't want to argue with him. "Oh Sidney, just go to bed. I'll be in soon."

As she turned away to go to the other room, Sidney said, "Don't you turn away from me while I'm talking to you!" He lunged at her with the chisel and chipped a small piece of marble off her upper back.

Stella cried out in pain and turned around.

"That's it, Sidney," she said. "You need to leave. We can talk tomorrow when you're not so angry and drunk."

Sidney didn't want to leave, but Stella threatened to call the police. He slammed the door as he left.

Sidney muttered, "I didn't mean to hurt her, and I only chipped away a little. It can be fixed. It's such a small chip."

The next day Sidney rang the doorbell and Stella opened the door. Sidney was holding a dozen roses and he had tears in his eyes.

"Oh Stella," he said as he handed her a dozen roses. "I really messed up. I'm sorry I hurt you. I couldn't sleep and was up all night at the thought of losing you. Please don't make me leave. I love you and can't live without you. I don't know what came over me. I promise to work on my temper and I will never hurt you again. Please let me come back."

Sidney pulled Stella into his arms. She could feel his tears on her marble. She could tell how sorry he was. Her heart softened. Stella took the roses and cried as Sidney held her.

"I don't want to ever lose you," said Sidney as he pulled out a ring box and got down on one knee. "I'll make it up to you if it takes the rest of my life. Stella, you are the love of my life. Will you marry me?"

Stella had hoped that Sidney might propose soon but not under these conditions. She wanted to share her life with someone and did not like being alone. She loved Sidney, but now she had doubts about whether he could control his temper.

She said, "I love you Sidney, and you can move back in, but I need to think about your proposal. When I decide to marry someone, I don't want to have any doubts. I'm having doubts about your temper and how you treat me when you're mad."

Stella let Sidney move back in, and for a while things were almost back to normal. Sidney thought, "I'm sure that in time I can convince Stella to marry me. This will pass and she will forget."

But Stella held firm on needing more time to make up her mind about the proposal. Sidney started to feel resentment toward Stella. "I know I messed up but it was only the one time. She needs to get over it and move on. She won't find another guy as great as me, and we belong together."

Slowly and surely Sidney's anger grew. He was annoyed on bowling night when Stella came home at 9pm. He was furious when Sue called to talk to Stella and would hardly give him the time of day. He was really steamed when Stella got on Facebook to message an old friend from high school. She reassured Sidney that they were only friends but Sidney thought otherwise. Stella did not understand why Sidney was so jealous. After all, her old friend was gay! Sidney didn't believe that, either.

"Maybe she's cheating on me," thought Sidney. "If she thinks she can leave me for someone else she has another thought coming."

That night, after bowling, Sidney checked Stella's messages. Aha! There was one from the old friend. It said, "I can't wait to see you next week. Goodnight, darlin', hugs and kisses, love ya."

Sidney flew into a rage. There was his proof that Stella was cheating on him!

Sidney took the chisel and mallet and flew at Stella as she arrived home and came in the door.

"Take that!" he said as he chipped away at her hands, her breast, her cheeks, her arms. "Crack!" went one arm under the force of the mallet. Soon there were large gouges all over her body.

"No one will want you when I'm done with you!" shouted Sidney. Stella screamed and cried but she was no match for the strong Satyr.

She finally pulled away and escaped through the door, but the damage was done.

As he watched her run off, Sidney knew he had crossed a line. Stella had left him, and maybe for good.

"This time I *really* messed, but maybe in time Stella will forgive me," thought Sidney. "The gouges, cracks and chips can be fixed. A good doctor can repair the damage. But she should have known better than to cheat on me."

You and I know that Stella's gay friend was no risk to Sidney. It might seem crazy that Sidney was still blaming Stella for his violence and you would be surprised if she ever went back to him. But abused women do go back time and time again, hoping for *true love* or someone to pay the bills.

Stella went to stay with Sue, who called the police to arrest Sidney when Stella showed up at her house that night. Stella found a good doctor to help her recover and her gay friend gave her lots of emotional support. There's no *happy ever after ending* to this story, at least not yet. Maybe in time Stella will find *true love* but for now she would learn to take care of herself. After all, being alone is better than being with a jealous old goat.

THE BOTTOM LINE: Never Seek Love With a Jealous Old Goat!

Food for Thought Questions:

- How are you like Stella? _____

    _____

- Who in your life reminds you of Sidney? _____

- Why does Sidney keep promising to change? _____

    _____

- What does Sidney need to change? _____

    _____

- Do you believe Sidney when he says he is going to change? Why or why not? _____

    _____

    _____

- What does Stella need to change in terms of her thinking? _____

    _____

- How does this story represent a cycle of violence? _____

    _____

Note

1 From *Outsmarting the Riptide of Domestic Violence: Metaphor and Mindfulness for Change,* by P. Pernicano, 2011, Lanham, MD: Jason Aronson. Reprinted and adapted with permission.

CHAPTER 18

PARENTING ISSUES

Story 44: Protectiveness with Children

Purpose(s) and Goal(s): ☒ Psychoeducation for caregivers about boundaries around other adults, as well as a safety-planning focus. ☒ Treatment Intervention: for safety planning with children and caregivers. This is an excellent resource for caregivers who expose children to unsafe adults or experience *blind spots* with regard to their friendships or dating practices. It is a good story for caregivers who use drugs or alcohol or move from one adult partner to the next. The story may be used in group, individual, or family session.

Adults sometimes do not pay attention to what they do around kids and they make decisions that are not safe. They take their kids to places that aren't safe or they let strangers be around their kids. This is a true story about a parent that was very careful about taking her children around dogs but not careful in taking her children around people. This story shows the kinds of questions kids and adults can ask in order to stay safe.

Does He Bite?

A mother was pushing her child in a stroller through the park. The mother saw a large collie dog coming toward them, on leash, with its owner walking behind it. The child really liked dogs. As the collie approached, the child climbed out of the stroller and started to run forward.

"Stop," said the mother. "Where are you going?"

"Mommy, I want to pet the doggie," replied the child.

The mother said, "Wait. We need to find out if the dog is safe. And let me hold your hand."

When the dog and owner got close, about three feet away, the mother asked, "Is your dog friendly?"

"Yes," said the owner. "My collie is very friendly."

The child moved forward, ready to pet the dog.

The mother said, "Stop. I have another question." The child stopped.

The mother asked, "Does your dog like children?" and the owner replied, "Yes, my dog likes children."

The child moved toward the dog.

"Wait," said the mother, smiling as she stopped her child. "Before you can go near the dog, I have another question. Probably the most important question of all."

"Does he bite?" she asked the owner.

"No," said the owner. "My dog does not bite."

"Now, Mommy?" asked the child.

The mother smiled at her child and said, "The dog is friendly, he likes children and he doesn't bite. It should be safe to pet him."

The child smiled. The collie was very gentle and sat still while the child petted him. Then the child got back into the stroller, and the mom and child continued their walk.

A little way further down the path, the mom and child saw another dog approaching with its owner. It was a cute little Maltese, fluffy and white.

The child said, "Look at the cute little doggie, Mommy! I want to pet it!"

The mom said, "I'll hold your hand, and this time you can ask the three important questions."

The child climbed out of the stroller and toddled over to the dog and its owner.

The little dog growled. The child stepped back and asked, "Is the doggie friendly?"

The owner said, "Sometimes the dog is friendly and sometimes it is not friendly. Today, it seems, the dog is not feeling friendly."

Then the child asked, "Does your doggy like children?"

The owner replied, "Well, he doesn't really like small children. They move too fast and make him nervous. He does better with older kids."

"I have one more question," the child said. "My mommy says it's the most important question. Does your doggy bite?"

The owner answered, "Sometimes he bites when he is scared or when young children are around. I don't think you should come any closer because he growled at you. Maybe he is scared, or maybe it is because you are a stranger. I'm sorry."

"That's OK," said the child.

"You did a good job!" said the mother as she put her child back in the stroller. She walked her child a bit further into the park until they reached a play area. The child asked, "Can I swing and play on the slide?"

The mother agreed the child could play and she sat down on a park bench to watch. Pretty soon a nice-looking man came up to her.

"Do you mind if I join you?" he asked. "I saw you sitting here alone."

"My child is playing," she replied. The mother was lonely and the man was cute. Without a pause she said, "Sure, you're welcome to join me."

He sat down on the bench beside her and started to flirt. He had a six-pack of beer with him and offered her a can. She accepted, and they laughed and talked while the child played. One beer led to another.

"Which one is your kid?" asked the man as he put his arm around the mother. She thought about pulling away but it had been a long time since a man had paid attention to her.

The mother pointed toward the slide, and the child waved at the mother from the top of the slide.

The child went down the slide then ran over to the mother with a worried look.

The man smiled at the mother, his arm still around her shoulders. "What a cute kid—takes after you! I don't have any kids, but I love them."

He was such a flirt, but the mother kind of liked it.

"Come here, darlin' and give me a hug and a kiss," the man said to the child.

The child gave the mother a look.

"It's OK, honey," said the mother to the child.

The child stepped away and said, "But mommy, you forgot to ask the most important question."

The mom looked confused for a minute. "What do you mean?"

The child asked, "Mommy, does he bite?"

The mother's heart skipped a beat.

She reached down and picked up her child and said, "You're right. I didn't ask any of the important questions. Thank you for reminding me."

The mother put the child in the stroller and said to the man, "We need to go home."

"Can I have your name or phone number?" the man asked. "Or tell me where you live and I'll stop by sometime."

The mother said, "No." After all, at a park you can't tell the difference between Jack the Ripper and Charlie Brown.

She put her attention back on her child, where it belonged.

"Mommy," said the child as they headed home, "He was a stranger. Don't mommies have to stay safe too?"

"Yes," said the mother as she gave her child a big hug. "Mommies need to stay safe, too. It's my job to keep us both safe!"

Children and adults need to be safe around dogs and strangers, but sometimes they forget to ask the important questions.

THE BOTTOM LINE: Ask the Important Questions.

Food for Thought Questions:

- Which dog was safe—the big one or the little one? How could you tell which dog was safe? __
  _____
  _____

- Why did the mommy forget to ask the important questions? _____
  _____

- Give an example of how someone can act friendly but not be safe. _____
  _____

- What is OK and *not* OK to do with strangers? _____
  _____

- What are some clues that an adult is not safe to be around? (For example, they might be drunk or high and driving. What else?) _____
  _____

- Write down any other questions you think a mommy should ask when thinking about her child's safety._____
  _____
  _____

Story 45: Parental Risk-Taking

Purpose(s) and Goal(s): ☒ Psychoeducation about exposing children to fearful events and parental blind spots. ☒ Treatment Intervention: individual or group parenting intervention to reduce risk-taking behaviors in parents and understand the impact of their behavior on children.

Some parents are risk-takers and seek excitement, getting high off danger and doing things for the adrenaline rush. They seem to thrive on crisis and don't understand that exposing children to these kinds of risks is destabilizing. Children desire secure consistency and overstimulation can lead to overly high levels of arousal or stress.

The Balancing Act[1]

It was the opening night of the circus.

"GASP!" went the crowd. Fannie Flamingo was dancing across the tightrope, one leap at a time. She was on the high wire *without a safety net*.

Fannie wobbled, swayed, and slipped. She finally made it to the platform on the other side.

"Why isn't she using a net?" asked the worried parents and children.

The truth was that Fannie Flamingo had refused to use one.

"Dancing on the high wire without a net gives me a real thrill," said Fannie. "I like the excitement."

The circus manager said, "I don't want children and parents to see you fall to your death!"

"I'm willing to take that chance," said Fannie.

"Well, I'm not," said the manager. "Next time use the safety net!"

There was a big crowd for the circus the next day. Parents and children were eating popcorn and cotton candy, and everyone smiled at the elephants and the dancing dogs. Then it was time for Fannie's big act. Out she came, tall and pink in a sparkly costume.

"Oh look!" the crowd cried out. "What cute little flamingo babies."

It was true. Fannie had brought her two babies with her.

"Sit here and watch Mommy," she said as she led them to the front row of seats. "Mommy is going to dance on the high wire."

"Where is the safety net, Mommy?" asked her oldest child.

"Pish-posh!" said Fannie. "I don't need a safety net. I'm not afraid of anything."

"Don't cry!" she said as she saw tears in her children's eyes.

As her babies and everyone watched, Fannie climbed the tall ladder, stepped out on the tightrope and began to dance across.

Slip! "GASP!" Slip! "GASP!"

"Please stop, Mommy!" The small, tearful voice came from the front row.

Fannie ignored the cry and leaped across the wire. Right before she got to the other side, she started to wobble, first right, then left. Swan leaned over, grabbed her and pulled her to safety.

The crowd gasped in relief.

Fannie took a bow, then climbed down the ladder and went to where her children were sitting. She put a baby flamingo on each shoulder, and headed back toward the ladder.

"What is she doing?" murmured the worried crowd.

Fannie grabbed the microphone: "Yes, it's what you've all been waiting for! A family flamingo act with no safety net! You won't believe your eyes!"

She climbed the tall ladder with two scared babies on her shoulders. They clung to her and hid their heads.

"Don't worry," Fannie whispered. "If we fall, I promise someone will catch us."

"But Mommy," whimpered the babies. "We don't *want* to fall. Please don't take us out on the high wire."

Fannie had crossed a line. She was putting her own fun and excitement before the needs of her children.

At the top of the ladder, Swan blocked Fannie's way to the wire.

"Get out of my way!" said Fannie.

"No," said Swan. "I won't let you put your children at risk."

Fannie grumbled and groaned, but she knew that Swan was right. She climbed down the ladder and put her children back in their front-row seats.

"You can just watch," said Fannie to her children. "Sorry I put you through that. . ."
Then Fannie called for the manager. "I'll use the safety net for the sake of the children.
You understand that if it was just me, I would continue my act without it."
"Fannie," said the manager. "*Life* is a real balancing act, so always have a safe place to land!"
THE BOTTOM LINE: Everyone Needs a Safety Net!

Food for Thought Questions:

- Who in your life does Fannie remind you of?_____
  _____

- Why does someone show off or need a lot of attention?_____
  _____
  _____

- Give an example of a time you showed off to get attention? _____
  _____

- Describe a time when you did something self-centered for fun or excitement that put your children at risk or scared them? _____
  _____

- What do Fannie's children want from her and why? _____
  _____
  _____
  _____

Story 46: Attachment Needs

Purpose(s) and Goal(s): ☒ Psychoeducation for caregivers about the attachment needs of infants and young children. ☒ Treatment Intervention: to be used with caregivers to identify adult behaviors which interfere with development of secure parent–child attachment.

Some parents have a lifestyle that results in emotional or physical neglect. The parent's own needs over-ride those of the child. This story will help parents better understand and respond to the attachment needs of very young children.

Velma Crowe's Sticky Situation[2]

Velma had grown up in a crowded nest with ten brothers and sisters. There were never enough worms to go around. Her mother pushed her out of the nest almost before she could fly. She was glad when she was finally old enough to have a nest of her own.

Velma was a resident of Bird Town, a very nice place to live if you are a bird. The ground in Bird Town is full of worms and grubs, and there are plenty of crickets and bugs. Every morning at dawn, you can hear the Bird Town Chorus singing merrily as the sun rises. What more could a bird ask for?

Velma, at that very moment, was asking for more. "Keep it down!" she screeched at the singing birds. "I'm trying to sleep. I had a late night and my head is killing me."

Velma liked to have fun. She loved to party with her friend Hummingbird. They danced late into the night at the Bird Town Disco. On Friday nights Velma went to late-night karaoke with her friend Hound Dog. Hound Dog could really howl up a storm!

But now Velma was going to become a mother. Soon she would have to share her nest with baby birds. She had laid five eggs, and any day they were going to hatch.

Hummingbird and Hound Dog were worried. They didn't think Velma was ready to be a mother. They knew that baby birds would change Velma's fun-filled life.

On Friday night, as usual, Hummingbird and Velma were listening to Hound Dog howl out a great *Proud Mary*.

Hummingbird leaned close. "Vel, you'll need to change your lifestyle when your babies hatch. You know, settle down a little."

"Nah," said Vel, taking a sip of her drink. "I can have babies and have fun too!"

"You'll be a *mother*, Vel," replied Hummingbird. "Fun will come second. You'll need to put your family first."

"I'll be a good mother," said Vel-Crowe. "There's nothing to it!"

Hound Dog came back to the table after a round of applause. "We were talking about Velma becoming a mother," said Hummingbird.

Hound Dog said, "Hmmm. . . I've been thinking about that, too. Velma, you'll have to stay home more. You can't leave baby birds alone. Babies need to be cuddled and taken care of."

Velma replied, "I've never been the cuddly type."

She added, "When I go out, I'll leave them some worms so they won't get hungry."

"But baby birds can't feed themselves," said Hound Dog.

"No one took very good care of me," Said Velma. "I turned out OK, didn't I?"

"No comment!" said both Hummingbird and Hound Dog, at the same time.

Velma got back to her nest about 2am, and an hour later the eggs hatched. She had five beautiful baby birds.

"Come on," said Velma to her babies. "Let's go celebrate your birthday! I'm taking you out to eat."

The babies climbed on their mother and tried to hold on. Velma flew out of the nest. All five baby birds slid off their mother, dropping to the ground below.

"Look at that!" said Velma fondly. "Those little buggers are accident-prone, just like me."

It was true that Velma was accident-prone. But her babies were just not old enough yet to hold on.

On the ground, the baby birds began to cry and chirp.

"Chirp, chirp, chirp," cried her five hungry children. Velma hunted for some worms but could only feed one baby at a time.

One very loud baby stuck his beak up to try to grab a worm, and Velma brushed him away with her wing. "You have to wait your turn," she said. I can't feed all five of you at once!"

Then the babies started to explore. Velma saw five baby birds hopping off in five different directions.

"Look," she said. "My babies are independent—just like me! Don't go too far," she called out. She pointed with her wing. "There's a mean owl that lives over there in an old tree. Stay away from him if you can."

The baby birds did what babies do: They continued to cry, with their hungry mouths open, and they did not listen to their mother. All five hopped away.

"Oh well," said Velma. "What can you do when your children won't listen? They'll have to learn from the school of hard knocks, just like I did!"

Velma was tired from flying around and trying to feed five busy baby birds. She perched on a tree limb to rest for a minute. Then her head dropped down onto her wing, and she fell sound asleep.

As if out of a fog, Velma heard, "Velma, Wake up! Where are your babies? The nest and eggs are empty!"

She woke up to find Hound Dog staring at her.

"Did you say something?" asked Velma. "Why did you wake me? I was up all night and need to get some sleep!"

"Where are your babies?" asked Hound Dog. "You can't sleep while they are up and around. You need to keep an eye on them!"

Velma rubbed the sleep out of her eyes and said, "Don't worry. I'm sure they are fine. They can pretty well look out for themselves."

"No they can't," said the Hound Dog. "Baby birds need care and protection, 24/7."

"It's not my fault," said Velma. "They wouldn't listen to me."

With that, she went back to sleep.

"I'll get back to you after I find the babies," said Hound Dog. He ran off sniffing at the ground, because that is what hound dogs do when they are trying to solve a problem. Soon he found all five baby birds. He gently picked them up in his slobbery mouth and carried them back to their mother. He nudged her awake.

"Velma," said Hound Dog, "You don't know how to take care of babies."

Hound Dog quickly ran to the store and came back carrying a large package in his mouth. He dropped it at Velma's feet.

"What's this?" asked Velma as she opened the package.

"It's a present for the babies," he replied.

Inside was a coat covered in Velcro.

"Wear this," said Hound Dog. "The babies will stick to it.'

Velma did not want to wear it, but it was a gift after all. She put on the coat, one wing at a time. "OK, kids," she said, "Climb aboard!"

The baby birds flung themselves at her and stuck to their mother's coat. They chirped happily as they snuggled into Velma.

"I don't know about this," said Velma. "I won't have much privacy with them right here under my beak."

"They need to be attached to you—where you can keep an eye on them—until they're a little older," said Hound Dog.

It was a *very* long week. Velma wasn't used to being surrounded by babies.

"Chirp, chirp, chirp," they went, day and night, except for when they were sleeping. They were always hungry, and Velma could not get a full night's sleep.

A week later, Hound Dog came by to babysit. Velma looked very tired, with circles under her eyes.

"Hound Dog," said Velma. "Those babies cry day and night. I never get a full night's sleep. They wake me up too early and won't go back to sleep. All that crying really gets on my nerves."

"All babies cry," said Hound Dog. "That's what babies do. Believe me, they will cry less if you take good care of them."

"I'll take your word for it," Velma replied. "I guess life's hard enough without having to find your own food or take care of yourself when you're little."

Velma got used to having noisy babies around. She slept when they slept and took them with her wherever she went. When she wanted a night out, she got a babysitter. And even when the babies woke her up too early, she got up with them. She fed them worms when they were hungry and played with them when they chirped for her to pay attention to them.

Hound Dog was right. Her babies depended on her to care for them. She knew they would leave the nest when they were older, and then she would have more time for herself.

It would be worth waiting for.

THE BOTTOM LINE: Children Need to Attach.

Food for Thought Questions:

• How are you like Velma? _____

_____

• Who in your life reminds you of Velma's friends? _____

_____

_____

• If you sent Velma to Bird School, what three skills would you want her to learn? _____

_____

_____

• What will happen to Velma's babies if she forgets to take good care of them while they are young? _____

_____

_____

Story 47: Empathy vs. Blame

Purpose(s) and Goal(s): ☒ Psychoeducation for caregivers about the need to provide empathy toward children and to reduce criticism and blame. It is intended for the caregiver who has trouble offering help or noticing distress in his or her child. ☒ Treatment Intervention: to be used in family treatment with adolescents and caregivers or in a parent session to discuss lack of empathy. The story opens up discussion about parent–child communication.

Some caregivers have difficulty empathizing with children. They use words that imply a child needs to *be punished, learn a lesson,* or *was responsible for what happened to him or her.* They do not notice or respond to children's feelings and instead of displaying empathy, they lecture, teach, reject, or punish the children in their care. A blaming caregiver might let a child sort of *wallow* in pain when the adult judges that the child made a mistake, did not use good judgment, or *caused* the difficulty. In the midst of the child's high distress (sometimes immediately following a disclosure), such caregivers might ask a lot of questions or start in with problem solving. They seem unable to mirror the child's level of distress and have trouble sharing their own emotional response. The following story is helpful as a parenting lead-in with the goal of increasing caregiver empathy.

First Things First[3]

Once upon a time, three young spider monkeys were walking down a long, muddy path in the middle of the South American rainforest. Harry, Larry, and Mary were very tired from their busy day, and Harry was carrying a long rope. They had used the rope to play "Drop in the River." That is a game where monkeys take turns swinging out over the river and then dropping into the cool, refreshing water. They then have to swim really fast back to shore before the hungry crocodiles catch them.

What fun the monkeys had that day at the river! They played "Drop in the River" over and over until they started to shiver in the breeze that was blowing. The next thing they knew, all three monkeys were very hungry. "Let's go eat our picnic lunch," suggested Mary. So the three monkeys sat down under a banana tree and had a yummy feast of bananas, honey, fresh green leaves, and termites.

Now, they were on their way home. Harry, Larry, and Mary were too tired to swing from tree to tree and decided to walk. It had rained hard for three days, which it often does in the rainforest, and there were many deep puddles along the way. The monkeys tried leaping the puddles but often did not make it.

Jump, plop, splash! Jump, plop, splash! Into the puddles they went!

Now, in addition to being very tired, they were very muddy. As they came upon a particularly muddy section of the path, Mary tried to jump over the thick mud.

Jump, plop, GLUG! GLUG?

Harry and Larry thought, "Oh my!" as they realized Mary had landed right in the middle of the mud. And, as they watched, Mary started sinking, just where she had landed. Soon the mud was up to her ankles. She pulled and tugged, but her feet would not come loose.

"Look there," said Harry to Larry. "Mary is sinking into the mud. I wonder if that is quicksand."

"It might be," said Larry. "Harry, go ahead and throw her the rope so you can pull her out."

Harry, instead, went over to where Mary was stuck and looked down at the mud. He got down on his hands and feet, leaned over, put one hand into the mud and felt around. No bottom.

"Yup," he said to Larry. "It's quicksand."

By now Mary was calling out loudly, "Please help me! I'm sinking!" Mary had sunk down to her knees and was thrashing around wildly in the sucking, slurping quicksand, which gripped her tightly.

Larry said, "Harry, just throw her the rope and pull her out."

Harry instead said, "Mary, if you keep thrashing you'll go in deeper. Don't you know that in quicksand you need to stay still and move slowly? The more you struggle, the faster you will sink. And you should have known better than to jump in wet mud in the middle of the rainforest. There is a lot of quicksand around, you know."

Larry said, in a stern voice, "Harry, it was an accident. Quit being such a know-it-all! Just throw her the rope and pull her out!"

But Harry liked being a know-it-all and said to Mary in a know-it-all voice, "Mary, if you lie on your back in the quicksand, your feet will come up and you can float until someone rescues you. That's what you need to do. Float on your back, let your feet come up, and then I will rescue you."

Mary did not know how to float, and now the thick mud was up to her neck. She was still sinking. Her face was tilted up, and she was trying hard to stay above the surface. Any minute now, she was going to sink.

Larry said in an insistent voice, "Harry, throw her the rope, NOW. This is not the time to give Mary a lecture. She needs your HELP!"

At this point Harry finally noticed that Mary was very red in the face and tilting up her face to keep her nose and mouth above the surface. "Maybe," he thought, "I should help Mary, since she is doing all the wrong things. She has sunk down so deep that nothing she does on her own will save her. I *could* throw her the rope and pull her out."

But at that very moment, Harry felt the rope suddenly jerked out of his hands. He watched as Larry raced over to the muddy quicksand and threw the rope to Mary, who was now gagging on the muddy water. She grabbed it and held on tight. Mary leaned back with great relief as Larry tugged, and ever so slowly she floated up to the surface. As the suction broke, Larry gently pulled Mary back to hard ground.

"Whew!" said Larry. "That was a close call!" He gave Mary a big hug and turned to Harry with a frown of annoyance. "Harry," he said, "What were you thinking of? When someone in real trouble needs your help, you help first and talk later!"

Harry replied, "But I was right about the quicksand."

Larry pointed out, "Right and wrong don't matter when someone needs your help."

"OK," said Harry, "I get the point. There are more important things than being right."

He turned to Mary and said, "I'm sorry I didn't throw you a rope. I was too busy giving advice and judging you."

"Harry," said Mary, "I understand that you like to be right, but I wish you could have seen how scared I was and how much I needed your help. Thanks to you, at least I know what to do the next time I get stuck in quicksand." She added, "I am very glad, though, that Larry was there to save me." Mary gave Larry a big hug of thanks.

Larry, Harry, and Mary continued on home. This time, Larry carried the rope. You never know when you might need a rope to help a friend in trouble.

THE BOTTOM LINE: First Things First!

Food for Thought Questions:

- Are you more like Mary, Harry, or Larry and why? _____
  _____

- Describe a time when you needed help but had trouble getting it or no one listened to or believed you. _____
  _____
  _____

- Describe a time when an adult criticized you instead of listening to your feelings. _____
  _____
  _____

- Re-write parts of this story to change Harry's response to Mary. In the new version, he understands her feelings and helps her get out of the quicksand.

Notes

1 From *Outsmarting the Riptide of Domestic Violence: Metaphor and Mindfulness for Change,* by P. Pernicano, 2011, Lanham, MD: Jason Aronson. Reprinted and adapted with permission.
2 From *Family-Focused Trauma Intervention: Using Metaphor and Play with Victims of Abuse and Neglect,* by P. Pernicano, 2010, Lanham, MD: Jason Aronson. Reprinted and adapted with permission.
3 From *Family-Focused Trauma Intervention: Using Metaphor and Play with Victims of Abuse and Neglect,* by P. Pernicano, 2010, Lanham, MD: Jason Aronson. Reprinted and adapted with permission.

PART V

CHILD'S GUIDE TO TRAUMA

CHAPTER 19

INTRODUCTION FOR THE CHILD READER

This Child's Guide is about how abuse changes your brain, your behavior, your moods and your relationships. If you have been abused, this handbook is for you. It was written for abused kids aged nine years and above (even young teens will find it helpful), and it is written in words kids can understand.

Kids sometimes have a hard time getting over abuse. According to Dr. Perry, who wrote the book *The Boy Who Was Raised As a Dog*, an abused child has a brain that remains in a state of fear (Perry, 2004a, 2004b, 2006, 2009; Perry & Hambrick, 2008; Perry & Pollard, 1998). It is hard to have good relationships and live a normal life when you are in a state of fear.

So what does it mean for someone's brain to remain in a state of fear? You probably know that all kids (and grownups) have *fears* and *freak out* sometimes. Kids might be afraid of things like singing a solo in the chorus, having a spider crawl on them or riding in a car during a bad storm. But these types of things don't last too long, and a kid can calm back down after they are over.

An abused kid's brain gets changed by the abuse, because abuse is *very personal, very scary, and sometimes it goes on for a long time*. The kind of fear that comes from abuse is big: It is more like a broken fire hydrant than a leaky faucet; the water gushes out over the pavement and pretty soon it floods the road.

That kind of fear makes abused kids go into *Freak Out, Freeze, Flight* or *Fight* more than other kids. All through this book you will read about *Freak Out, Freeze, Flight* and *Fight*. You might call them the four "F" words!

After abuse, you are very *watchful* because you believe something bad could happen again. Another word for *watchful* is vigilance—a state of high arousal or high stress. You are on *alert* and easily startled by anything that *triggers* your fear. Another word for a trigger is a *trauma reminder*.

Freak Out means that your stress increases when your fear is *triggered by a trauma reminder*. A trauma reminder can be anything that reminds you of past abuse, such as a sound, smell, sight, emotion, season, person, place, touch, taste, or tone of voice. You *freak out* when you are triggered by the reminder and think something bad is going to happen.

Freeze means you are too afraid to even move or talk if and when something bad starts to happen. You are *alarmed* and might become very *emotional*.

Flight means that you are so scared that you try to get away from the danger.

Fight means you fight back to protect yourself. You are in a state of terror.

You will learn more about these four Fs if you decide to read this guide.

So why read on? Well, there are books about trauma written for therapists. Therapists use books to help kids get over abuse. There are also some good books (see Appendix A) written for kids and parents that help you understand and talk about things like . . .

- No one should touch you on the private parts of your body.
- No one should ask you to keep abuse a secret.
- Abuse is never your fault.
- It is OK to talk about your abuse.

Then there are science books about what abuse does to the brain. This is called *neurobiology*. But most of the stuff written by scientists is hard to read and boring for kids.

This Child's Guide to Trauma explains the science of abuse and helps kids know why they feel and act the way they do after abuse. The abused kids I know have questions like . . .

- Why do I feel sort of *crazy* after being abused?
- If the abuse is over, why do I still feel scared?
- Why do adults sometimes think I am being "bad" when I am trying to cope?
- Why do adults sometimes do things to get me more upset?

Abused kids need answers to their questions. They need adults to be open with them about abuse and what kids can do to get over it. They need adults to listen to them and not judge them. This book will help abused kids talk to adults about abuse and what they need to get over it.

If you accept this *mission*, you will learn . . .

- How abuse changes your brain, and what you can do to fix that.
- How your brain tries to protect you when you are scared.
- Why some abused kids have trauma symptoms or PTSD (Post-Traumatic Stress Disorder) and others don't.
- How to talk about your memories, thoughts and feelings and why this helps.

Each chapter has questions to answer about your abuse, your behavior, your emotions, and your relationships. There is also a section about the three Cs (Calming Down, Connecting, and Conquering), all of which are tools to help you change thoughts, feelings, and behavior to get over abuse.

As you read each chapter, you can say, "Yes, this is *like me* (or *not like me*). This is how *my abuse affected me*. This is *how I changed*. This is what I need to do to *get over my abuse*."

There are also stories that go along with the stuff in the chapters. The stories are *not the answers* to your problems, but they might help you see things in a new way and talk about your problems. They have information about abuse and how kids think and feel after being abused. The characters in the stories are like abused kids and families I have worked with in therapy. As you read the stories, you might even have an "aha" experience if something reminds you of what you went through and gives you new ideas.

You and your therapist and caregiver can use the stories to talk about problems and set goals for treatment. The stories will help you learn coping skills and get along better with others.

Abuse usually ends because:

1 a child tells a teacher, friend, parent or caregiver;
2 a child leaves clues and someone figures it out; or
3 the abuser is caught hurting the child.

Ending abuse is important. After abuse ends, adults need to help a child find treatment. As you probably know, most abused children do not just *get over it* by themselves.

Before you start reading I want to let you know that when I use the word *he* for an abuser, I do not mean to say that all abusers are men. Abusers can be men, women, or children older than you.

The last thing I want to say to you before you start reading is that you are an expert about yourself and your abuse. You know yourself better than anyone! So, if you read something in this book that seems like a good idea or sounds like you, I hope you will share it. Other kids have been helped by the ideas in this book and I hope you will be too!

CHAPTER 20

THE IMPACT OF ABUSE

Being abused is a little like being overpowered by a force of nature: a riptide in the ocean, a destructive tornado, a powerful flood, a terrifying hurricane, an unbalancing earthquake, or a blinding blizzard whiteout. Wherever you live, you have probably heard about or experienced one of these forces of nature.

Do you know what a riptide is? It is a strong current in the ocean that can overpower you and pull you out to sea.

A tornado can form suddenly and it goes where it pleases, tearing down anything in its path. You have to take shelter until it passes, hoping that you do not get hurt or have your home destroyed.

A flood is a dangerous thing indeed; a tidal wave washes ashore, a river rises, or a dam breaks, and before you know it everything is under water. You have to wait until the water levels go back down and hope that you don't drown before someone rescues you.

An earthquake starts with a small rumble or shaking of the ground beneath you. You feel yourself getting off balance and realize what is happening. You go outside to avoid falling objects and if you are in a car, you have to avoid the buckles in the pavement.

A whiteout in a blizzard (or thick fog or a huge dust storm) is really scary. One minute you can see and the next minute you are blind to what is up ahead. You have to go inside or pull off the road if you are driving. A whiteout can cause a big pile-up in traffic and strand people on the highway.

All of these forces of nature can leave people feeling helpless, out of control, and scared.

Let's use the riptide example. One minute you are having fun playing in the waves of the ocean, laughing and having a good time. Suddenly you feel a very strong current, a riptide that pulls you off your feet. You are startled and scared—you start to *freak out!*

You try to escape the pull of the riptide but it holds you fast. Next, you might *freeze*. You don't know what to do and can't think. So for a few moments, you don't do anything. You might think, "What is going on? The water is pulling me away from shore!"

Then you decide to be *strong*. You are a good swimmer so you fight against the current. But the current is very powerful. If you *fight* or try to swim against a riptide, it will overpower you.

Soon you are too tired to fight any more. You might decide to float and stop fighting. But if you give up and stop fighting (*flight*), you will end up in deep water. You might even be carried out to sea.

It's easy to drown in a riptide. If you want to survive one, you have to *outsmart* it. You must move *sideways* until you are out of the current. That is the only plan that will work.

Each force of nature mentioned above requires a different safety plan to survive.

But you want to do more than *survive* a force of nature. You want *to be ready the next time* it happens. You want to *be prepared just in case it ever happens again*. You want *to face your fear*. So you use your brain and come up with a good plan.

Abuse is like that: When it happens, it overpowers you just like a force of nature. Someone bigger, older, or stronger than you hurts your body, your mind, or your feelings. After the abuse is over, you want to get over what happened and to heal. You might be a little nervous to talk about your abuse, but you decide to face it. After all, you want to do more than just survive abuse; you want to conquer it. You go to therapy, learn new coping skills, and come up with a safety plan. The chapters that follow will help you face your fear and conquer the abuse.

CHAPTER 21

FREAK OUT (VIGILANCE)

You *freak out* when:

1 *something scary and bad happens* to you;
2 *you think something bad is going to happen* to you; or
3 when there is a *trauma reminder* and your fear is triggered.

Some bad things make you think your life (or the life of someone you love) is in danger. This type of bad thing is called a *trauma*. The bad thing could be a riptide, a tornado, a car accident, or getting abused. The bad thing could be hearing or seeing someone you love get hurt. After a trauma, you stay *on alert*, because at least part of you is afraid that the bad thing will happen again. Another word for being *on alert* is *vigilant*.

Here is an example of *freak out*. I was driving to work on a rainy morning. I heard a *loud bang* (someone rear-ended my car) and the car started spinning. The loud bang startled me and my heart started to pound. Before I knew it, my car was on the other side of the highway—going the wrong way. I thought I was going to die. Luckily I got off the road before anyone else hit me. Later, I could not remember exactly what happened. A few weeks later I was driving on the same highway and it started to rain. That *triggered* my memories of the accident. I *freaked out* a little because I remembered the accident and didn't want to have any more car accidents. I drove slowly and looked in my rear view mirror. I was *vigilant*. The word *vigilant* means I was watching for danger (other cars) and being extra careful.

Here is another example. Let's say a mom filed for divorce after the dad hurt the mom. The kid had often heard his parents fighting at night and had seen the dad hurt the mom. That is called interpersonal partner violence (IPV). Then his mom changed her mind about the divorce and let the dad move back in. After the dad moved back in, the kid had trouble getting to sleep at night—he was being *vigilant*. The kid was afraid his parents would fight and that his mom would get hurt again. One night the parents had a loud argument and woke the kid up. Their argument was a trauma reminder. The loud voices *triggered* his memories of the IPV. Of course the kid *freaked out*. He even got out of bed to check that everything was OK.

So what is it like to *freak out?*

- You might get a bad feeling in the pit of your stomach (fear, dread, nervousness).
- Your heart might pound and make it hard for you to breathe.
- You might start to cry or feel dizzy.
- Your head or stomach might hurt.

Kids can *freak out* during or after abuse. During abuse, you might *freak out* and think, "This can't be happening!" After being abused, you might *freak out* whenever you fear someone is going to hurt you.

Past abuse makes you *vigilant* or very alert to signs of danger. When you are *vigilant* your eyes, ears, and senses check things out because you want to stay safe.

21.1 My Own Freak Out

Below is a list of things or situations that make some kids *freak out*. Circle any of the things that apply to you.

- Creepy crawlies like bugs, spiders
- Being in the woods and afraid you might see a snake
- Going across a bridge in a car
- Being in high places
- Being in an elevator
- Being around dogs
- Loud noises that startle me
- Fireworks
- Thunderstorms
- Sleeping in the dark
- Being around strangers
- Being in a crowded place
- Being in or near the place where you were abused
- Being around your abuser
- Being around older kids
- Being around adults that are drinking
- Being around adults that are using drugs
- Being left alone in the house
- Wondering if your parent is going to hurt you
- Wondering if someone else is going to hurt you
- Wondering if your abuser is going to hurt someone else
- Your parent is sleeping and won't wake up
- A stranger tries to hug you
- Someone is following you
- Someone grabs you and you can't get away
- Someone yells at you and startles you

- Someone gets in your face (comes too close)

- Someone shakes a finger at you

- Someone threatens you

- Other: _____

- Describe a specific time when you were *vigilant* (on the lookout for danger or scared that something bad was going to happen). _____

    _____

    How did you think, feel and act? _____

    _____

    _____

    _____

- Which of the things you circled make you *freak out* the most? _____

    _____

    _____

- Write about a time when you *freaked out*. Describe what happened and what you were thinking and feeling._____

    _____

    _____

    _____

    _____

    _____

    _____

    _____

    _____

    _____

CHAPTER 22

FREEZE OR HIGH EMOTION (ALARM)

Freeze is a mix of surprise and fear. *Freeze* is what you do when you are caught off guard, when you feel like a deer in the headlights of a car at night. First the deer is startled by the headlights. It hears the car and senses danger. When it *freezes*, it stops in its tracks and stands still as a statue. It can't move, even though it might get hit by the car.

A few years ago, I went camping in the woods. In the middle of the night, I heard noises outside the tent. I *froze* and listened very carefully. I held my breath and grabbed my flashlight. I was almost too scared to get out of my sleeping bag and look outside. Finally I went to the door of the tent, turned on my flashlight and took a look. There was a family of skunks walking down the path! I stayed really quiet and did not disturb them.

You might *freeze* if an abuser sneaks up on you or comes into your room when you do not expect it. It shocks you—you are so scared you can hardly breathe. You might even feel *really emotional* and start crying. You can't think or talk. You don't know which way to move or how to protect yourself. So like the deer, you *freeze*.

When you look back on your abuse you might wonder, "Why didn't I just run?" but in the moment you could not move. If someone tries to tell you what you "should have done," remind them that a kid in *freeze* can't move; it really is just like being frozen, hence the name.

If you were abused in your bedroom, you might *freeze* when you hear someone coming down the hall after you go to bed. You might hold your breath and stay very still. When you *freeze*, you might feel very small or wish you were invisible. *Freeze* is automatic.

Fear (memory of the abuse) makes you *freeze*. A memory can be a sound, sight, smell, feeling, or thought of past abuse. Ask your therapist to help you make a coping card. When you freeze, you can use your coping card and practice coping skills such as distraction, deep breathing, humor, pretending to be a brave lion tamer, or relaxing. Think of a funny story or practice being a floppy rag doll. Do what you need to do to *unfreeze*.

22.1 My Own Freeze: Practicing Freeze and Unfreeze

22.1.1 Playing the Statues Game

Ask someone to play *Statues* with you. All you will need is some music to turn off and on. The other person is in charge of doing that, while you are in charge of listening carefully. When the music plays, you dance or move around like a rag doll. Let your muscles go limp and loose. When the music stops, the other person calls out "freeze," and you hold your pose and try not to move. If the other person catches you moving, you will be "out." Then you get to turn the music on and off.

Questions for After You Finish Playing:

What was it like trying not to move when the other person said *freeze*?_____
_____
_____

When you *freeze*, are you tense or relaxed? How can you tell?_____
_____
_____

When you are tense, where do you feel it in your body? _____
_____

Do you breathe freely or hold your breath when you are trying not to move? _____
_____

Are you tense or relaxed as you move freely? How can you tell? _____
_____
_____

Do you breathe or hold your breath while you are moving?_____
_____

22.1.2 Ice Sculptures: *Freezing* and *Thawing*

Pretend that you are an ice sculpture (carved piece of ice). You are frozen in a pose, like a block of ice. Make any pose you like. You are cold and stiff.

- Describe how you feel when you are frozen. _____
  _____

- What would help you thaw?_____
  _____

- Pretend you are doing something to help you thaw.

- Imagine you are thawed out. How do you feel now?
  _____
  _____
  _____

22.1.3 Stand-Up Comedian

It is not possible to be laughing and *frozen* at the same time. During this activity, you will pretend you are a stand-up comedian.

- Make a Joke Collection. Every stand-up comedian needs good material. Ask each of your friends and the adults you know to tell you a good joke. Write down the ones you like best. Go to a kid's Web site for jokes or riddles and pick some you really like.

- Perform. Invite some friends to your comedy performance. Serve lemonade and cookies. Tell your best jokes, using lots of expression and pausing at all the right places. They love you! They clap and cheer at your funny jokes. Notice how you start to unfreeze as you tell your jokes and listen to the laughter.
- When you get nervous, think of the funniest jokes in your collection and pretend you are on stage telling them to the audience.

22.2.4 Sing Aloud!

When you sing, it is hard to stay *frozen*. Put on a CD or DVD and sing along, or pretend you have a microphone and sing your favorite song as loud as you can. Take a deep breath before you sing each line of the song. Notice how you *unfreeze* as you are singing.

CHAPTER 23

FLIGHT (ESCAPE)

Flight is what a kid does to get away or escape because he or she is afraid. This can happen during abuse; or it can happen when there is a trauma reminder (trigger) after being abused. *Flight* can happen in your mind (tuning out) or behavior (running or hiding).

23.1 Running or Hiding

It is easy to understand why an abused kid runs away or hides from an abuser or someone who *could be* an abuser. *Flight* is like a scared rabbit: If it hears the slightest noise, it jumps away to find a hiding place. A kid might run out the back door when the abuser's car pulls in the driveway. The kid might go spend the night with a friend when the abuser comes to visit. A kid might hide when he hears the abuser coming down the hall. And a kid might run or hide if an adult gets very angry and threatens him or her. All these reactions can be called *flight*.

23.2 Dissociation: A Special Kind of Flight

Some kids tune out during abuse. This is called *dissociation* and it is a coping technique to deal with the horror of what is going on. It happens when the kids can't stand to feel, think about, or remember abuse because it was so bad. When kids tune out, their eyes go sort of blank and they might stare straight ahead. The kids might think about something else or tune out in their mind (*dissociate*) when someone asks about their abuse. Other people might think the kids are ignoring or not paying attention, but they are dissociating. Some kids who dissociate hear voices in their heads or behave younger than they actually are; grownups tell them to *act their age*, but those kids are afraid and need a grownup to take care of them like when they were little.

Dissociation protects abused kids from hurt and pain. It keeps memories safely locked away in their brain. Later, when the abuse has ended and the kids are safe, memories of abuse may start to come back in dreams or what is called a *flashback*. A *flashback* feels like the abuse is happening right now even though it took place in the past.

Dissociation is a little like sleepwalking; you are awake and asleep at the same time. After the abuse ends, kids might keep dissociating, especially under stress. They might do it if the abuse starts up again, or when they are reminded of the abuse and experience strong feelings as a result. Some kids dissociate too much and don't know how to stop, which can prevent them from understanding what happened to them.

When kids are finally safe from abuse, they can learn (in therapy) how to stop dissociating and start talking about the abuse memories. You should let your therapist and caregiver know if you dissociate so that they can help you cope in new ways.

23.3 My Own Flight

- Where do you run or hide when you are afraid? _____
  _____
  _____

- Tell about a time you used *flight* (ran or hid) to cope with fear or abuse.
  _____
  _____
  _____

- It is not a good idea to go into flight unless there is real danger. What are some signs of real danger?_____
  _____
  _____

- The opposite of *flight* is facing your problem or getting help from someone when you are having a problem. Pretend that you feel like running away from an *abuse monster.* Instead of running away, stand on a tall platform, like an orchestra conductor uses. Stand as tall as you can. Puff up your chest, raise your head high, and hold a megaphone up to your mouth. If you don't have a megaphone you can make one. Now give a speech to the abuse monster (write what you will say before you give the speech). Tell the monster in your own words why you are not going to run any more. Tell the monster to quit picking on you. Tell the monster that the abuse is over and it is time to stop running. Tell the monster that you are safe now and that you know how to stay safe. Now go and get help from an adult you trust.

CHAPTER 24

FIGHT (TERROR)

It is easy to understand why abused kids are ready to *fight*. Many of them overheard adults fighting or got yelled at a lot. Now they think they have to fight to protect themselves—to survive. *Fight* is like an injured dog. When someone comes near an injured dog, it expects to be hurt again, so it snarls and bares its teeth in pain and fear.

During abuse, a kid might bite, kick, hit, or scream to get the abuser to stop. The kid is usually not able to fight off the abuser, who is usually bigger and stronger. And sometimes fighting makes the abuser even meaner. That is not very safe for the kid.

After the abuse, kids have lots of reasons to be mad. First, adults who abuse kids are very selfish.

- The abuser thinks only of himself and what he wants but not about the kid. It is like the abuser baking peanut butter cookies (because he likes peanut butter) when the kid is allergic to peanuts. The abuser offers to share the cookies, but only he can enjoy them.
- When a kid asks an abuser to stop, the abuser does not listen and does not stop. The abuser wants to have things *his* way.
- The abuser might say that *it* (the abuse) is a way of showing *love*. But *love* does not ignore a kid's feelings. Love should not hurt or confuse someone.
- An abuser also might threaten to hurt or kill a kid if he or she tells, to scare the kid into not telling. The abuser is trying to make the kid go along with what he wants. That is bullying. It is wrong for someone bigger and older to make a kid go along with abuse and tell that kid to keep it a secret.

After the abuse, kids might be mad that it happened. Or mad that no one noticed. Or mad that they could not stop it. Some kids don't feel safe, even if they are in a safe place. They hit, curse, and shout more than other kids who were not abused. They may not know how to stop fighting, because fighting feels better than getting hurt. Abused kids might even fight people that try to help them.

So how do you stop fighting? When you are mad and feel like *fighting*, you might try doing *the opposite*. This is an idea that comes from an adult therapy called Dialectical Behavior Therapy (DBT) (McKay, Wood, & Brantley, 2007). Doing the opposite helps you let go of your anger. For example, if you get mad and want to curse at someone, think about something you can say that is the opposite of cursing. It sounds silly, but you might go write a gratitude note in a journal (what you are thankful for or grateful for) or tell someone you love them. Or instead of cursing, you could blow bubbles with your mouth, or sing a silly song as loud as you can. If you want to throw something, think about something you can do with your hands that is the opposite of throwing. You might go clean the kitchen counter and scrub it really well or play catch with someone.

Another thing you can try is called thought-stopping with problem solving. You *STOP* and think when you are *starting* to get frustrated or angry. Don't wait until you get so angry you can't think. You already know that anger comes on fast, like lighting the fuse of a grenade and waiting for an explosion, so the minute the fuse is lit, you have to stop and think. Some kids carry around a little STOP sign to remind them to do this. The steps of STOP are Stop, Think, Observe, and Plan.

Here is how this works. When you start to get angry or frustrated, before you lose your temper or say anything, think *STOP!*

Now get your brain in gear to think about the situation. While thinking about the problem, you **t**alk to yourself.

Ask yourself some questions like, "What about this situation upsets me? What are my choices? What am I doing to make it worse? Am I basing my feelings on the facts? Do I have all the facts? What can I do to stay calm?" Most situations are a bit like stepping stones, where one stone leads to the next. Try to see the big picture.

Observe your feelings, your body's physical response, and your stress level. **O**pen your eyes and ears to observe all the facts.

Now, based on the facts, come up with a **p**lan. You need to think about the pros and cons of your plan, so weigh the risks and benefits of each thing you might do or say. When you are angry you probably feel like yelling, shouting, throwing, being mean, cursing, hurting someone or yourself, or breaking something. These behaviors have risks and could get you in trouble.

If you are really upset and might do something to get yourself in trouble, then do the opposite. The opposite is anything that resolves the situation or calms you down. A good plan does not cause trouble for you or anyone else. This may sound strange to you, but by *doing the opposite, you can gain a little time and calm down.*

24.1 STOP Practice

- **S**omeone at school is teasing you. They might be trying to get you mad so that you will do something and get in trouble. You feel like hitting that person.

- **T**hink, "This person is trying to get me mad. He or she wants me to blow up. Then I will get in trouble."

- **O**bserve, "My chest feels tight and my face is turning red. I need to calm down."

- **P**lan. What is the opposite of using your hands to hit (think of something you could do with your hands that is not aggressive in any way and is comforting or helpful)?

  _____

- If you said, "Using your hands to be gentle, like putting lotion on your arms," you are right. If you said, "Doing push-ups or throwing hoops with a basketball" you would be right because those things are other ways to use your hands that are not hitting.

- What is the opposite of saying something mean? _____

  _____

- If you said, "Saying something kind or supportive, like a compliment," you are right. If you said, "Telling a good joke and laughing," you are right, because that is using your words to say something funny, not mean.

- If you said, "Say something that totally surprises the other person," you are right, because that is not what the person expects you to do.

It is a mystery, but when you do or say the opposite of what you feel like doing when you are mad, it helps you feel less mad. Now let's move on to some other questions.

24.2 My Fight

- What makes you mad about being abused (or about watching your parents hurt each other)?
  _____

- What do you feel like _doing or saying (words and behaviors)_ when you get mad or become so scared that you want to fight to protect yourself? _____
  _____

- What is the opposite of doing these things? _____
  _____

- Have someone do or say something to upset you and scare you enough to make you mad. Describe what you feel like doing. Then practice doing the opposite.

CHAPTER 25

ABUSE AND TRAUMA

25.1 Trauma Event

A *trauma event* is something that puts you or someone you love in danger. It is something that actually hurts you or makes you think you are going to be hurt. Abuse is a type of trauma event. A trauma event can also be something you *witness* (see, hear, or know about). So if you see or hear someone close to you being hurt, it is a trauma event. It is very scary to be around someone who might hurt you or hurt someone you love.

25.1.1 Neglect

Neglect is also a trauma event, especially when you are very little. That is because when you are very little, you can't take care of yourself or survive without your parents. Neglect is when someone does not take good care of you or expects you to look after yourself when you are too young to do that. This can be about not having food when you are hungry. It can be about a parent sleeping when a baby has a wet diaper and starts crying. It can be about not having a safe place to call home. It can be about a parent who is too drunk or high on drugs to notice what you need. It can also be about someone leaving you alone too much. It can even be about someone ignoring you when you are scared, lonely, in pain, or in need of comfort. Not being cared for threatens your survival.

25.1.2 Abuse

Abuse can be physical (bad touch like hitting, shoving, burning, etc.), sexual (someone touching you in private areas or asking you to touch their private parts), or emotional. Emotional abuse is hard to describe—it is usually when someone says things to scare you or makes you feel really bad about yourself. It might be name-calling, making fun of you, laughing at you in a mean way, cursing at you, telling you that you are *no good* or calling you a *failure*.

25.1.3 Problems after Being Neglected or Abused

After you get abused or neglected, you might really feel "crazy" but you aren't. It is *normal* to react to abuse or neglect. There are lots of ways that feelings and behavior might change after abuse or neglect. Below are some examples—you might want to circle the things that sound like you.

- One boy felt empty and numb. He said, "I feel like a robot that can be turned on and off. I don't feel anything."

- Some kids blame themselves for the abuse. They think it was their fault or that they should have stopped it.

- Some abusers tell kids they *wanted it* and the kids start to believe them.

- Some kids get really mad and have temper tantrums. They hit, yell, bite, or curse. Some even break their own toys.

- Some kids have trouble concentrating or paying attention at school. Their grades might drop during or after the abuse.

- It is pretty common for kids to cry more or feel sad.

- Some abused kids are tired all the time.

- You might *tune out* or *dissociate*. When you do this, you go somewhere else in your mind. It is a little like being asleep and awake at the same time.

- Some kids have flashbacks. That is when it *feels like the abuse is happening all over again*.

- Some kids think about or dream about the abuse and are afraid it will happen again.

- You might think you are in danger even when you are safe.

- You might not want to be alone or sleep alone. You try to be a watchdog, 24/7.

- You might think someone is mean or "out to get you" even when it is not true.

- Some kids take things that don't belong to them.

- Some kids worry about germs or getting sick.

- Some kids want to be left alone and stop hanging out with their friends.

- Some kids feel different and think they don't fit in.

- Some kids pee or poop in their pants.

- Some abused kids can't sleep at night—they worry about what might happen.

- Some abused kids get more *hyper* and can't be still.

- Some kids touch their own or other kids' private parts. One girl we knew touched her private parts a lot after being abused. She hated it when grownups asked her, "Why are you doing that?" She didn't know why.

- If you were abused when you were really young and it lasted a long time, you might even hear voices in your head—angry or mean voices that make fun of you or call you bad names.

- Some kids start to hurt themselves (cut, bite, bang head) or think about suicide or dying. This is a very serious problem and a kid needs to tell an adult right away when this happens.

- Some kids can't talk about it, but they say they are *over it* (even though they aren't) and don't want others to talk about it.

- Some kids start to have *eating problems*. They stop eating, eat too much, or throw up after eating. Others *hoard (hide) food* in secret places just in case they might need it later.

You might want to show someone—a therapist, teacher, counselor, parent, or foster parent—your list. It is very important for you to let a caregiver know what you are going through.

CHAPTER 26

POST-TRAUMATIC STRESS DISORDER AND COMPLEX TRAUMA

26.1 Post-Traumatic Stress Disorder (PTSD)

Some abused kids end up with something called Post-Traumatic Stress Disorder (PTSD). *Post* means *after*, so here it means *after the abuse is over*. *Traumatic* means something really horrible—usually so horrible that you think you might not live through it. *Stress* is what you feel when and after you go through something horrible.

PTSD is usually tied to a specific abuse event. With PTSD, you might keep thinking about what happened. You might dream about it or have a *flashback*, which means you remember what happened in a way that you are reliving it. When you remember the event, it really upsets you. You might go numb. You try not to think about what happened and you might avoid things that remind you of what happened.

26.2 Complex Trauma

If you went through more than one type of abuse or neglect, it might be hard to remember when your problems started. Maybe your life had one bad thing after another. Maybe you were neglected as a baby, but you don't *remember* that. Or the adults in your house used drugs and alcohol so they ignored you or yelled at you when you cried.

You might have what is called *complex trauma* if there is more than one trauma event. It is more *complex* than PTSD. Most kids with complex trauma have been neglected and abused for a long time and it started when they were very young. There is not one single event that makes them feel bad, but a whole bunch of bad things all blended together, like the ingredients of a stew.

You might wonder why some kids get over abuse or neglect more quickly and others don't. Well, if something bad happens once or is not too bad, the child might get over it by talking to a school counselor or a friend. But there are some things that make it likely a child will have problems after abuse or neglect:

- if the abuse or neglect is really severe;
- if the abuse or neglect happens over and over;
- if the neglect or abuses start before you can talk or before they are old enough to go to school;
- if the abuser or neglecting person is someone they know and love, especially their mom or dad.

When things like this happen, trauma is harder to get over, and the child might end up with symptoms or problems coping. It is just like what happens to a brand new pan when you forget about it on the stove—the food burns. The first time, you might get the pan clean again if you let it soak a long time and then scrub really hard. If you burn things over and over in that pan, it is harder and harder to get the pan clean.

So how do you know if a kid has trauma-related problems? First, the problems start during the trauma, get worse after it, and don't go away after it has ended. A kid might go into *freak out, freeze, flight* and/or *fight*. The problems (like the ones listed before) can happen at school or at home. And the problems *keep the kid from being happy or enjoying life*. Most kids say they feel *changed* after the trauma. They feel different—some say they feel broken or wounded. Part of therapy is to help a kid feel *whole* again.

26.3 My Trauma

- Do you think you have trauma-related problems? Why or why not?_____

  _____

  _____

- Do you think you have PTSD or complex trauma? _____

  _____

If you have problems related to your abuse or neglect, it helps to talk to your therapist. You can also talk to a teacher or other adult you trust. It is hard to get over trauma, but it is worth it to try. *You* are worth it. The only way to deal with trauma is to outsmart it so that you can stop *freaking out, freezing*, going into *flight*, and *fighting*.

CHAPTER 27

HOW STRESS AFFECTS KIDS

Here are a few things about stress that many people don't know . . .

- Babies can have stress before they are born.
- A little kid can tell when an adult is stressed (by listening to the adult's voice, by looking at the adult's face, and by looking in the adult's eyes).
- Abuse and neglect raise a kid's stress.
- Seeing (or hearing) parents hurt each other raises a kid's stress.
- Stress is not good for your health.
- Stress can make it hard to think, cope, and sleep.
- Stress can make you tired and grouchy.
- Stress is *contagious* (contagious means you can *catch* something from another person, like a cold or the flu); kids can *catch* it from their parents. If the parent cries, the kid might cry; if the parent yells and hits, the kid might yell and hit; if the parent is scared, the kid might get scared.

A little stress is OK, like when you want to raise your grade in a hard school subject; that kind of stress might get you to do your homework or study for a test. But too much stress is not good for anyone. Living in an abusive home is *really* stressful and some kids stay stressed even after the abuse is over. When you are *stressed*:

- You might be tired all the time or feel tense.
- Your head might hurt or your chest might feel tight.
- You might get grouchy over little things.
- It is hard to get a good night's sleep.

27.1 Your Own Stress

- What stresses you out?_____
  _____
  _____

- How can you tell when you are stressed (think about how you feel and act)? _____
  _____
  _____

27.2 Stress and Babies

Before you were born, you floated in warm water in your mother's womb. You heard her voice and felt her heart beat. Until a baby is born, everything good and bad comes through the mother's body to the baby—even stress.

After the baby is born it needs a home with low stress. If a home is full of stress (noise, shouting, hitting), it is hard for the baby to relax.

A baby looks at the mother's face while being fed. When the mother smiles at the baby, the baby relaxes. A baby listens to the mother's voice. A calm voice makes the baby feel calm.

27.2.1 You as a Baby

- Ask someone to tell you your birth story and what you were like as a baby. Write down your favorite parts of your birth story and what you were like as a baby.

  _____

  _____

  _____

  _____

  _____

- How did you show your feelings (happy, scared, and mad) when you were a baby?

  _____

  _____

- Imagine being a baby again. Pick a blanket and stuffed animal to hold. Curl up somewhere comfortable, maybe even inside a sleeping bag. What would you like your caregiver to do to show love? _____

  _____

  _____

  Imagine something upsets you. You start to cry. What would you like your caregiver do to comfort you? _____

  _____

  _____

  _____

  _____

27.3 The Needs of Young Children

Once you could talk, you asked for what you wanted. If you were hungry, you asked to be fed. If you were scared, you asked someone to hold you. A parent shows love by feeding a hungry child or cuddling a child who is crying. When your needs are met, you are less stressed.

27.3.1 You as a Little Child

- Imagine yourself as a little child. Pretend that you and your caregiver are doing something together that makes you smile. What are you doing together?

  _____

  _____

- Make mad, happy, sad, grossed out, shocked, and scared faces with someone—see if you can guess each other's feelings. Which feelings were easiest to guess? _____

  _____

  _____

  _____

- How can you tell when your caregiver is feeling each of the following?

  Mad: _____

  Happy: _____

  Sad: _____

  Scared: _____

  Stressed: _____

27.3.2 The Mirror

- Carry around a hand mirror for a day. When you are having a good feeling, look at your face in the mirror and see what your face looks like. When you are having a bad feeling, look in the mirror and see what your face looks like.

- When your caregiver makes a face (happy, mad, sad, scared) ask him or her to look in your mirror and see what that looks like. Talk about what you see in your caregiver's face.

27.3.3 Pretend Play

- Imagine you are a scared little child. Ask your caregiver to do something to help you feel safe again. _____

  _____

- Pretend you are a small child playing make-believe with someone you love. Who are you playing with and what are you doing together? How does it make you feel?

  _____

  _____

  _____

- Sit with your caregiver and blow bubbles for each other. Watch the bubbles float down from above your head. Relax. Pop them right before they reach your faces.

27.3.4 Love Letter

- Write a letter to someone you love. Tell that person what he or she does that makes you feel happy, sad, mad, or scared. Your letter:

  _____
  _____
  _____
  _____
  _____
  _____
  _____

- Now pretend that the person you wrote to has sent you an answer to your letter. Write down exactly what you would like that person to say to you:

  _____
  _____
  _____
  _____
  _____
  _____
  _____

27.4 How Parents Raise Stress in Kids

Every kid has some stress—believe it or not, it is part of life! But there are things parents do that raise it in kids. Abused kids do not need adults to do things that bring extra stress, but often the grownups do things that increase it. Circle the things adults in your life have done to raise your stress.

27.4.1 Things Adults Do That Raise Stress in Kids

- They yell, curse, or fight around their kids.
- They blame kids for things that aren't their fault.
- They forget to praise their kids.
- They act like they want kids to be perfect.
- They criticize too much.
- They forget that kids are human and make mistakes.
- They forget that kids have feelings.
- They don't pay attention to *good* behavior.
- They call their kids *bad*. (Kids are never *bad*: They might make bad choices or misbehave, but they are good people.)
- They compare them to someone else ("You are just like . . ." or "Why can't you be more like . . .").
- They go out and leave their kids alone. If something happens (for example, the kids run out of food or someone gets sick), the kids don't know what to do.

- They sleep when their kids are awake.

- They drink too much or take drugs. This changes how parents behave around their kids. Kids have trouble getting their needs met when their parents are drunk or high. Parents' eyes and faces even look different when they are drunk or high, and this is stressful for a baby or young child.

- They punish kids in mean ways like locking them in a room or punching them.

You might want to share your list with an adult you trust. Sometimes adults don't know that they are causing you extra stress. Other times they know what they are doing but don't care or don't understand that it is hurting you. You might want to talk with someone about the things on your list. Grownups make mistakes too—even grownups who love you! They would probably like to know how to help you with your stress.

27.5 When Stress Gets Too High

Too much stress is like throwing a kid who can't swim into the deep part of a swimming pool, or like trying to paddle over a waterfall on a leaky air mattress! Nobody copes well when stress is too high. So how can you tell when a kid has *too much* stress? Well, here are some clues. Circle any clues that sound like you.

27.5.1 Clues That a Kid has Too Much Stress

- Gets stomachaches a lot

- Grades fall at school

- Whines or cries most days

- Stops eating or eats too much

- Gains or loses a lot of weight

- Hides food

- Starts taking things that don't belong to him

- Loses his temper a lot

- Has trouble sleeping or many bad dreams

- Needs more attention than usual

- Has accidents during the day (poop or pee)

- Other: _____

Show your stress list to a grownup and talk about it. It is important to lower your stress when it is getting too high.

27.6 Lowering Your Stress

- Imagine having a special, safe place where you feel no fear and no stress. Describe it. What are the colors, sounds, smells, sights, temperature, etc.?

  _____

  _____

  _____

  _____

  _____

- Draw a picture of your safe special place.

- Pretend that you go to your _safe place_ to relax. What will you do while you are there? _____

  _____

CHAPTER 28

MEMORY OF ABUSE

Kids don't remember everything that happens to them. They tend to remember things that *stand out*, like getting stitches, moving to a new house, or a special birthday. You might remember a house you lived in or where you went to school. Scientists show that some kids remember their abuse and some do not. Even if you remember your abuse, the memory might not be clear or complete. You might even have memories that are pictures without words, or bad dreams.

Many people think kids won't remember their abuse later, because they were *too young at the time* it happened. It isn't true that little kids don't have memories. Little kids have memories, but their memories are different.

A memory of early abuse is like . . .

- A scar. A scar can be sore long after the wound has healed.
- A tattoo. The ink is under the skin and you can't scrub it away.
- A computer *virus*. If you want to get rid of it, first you have to find it in the computer and then you have to do something to erase it. Ignoring it won't make it go away. If you leave it there, it can even damage your other documents.

28.1 Your Own Memory of Abuse

Draw a picture of a scar, tattoo, or computer virus. On the picture, write down a memory of abuse or neglect that is hard to get rid of.

Your earliest memories are made before you can talk (pre-verbal) and they are often *sensory*. *Sensory* refers to your senses: hearing, sight, taste, touch, smell, or feeling. A sensory memory is in your body.

Here are a few examples of sensory memories:

- a sound, like a car door slamming or a loud voice;
- a smell, like perfume or body odors;
- a taste, like soap in your mouth;
- a touch, like a strong hand gripping your wrist or sweaty skin;
- a sight, like a picture in your head of something in the room;
- a feeling, like the feeling of floating above your body during the abuse or the feeling of wanting to throw up.

After kids learn to talk (become verbal), they have words to talk about their memories. Some adults think kids get over abuse if they forget about it and don't talk about it. That is not true. You can stop thinking about a memory, but your body does not forget.

Let me tell you a true story about a boy with a sensory memory. A three-year-old boy screamed and cried in the car one day as an ambulance passed the car he was riding in with his mother. He cried until she took him home. From that day on, he cried when he heard a siren. He also was scared of the color red and cried when his dad wore a red shirt. When his parents asked him what was wrong, he said, "I don't know."

It turned out the boy was in a car accident with his mother when he was one and half years old. His mom hit her head during the accident and there was blood on her. She went to the hospital by ambulance to get stitches. The boys seemed calm through the whole event. His parents thought he did not remember the accident.

You have probably guessed that the boy had a *sensory* memory of the red blood and the sound of the siren. He hadn't really been calm during the accident—he was in *freeze*. Sometimes memories stay *asleep* until something triggers them or wakes them up. The ambulance siren the boy heard later when he was three triggered or *woke up* the old memory.

28.1.1 Your Sensory Memories

We all have sensory memories. Using our senses can help us recall things in more vivid detail. Smells, sights, tastes, colors, or sounds can make you feel good or bad. This writer got a fishbone stuck in her throat when she was six. Now, many years later, she does not like the taste of fish. She loves the smell of garlic bread, though: Her mother served it with lasagna on her birthday, so it is a smell that makes her feel good.

- Write down smells, sights, tastes, colors, or sounds that make you feel bad or gross you out:
  _____
  _____
  _____

- Write down smells, sights, tastes, colors, or sounds that make you feel good:
  _____
  _____
  _____

- Which sense or senses (tastes, sounds, smells, touches, or colors) come to mind when you think of your abuse? _____
  _____
  _____
  _____
  _____

- Close your eyes and think of a happy memory. What do you see, smell, hear, and taste?
  _____
  _____
  _____

Your therapist might ask you to talk about your abuse. Some kids are afraid to talk about the abuse and worry that talking about it will make it worse. What they don't know is that until they talk about the abuse, it is still *in charge of* them. It is stressful to push back bad memories. Kids need to *take charge of* the abuse and talk about it. Talking about your abuse gets easier the more you do it. And you get over trauma by talking about your abuse. Don't try to deal with abuse alone—talk to a therapist or a caregiver. Get it out and be in charge of your life. No more secrets, and no more silence!

28.1.2 Memory of Your Abuse

- On a scale from one (very little) to ten (all), how much of your abuse do you think you remember?

  _____

- Draw a sponge with holes in it.

  The holes in the sponge are the *things you don't remember* about your abuse. It is OK that you don't remember everything that happened. It was still real. The solid part of the sponge is things you remember. Write some of the things you remember (using your senses) on the solid parts of the sponge.

CHAPTER 29

HOW ADULTS CAN HELP (OR HURT) ABUSED KIDS

There are some simple things adults can do to help kids lower their stress and get over trauma. As you read, you might want to circle the things that your caregiver does for you.

29.1 Ways Caregivers Can Help

- Feeding you yummy foods
- Giving you treats on a bad day
- Giving hugs and praise
- Using a quiet voice
- Helping you practice coping skills
- Doing fun things with you like _____
- Being willing to listen when you want to talk
- Believing you about the abuse
- Taking you to a therapist if you have coping problems
- Asking you what would help you feel more safe and secure
- Doing things to keep you safe
- Giving you time to calm down when you are upset
- Tucking you in at night
- Feeding you breakfast
- Giving you a snack after school
- Helping you clean your room
- Being there when you need them
- Other: _____

We know that abused kids can get upset (scared and stressed) *really fast* when they think something bad is going to happen. They try to cope with their fear by protecting themselves. Adults need to notice when kids are stressed and help them calm back down. Kids calm back down when adults do the *right thing;* they get more upset when adults say or do the *wrong thing.*

The *right thing* is anything to help the kid calm down. Some things work better than others. The *wrong thing* is anything that makes the kid more stressed. If you look at the Appendix B in the back of the book, you will see an example of a parent doing the wrong thing and what happens. This is an example of trauma related state-dependent functioning (Perry, 2004a,b). You probably already know that *a kid's behavior goes hand in hand with his level of fear or stress.*

When an adult does the *wrong thing*, a kid might have a *trauma chain reaction*. Do you know what a chain reaction is? Imagine 100 dominoes set up in a row on a long table. If you push the first domino, it sets off a chain reaction by knocking down the others and unless you stop it, all the dominoes fall down, one after the other. A *trauma chain reaction* is like that. It is set off by fear. An adult (usually not on purpose) *pushes a kid's fear buttons.* A *trauma chain reaction* starts with nervous fear and it ends with *terror*, a type of fear that looks a lot like rage.

The *PTSD chain reaction* of *freak out, freeze, flight, or fight* is a little like going from a dark, cloudy, rainy day to a tornado touch-down. As the storm builds, the wind gets stronger and the sky gets darker. Then rain and hail come down hard. The thunder and lightning crash, so much so that you can't hear your own thoughts. By the time the tornado touches down, you can't see or hear anything but the storm. Once a rainy day becomes a tornado, you need to take cover and stay safe, because a tornado can *destroy everything in its path.*

For a kid, if the chain reaction is not stopped once it starts, it ends with *a total meltdown.* During a total meltdown, part of your brain stops working, and you can't think at all. In fact, you fight to *survive.* After a meltdown, you might not even remember the things you said and did. That is because terror and rage shut off your thinking memory.

The chapters that follow discuss the *trauma chain reaction* in more detail.

CHAPTER 30

THE TRAUMA CHAIN REACTION: FREAK OUT

30.1 Calm: BEFORE the Chain Reaction

Abused kids are never as calm as other kids. That is because their brains are in a *state of fear*—fear that something bad might happen again (Perry, 2004a,2004b). They stay *alert* and *vigilant*. *Vigilance* means you are on the lookout for danger or keeping an eye out so that you don't get hurt again.

30.2 Freak Out

I call the first stage of the chain reaction *freak out* because that is what happens when you are startled by something. As you read the list below, circle what *you* do when something startles you and you start to *freak out*. Show what you circled to an adult.

30.3 Clues of Freak Out

- A kid's face might turn red.
- A kid might interrupt people and change the subject.
- A kid might start to frown.
- A kid might start to argue.
- A kid might start tapping his feet or hands, picking at skin, fidgeting, or biting his nails.
- A kid might get more *hyper* or restless, then run around or climb on things.
- A kid might start making lots of noise or laugh really wildly.
- A kid might start to bother others.
- A kid might ask to go to the bathroom.
- A kid might poop or pee his or her pants.
- A kid might ask an adult to stop talking about something or change the subject. If the adult doesn't stop talking, the kid might shout, "shut up!" even though he knows he will get in trouble.
- A kid might whine or complain more.
- A kid might get clingy and stay close to a parent all the time.

- A kid might stop sleeping in his or her bed.

- A kid might have trouble paying attention or concentrating at school.

- A kid might start eating more or less.

- Other: _____

As you read the next list, *circle the things* an adult could do to help you calm down when you freak out. Show the list to an adult.

30.4 How an Adult Can Help a Kid that Starts to Freak Out

- Stop lecturing or arguing.

- Lower his/her voice.

- Let the kid take a break (a few minutes to calm down).

- Say, "I'm sorry I scared you. I didn't mean to upset you."

- Point out what the adult sees. For example, "Wow, you seem really upset. You got really quiet all of a sudden?" or "Your voice is getting louder. What's going on with you?"

- Ask, "What would help you calm down right now?"

- Ask, "What's wrong?" or "How can I help?"

- Suggest things the kid can do to calm down.

- Let the kid leave the room or take a walk.

- Other: _____

If someone does not help you calm down (or does something to upset you more), you might enter the next step of trauma chain reaction.

30.5 Your Own Freak Out

- Name two adults that you trust. Write what they do to make you feel safe and help you stop freaking out.

_____

_____

_____

- What can you do (yourself) to calm down when you are upset?

_____

_____

_____

_____

CHAPTER 31

THE TRAUMA CHAIN REACTION: FREEZE

The next step of the *trauma chain reaction* is *freeze*. It is a *state of alarm* (Perry, 2004a, 2004b). I call it freeze like in the statues game when the music turned off. If an adult yells at you in a loud voice, you might freeze. That is because a loud voice scares you and you think you might get hurt. You might freeze if someone gets in your face and starts to order you around. You will probably freeze if someone threatens you. When you freeze, you sometimes start to cry or feel too scared to talk. When you *freeze*, it is harder for you to think and calm down. *Read the freeze clues below and circle the ones that sound like you. Show what you circled to your therapist.*

31.1 Clues of Freeze

- A kid might suddenly get really quiet.

- A kid might look away or look down.

- A kid might pull his coat or sweatshirt up over his head.

- A kid might suddenly stop listening.

- A kid might go somewhere (under a table, in a corner) and stay really still.

- A kid's eyes might go empty as she tunes out.

- It is hard to get the kid's attention—he/she seems in another world.

- Other: _____

When kids freeze someone needs to remind them that they are safe and offer comfort. Below is a list of things adults can do to help kids in freeze. Go ahead and circle the ones you might want adults to try with you.

31.2 How an Adult Can Help a Kid in Freeze

- Tell the kid what he sees going on, in a nice way. "I just saw you freeze there. You're OK—I'm not mad and I'm not going to hurt you. I'm sorry I scared you."

- Say, "Hey, I'm concerned about you, so why don't I just hang out until you feel better?"

- Move closer (not too fast) and talk to the kid in a calm, quiet voice.

- Use a gentle touch like putting a hand on the kid's shoulder. They should ask before they touch.

- Remind the kid that he is safe and point out the facts about that.

- Other: _____

Some kids tune out when they freeze, which to others can look a lot like ignoring. So if an adult doesn't notice you are in *freeze*, the adult might think you are ignoring him and get mad. If he gets mad and acts like he might hurt you, you could *go into flight* or *fight* to protect yourself. Like an animal in danger, you might run off or bare your teeth. It is *very* hard to think or calm down when you are trying to protect yourself.

Here is an example of a chain reaction where a teacher did not notice the child *freezing* and did the wrong thing.

- A kid is in class at school.
- A big boy that sits behind the kid threatens to kick his butt later that day. It is the same kid who beat him up two weeks ago. It alarms the boy that he might get hurt again and he freezes.
- The teacher asks the kid a question. The kid doesn't hear the teacher—he is thinking about how to get home from school without being beaten up. The kid starts to worry about getting hurt again.
- The teacher doesn't know the kid is in *freeze*. She thinks the kid is ignoring her (not listening or paying attention) and does the wrong thing. The teacher walks over to the kid's desk, puts her finger in his face and says in a loud voice, "Hey—I'm talking to you!"
- The teacher's behavior startles the kid and now he is scared of the teacher. At this point, the kid might *go into flight or fight*. Without even thinking, the kid might shout back at the teacher or jump up from his seat and try to leave the classroom.
- The kid will probably get in trouble, and no one even knew how scared he was .

31.3 Your Own Freeze

- Make a list of things that scared you and made you freeze. Be specific and give details. ___
  _____
  _____
  _____

- Write down two or more things adults did *that helped you calm down, listen, and pay attention* when you were in freeze. _____
  _____

- List things you plan to do (to calm down or communicate your feelings) when you become alarmed and start to *freeze*. Make a coping card. _____

CHAPTER 32

THE TRAUMA CHAIN REACTION: FLIGHT

Flight is when you panic and try to escape danger. Panic, the state word used by Perry in his training materials, is another word for very strong fear (Perry, 2004a, 2004b). When you panic, you want to get away because you think someone is going to hurt you. There are some clues that a kid is in flight. Circle any of the clues that sound like you.

32.1 Clues of Flight

* A kid might try to walk away or leave the room.

* A kid might hide.

* A kid might leave the house.

* A kid might pull away.

* A kid might tune out in his mind if he can't get away.

* A kid might run around the house really fast so that no one can catch him.

* Other: _____

A kid in *flight* is afraid and runs or hides to escape danger. Adults can do things to help kids calm down before they run or while they are running.

32.2 How an Adult Can Help a Kid in Flight

Circle the things you think would help you.

* Tell the kid, "Hey, I'm not coming any closer. No one is going to hurt you. But I need to stay near you so I know you are safe."

* Stay close enough to the kid so the kid won't get hurt. When a kid is in *flight, it is very hard to think clearly*. A kid might forget to look for cars and run across the street or go outside in winter without a warm coat.

* Stay between the kid and any danger.

- Stay calm and talk quietly.

- Suggest a walk or something fun the kid likes to do. "Want to swing outside? You seem to calm down when we swing."

- Call for help if the *flight* puts a kid in danger (running into a busy road or trying to jump out a window).

- Other: _____

During *flight*, the wrong adult behavior is anything that seems like a threat or makes a kid more scared.

32.3 Your Own Flight

- Kids tune out, run away or hide during *flight*. Describe a time you ran off or hid from someone.
_____
_____

- How did others react to your running or hiding? _____
_____

- List things you can do to calm down when you feel like tuning out or running. Put them on a coping card._____
_____

CHAPTER 33

THE TRAUMA CHAIN REACTION: FIGHT

You might *fight* to protect yourself if you can't escape someone or something that scares you. For example, if a teacher follows you after you leave the classroom and grabs your arm, you might hit or shove him without thinking. You *feel like* he is going to hurt you, even if it is not true. You act on what you feel, not on what is true (the facts). It is important to learn how to calm down before you start to *fight*. Fight behavior will get you into trouble and someone could get hurt.

When abused kids *fight*, believe it or not, they are *more afraid than mad*. The fight response is pretty automatic. That means it just happens. A kid in *fight* can't think or reason.

Think about what happens to you right before you start to fight. Circle the things below that sound like you.

33.1 How to Tell When a Kid Might Start to Fight

- A kid first looks shocked or startled (Alert or Alarm).

- A kid may back away and raise his fist (Flight).

- A kid probably sounds angry, curses, or says he wants to hit someone.

- A kid says something that sounds like a threat.

- A kid does something that says "keep away" (tips over a chair, throws something, breaks a toy, bites someone, hits a wall).

Other: _____

Next is a list of things that can help a kid calm down when the kid feels like fighting. Circle the things below that might help you calm you down when you feel like fighting.

33.2 How to Help a Kid Who Feels Like Fighting

- An adult can calmly say . . .

  ○ "I can tell you're getting upset. Think about what you can do to calm down."

  ○ "How can I help?"

- ○ "Do you want to (get a drink, take a walk, listen to music, play drums, rock in a rocking chair, hit a pillow, throw beanbags at the wall, do relaxation, or go somewhere you can be alone)?"

- ○ "I want you to be safe. I need to keep you safe."

- ○ "Please keep your hands and feet to yourself."

- • An adult can stop talking.

- • An adult can back off, be quiet and give the kid time to calm down.

Other: _____

Some grownups don't know when to stop talking. You probably know that makes things worse when a kid feels like *fighting*. There are two kinds of *fight*: verbal (where the kid starts to use angry words or threats) and physical (where the kid hits, bites, scratches, pushes, throws, or kicks). Another term for physical *fight* is a total *meltdown*. It looks like rage but is really fear. Total meltdown is like a *volcano erupting* or *a tornado destroying everything in its path*. During a total meltdown, you can't think. In *meltdown*, you fight *to survive*. Later, you might not even remember the things you said and did.

When you are in a meltdown, an adult needs to take charge to keep you safe. The adult needs to make sure you won't hurt yourself or anyone else. That adult might need to hold you, call 911, or get everyone else to leave the room. The adult might try to get you to a quiet room where you can stay until the anger/fear passes.

33.3 You in Fight

- • What *do you do and say* when you feel like *fighting?*_____
  _____
  _____

- • Who do you trust to help you calm down?_____
  _____
  _____

- • Who should not come near you when you feel mad? _____
  _____

- • Give an example of a time you started to *fight* or had a *meltdown* and an adult helped you calm down. _____
  _____
  _____

- • Describe a time you started to *fight* or *had a meltdown* and an adult did something that got you more upset. _____
  _____
  _____

- • Describe a time you started to fight then *you did something* to calm down. _____
  _____
  _____

- On a large index card, make a coping card of what you will do to calm down the next time you feel like fighting.

CHAPTER 34

YOUR OWN CHAIN REACTION

When you understand your own *trauma chain reaction*, you can help your caregiver understand you—how you think, feel, and behave when you are stressed. If you and your therapist understand what triggers your trauma memories and how you react, you can work together with your caregiver. After all, you are the expert on your own behavior.

Think of a time you went through a *trauma chain reaction* from start to finish. This would be a time when you saw or heard something that triggered fear (or anger, since you might feel your fear as anger). It might have started with a caregiver or teacher raising his or her voice, grabbing you, getting in your way, giving you an order, or criticizing you. It ended with a temper tantrum or *meltdown*. It is important that you think about what could have prevented or stopped the reaction at each stage.

34.1 Steps in Your Chain Reaction

- What were you doing before the chain reaction started (the *calm before the storm*)?
  _____
  _____
  _____

- Describe what startled, scared, or upset you. This is the *trigger* that started your *chain reaction.*_____
  _____
  _____
  _____

34.2 Mapping Your Chain Reaction

On the next page, you will *map* your chain reaction, one step at a time. Before you do this, read through Appendix B with your therapist or caregiver. To map your chain reaction, fill in the boxes from left to right. For each step, think about what could have helped you calm down and stopped the reaction.

In the boxes:

- Write how you felt during each stage.
- Write what you did or said during each stage of the chain reaction.
- Write what others did or said that got you more upset during each stage.
- Write what you and others could do to stop the chain reaction during each stage.

Table 34.1

*START HERE Freak Out (Alert) What could have helped you calm down when you got startled, scared, or upset?	Your Feelings and What You Did or Said	What Others Did or Said to Make it Worse
Freeze or Become Very Emotional (Alarm) What could have helped you calm down during freeze?	Your Feelings and What You Did or Said	What Others Did or Said to Make it Worse
Flight (Panic) What could have helped you calm down in flight?	Your Feelings and What You Did or Said	What Others Did or Said to Make it Worse
Fight (Terror and Meltdown) What could have helped you calm down when you started to fight?	Your Feelings and What You Did or Said	What Others Did or Said

CHAPTER 35

WHAT DOES YOUR BRAIN HAVE TO DO WITH IT?

You might want to skip this chapter if you are not interested in science, since it is about how your brain works.

If you look under the hood of a car, you will see the engine and all sorts of parts. There are hoses and wires in there with the parts. Everything has to work together for the car to run. A computer in the car also helps it run.

Your body also has lots of different parts that have to work together. Your brain is the computer that runs your body. Your brain also has lots of different parts, each of which has a job to do.

There isn't enough space here for me to tell you about all the parts of your brain, but I will tell you about some parts that are affected by abuse. I will keep it simple so that it does not bore or confuse you too much.

I will call the parts of your brain the Warning Brain (Watchdog), the Feeling Brain (The Spaghetti Pot), the Thinking Brain (Judge), and the Memory Brain (Computer Flash Drive). Let me tell you more about them.

The Warning part of your brain is like a Watchdog; its job is to sense danger, warn, and protect you. The Judge Brain is your Thinking Brain; it uses logic, words, and facts. The Feeling Brain (Spaghetti Pot) uses emotions and senses like taste, sound, smell, sight, and touch. The Memory brain stores memories.

35.1 The Warning Brain (Watchdog)

The Warning Brain (*Watchdog*) wants to keep you safe, so it warns you when it thinks you are in danger, like a dog that barks at an intruder. After you are abused, it might also warn you even when there is no real danger, because it doesn't take time to check out the facts.

35.2 The Thinking Brain (The Judge)

The Thinking Brain is like the Judge in a court of law. A Judge considers all the *facts* and makes a ruling based on the *evidence*. This part of your brain is not emotional; it is scientific and uses facts to solve problems and control your emotions.

When the Watchdog senses danger and sends a warning, you start to *freak out*. At that point, the Judge checks out the facts and decides whether you are safe. If you are safe, the Judge tells you to calm down.

But after abuse, the Feeling Brain takes over and the Judge Brain takes a court recess. During that recess, no one is sitting in the Judge's chair and the Judge is not available to consider the facts. When the Feeling Brain takes over, you can't think or check the facts.

35.3 The Feeling Brain (The Spaghetti Pot)

You don't want feelings to be too strong, but neither do you want to shut them off completely. If feelings get too powerful, they overwhelm you. If they are shut off, you can't feel anything. Feelings are a little like a pot of spaghetti cooking on the stove. It is important to keep the heat *just right*. If you don't do that, in no time at all the water starts to boil over. If you see white froth bubbling up in the pot, you can quickly turn down the heat and keep cooking the spaghetti. You don't want to turn the heat *off* because the spaghetti won't cook but you don't want it to get too high because then the water boils over.

After abuse, your feelings either shut down or boil over (you become very emotional). When your emotions (usually fear or anger) get too hot and spill over, you are likely to experience a trauma stress chain reaction.

35.4 False Alarms

After abuse, your Thinking Brain is not working properly, and you can't tell facts from fiction or danger from safety. Your *Feeling* brain is very sensitive—the *pot of water with your feelings in it is quick to boil over*. As a result, you may over-react to danger signals or *triggers*, and there will be *false alarms*. A false alarm is when you *feel* in danger but you are not. Even though you are not in danger, *you react as if you are*.

Let me give you an example of a false alarm.

- A kid is home alone. She heard about a break-in last week near her home. She is vigilant—ready to *freak out*.
- When she hears a noise outside the window, *she is scared and freaks out.* She thinks, "Maybe it is the robber."
- She *freezes* and holds her breath.
- She wants to hide or lock herself in her bedroom (*flight*).
- Before she has a chance to *go into flight, her mom comes home.* She tells her what she heard. The girl and her mom go to the window, pull back the curtains, and check the facts.
- The mom shows the girl a tree branch scratching against the window as the wind blows.
- Now the girl knows it is not a robber trying to break into her house. It was a false alarm.
- She takes a deep breath and calms back down.
- The girl tells herself that next time she will stay calm and check out the facts before she *freaks out.*

Here is another example.

- A boy gets abused by his grandpa over and over. He is really stressed.
- The Judge Brain goes on vacation. The Feeling Brain takes over.
- The boy starts to think all old men are abusive (not a fact).
- The boy starts to be afraid of all old men. He is *vigilant (very aware and watchful)* around older men.
- The boy goes to the park. He sees an old man approaching on the path.
- The boy's heart starts to pound and his mouth goes dry. Fear. Even though most old men are not abusive (the facts), the boy's feelings are *in charge*.
- When the old man leaves the path and walks over to the ice cream truck parked at the curb, the boy feels instant relief. He realizes that he was not in danger. It was a false alarm.

You can see how the Feeling Brain makes mistakes because it does not use the facts. During a *false alarm*, you might go into *Freak Out, Freeze, Fight* or *Flight*.

35.5 The Memory Brain (Computer Flash Drive)

Most kids today use computers, so I will compare this part of your brain to a flash drive. Your brain stores your memories, like a computer stores your documents. Storing memories in your brain is like doing *save* or *save as* on a computer or flash drive. Some memories go in a *temporary file* (short term) and others go into *permanent storage* (long term). Your memory files store the facts about the past. Abuse can damage your memory and make it hard for the Judge to check out the facts.

35.6 Your Own Brain (see Worksheet)

- On the triangle, write *Judge Brain* (Thinking) at the top point and draw a picture of a Judge. Write the words "check out the facts" by *Judge Brain*.

- Write *Feeling Brain* (Spaghetti Pot) and *Computer Flash Drive* (Memory) on the other two points of the triangle. Draw pictures that will remind you of these parts of the brain.

- Outside the triangle near the *Feeling Brain* write *Watchdog Brain*. Draw the Watchdog.

- Draw a line between the *Watchdog Brain* and the *Feeling Brain*. This line shows that they are connected. This is how the *Watchdog* sends a warning to the *Feeling Brain*.

- Draw a switch (//) on the line between the *Judge* and the *Computer Flash Drive* (Memory) Brain. This switch can block memories when it is turned on.

- Draw a switch (//) on the line between the *Judge* and the *Feeling Brain*. This switch can use facts to shut down (turn off) *Fear* and *Anger* in the *Feeling Brain*. This switch doesn't work very well (can break down) after abuse. Therapy helps fix it so it works again.

Now you have a pretty good picture of the parts of your brain that are involved with trauma and PTSD!

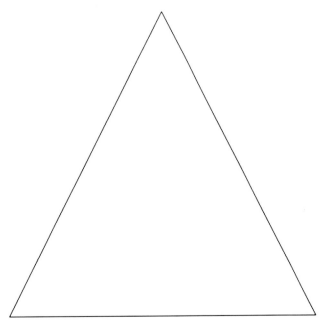

Figure 35.1 How your brain deals with stress and abuse.

CHAPTER 36

HOW STRESS CHANGES YOUR BRAIN

Really bad stress can change a kid's brain. As you know, abuse is a type of really bad stress, and it hurts your brain. Scientists show that these changes in the brain can lead to . . .

- memory problems (at school and home);
- speech delays (learning to talk later than other kids);
- hyperactivity (always in motion, like a motor running);
- not paying attention (tuning out);
- being too emotional (afraid or angry);
- doing things without thinking;
- trouble learning to read and write;
- slower *processing*;
- problems with attention and concentration.

An adult might think an abused kid has a *learning disability* or *attention deficit hyperactivity disorder (ADHD)* when in fact they have been through a *trauma-related change*.

A normal brain works like a railroad crossing; the crossing gate goes down only when a train is coming. Imagine a railroad crossing with a broken switch. If the switch is broken, the *gate might go down* when *there is no train coming*. Or the gate might *not* go down when a train *is* coming.

In abused kids, the danger signal is broken. Some abused kids see danger everywhere and they *freak out* too much. That is a very stressful way to live! Other abused kids ignore (deny) *real danger and can get hurt*.

The changes in your brain after abuse can be frustrating, but don't give up! When the abuse stops, and you feel safe, your brain can get better.

The next section of the book will be about things you can do to get over abuse. Remember, when someone is caught in a riptide in the ocean, it does not help to fight it or to float out to sea. To survive, you outsmart the riptide by staying calm, calling for help, thinking about what to do and then doing it (move sideways).

To survive abuse you stay calm, get help, think about what to do and then do it.

I call these smart skills the Three Cs:

1 Calm down: relax and control your emotions.
2 Connect: attach and trust.
3 Conquer: think, plan, and be safe.

CHAPTER 37

COPING SKILLS: CALM DOWN

It is important to learn coping skills to help you get over abuse. You already know that you can't change the past, but you *can change* how you think about the past and how you feel about yourself and others. You also can develop hope for the future and believe in yourself. Coping skills help kids calm down, connect with others, and conquer thoughts and beliefs that get in the way of change. You can call them the Three Cs.

37.1 Calm Down

The first thing you will want to learn to do is calm down (*regulate emotion and arousal*), because you know it is hard to think when you are too stressed. After being abused, it is hard to feel calm. Your body stays tense and your muscles tight. Your feelings are all stirred up. It is like a lake after a storm.

> - What does the water of a lake look like before a storm? _____
> - What does the water of a lake look like after a storm? _____
>   _____
>   _____

Yes, before the storm, the water is clear and blue. You can see down into the water. Right after the storm, though, the water is cloudy and dark. It is hard to see anything in the water when it is all stirred up. If you give the water time to clear, the *stuff* that got stirred up will settle back to the bottom. Abuse can stir you up inside, making you feel cloudy and dark.

After abuse, you might want to relax but don't know how. When you learn to relax your body, your Thinking Brain will work better. Things that relax your body don't require any thinking. Circle any of the things below that you do now or could do to relax. Pick a couple of these things and practice them, then try some new ones. Keep doing the ones that work for you.

> - Take a long walk or jog around the neighborhood.
> - Play with or hug your dog.
> - Take a hot bath or shower before bed or when you wake up.
> - Go to a safe place and yell into a pillow.
> - Sing at the top of your lungs.

- Blow bubbles.

- Cuddle with a really soft blanket or stuffed animal.

- Ride your bike as fast as you can for ten minutes.

- Practice slow, deep breathing. To do this, use a drinking straw to breathe in and out slowly. Put your fist in the middle of your chest below your breastbone—just under your ribs. You should be able to feel your fist move up and down as you breathe deeply. This kind of breathing is from your diaphragm (belly breathing). Breathe in while counting to five. Hold it for five. Let it out for a count of five. As you breathe out, think, "Out goes the stress" and picture the stress leaving your body. Once you can do this with a straw, then try it without. Breathe in slowly through your nose, hold your breath, and then breathe out by puffing as if you are blowing out five candles. With each puff, you should feel your belly move. For the last puff, let all the breath out in a long puff.

- Put on some relaxing music. Use headphones or ear buds. Pick music with a slow beat. While listening, pretend you are taking a trip to a very relaxing, peaceful place.

- Rock in a rocking chair until you have a steady rhythm—say a rhyme to the back-and-forth rhythm.

- Tighten and relax each set of muscles in your body, going from head to toe. Finish by tensing up and relaxing all your muscles at the same time.

- Sit and scan your body from head to toe for tension. Sit cross-legged quietly and focus only on your breathing. If a thought comes in, observe it and let it go. Scan your body with a *stress meter*. This will tell you where the stress is in your body— your head, face, neck, shoulders, arms and hands, chest, belly, pelvis (private part area), legs, and feet. If you find a high level of stress, let that part go limp like a rag doll. Keep breathing.

- Practice *guided imagery*. This is picturing something in your head. You might imagine you are . . .

  ○ Watching the flames in a fireplace and hearing the wood crackle.

  ○ Throwing stones one at a time into a calm lake so you can see the ripples.

  ○ Watching a sunset or sunrise.

  ○ Throwing leaves in a running stream and watching them float away from you.

  ○ Paddling a canoe down a slow-moving stream. Pay attention to each stroke and look at the rocks in the water.

- Imagine your mind is a bathtub full of stress. Pull the plug. Listen to and watch the water drain out. The water level gets lower and lower as the stress goes down the drain. As the water circles the drain for the last time, watch it go round and round. Take a deep breath and wrap yourself in a big, soft, warm towel.

- Smell something you really like—flowers, food cooking, etc.

- Eat a little chocolate (it is calming, especially dark chocolate).

- Imagine your favorite game/TV cartoon character moving through your body and chasing out the stress.

- When you are having bad thoughts, change the voice to the voice of your favorite cartoon character. Listen to that voice and see how it makes you feel. Do you believe what it is saying? Talk back to the voice.

- Do some yoga or stretching.

Other: _____

_____

Here are a couple of other *guided imagery* exercises to let go of stress.

37.2 Balloon Liftoff

- Draw a picture of a bunch of colored balloons. Each one is a different color. On each balloon, write something you worry about.

- Now close your eyes (or leave them open). Imagine the balloons are filled with helium. Helium balloons are the kind you tug on and they want to lift up into the sky.

- Pretend to hold the balloons. You will let go of the balloons, one at a time. Pick the first balloon you will let go of.

- Pretend to let go of the first balloon. There goes some of your stress. Watch it go up into the sky higher and higher, until it is just a dot of color.

- When you can't see the balloon any more, take a deep breath. Let all your muscles relax, as if you are a floppy rag doll.

- Keep letting go of balloons, one at a time. Each one holds a different worry. As you let go of each balloon, you let go of stress.

- When all the balloons are gone, take a deep breath and sigh as you breathe out.

- Notice what it feels like to let go of stress.

37.3 Narrative: Still Waters

- Imagine you are a lake. You are calm and clear. The sun is shining.

- A storm comes up and the sky turns dark. The wind blows.

- There are waves on your surface, big choppy waves.

- Finally, the storm passes.

- Your water is dark, cloudy, and all stirred up.

- Let all the stuff settle down that got stirred up by the storm. See it moving down, down, down to the bottom of the lake.

- Once again, your water is clear and blue. The sun is shining. Enjoy this feeling.

- A child on the shore tosses in a pebble. As it hits your surface, it makes a good splash. You see circles moving out around the place where the pebble hit the water. How nice! If you like this, ask the child to keep throwing pebbles so you can watch the ripples.

37.4 Reclaiming Hope

As time passes and you get over trauma, your memories of abuse (after you talk about them) will become less painful and bother you less. You will come to accept them as part of your past. Once you are safe and in therapy for your abuse, you realize that the abuse was not your fault and you will know who to trust and not to trust.

- Draw a picture of your journey, past, present, and future. Draw three things in the past that you want to leave behind. Draw three things in the present that you want to hold onto and keep in your life. Draw three things in the future that you hope will happen.

- What three things do you most want to leave behind? _____

- What three things do you most want in your future? _____
  _____

- What needs to change or take place for these three things to happen? _____
  _____
  _____

CHAPTER 38

COPING SKILLS: CONNECT

From the day you are born, you need someone to take care of you and meet your needs. You need someone to be there when you are scared or sick. You are a lovable valuable person.

A book called *Parenting from the Inside Out* (Siegel & Hartzel, 2003) says that the way we are raised affects us later in life.

A baby needs . . .

- To be loved (every baby is lovable).
- To be talked to and smiled at.
- To be fed.
- To be held and carried.
- To be played with.
- Other: _____

If a baby is cared for this way, the baby will feel safe and secure. If a baby is yelled at, hit, or ignored, that baby will not learn to trust. When your caregiver looks you in the eye, smiles at you, talks to you, holds you, and cares for you, it brings you pleasure and lowers your fear.

Attachment is a big word for trusting someone who loves you—someone you can count on.

38.1 Your Own Attachment

- Name two adults who love you or care about you.

  _____

- How do they show their love and care?

  _____

  _____

- Do you think adults are mostly kind or mostly mean?

  _____

- How are *kind* and *mean* adults different in how they treat children?

  _____

  _____

  _____

38.2 Trust and Bonding

The first two years of life is when babies and young children learn about love and safety. Babies need to have a *secure bond* with their caregivers. A *secure bond* (attachment) is when you trust someone to be there for you and meet your needs.

38.2.1 Your Ability to Trust

- On a scale from one to ten, how much do you trust other people (one is low and ten is high)? _____

- Name someone you really like and trust. _____

- What does that person do or say to make you feel good about yourself? _____

  _____

  _____

  _____

  _____

Some abused kids avoid others and are loners. Others cling to adults and avoid being alone. Abused kids can also be too *friendly*—they don't know the difference between strangers and friends. They might wander too far away from their caregivers even when they are very little.

38.3 How You Connect with Others

- Do you prefer being with others or being alone? _____

- Describe what you like to do when you are alone.

  _____

  _____

- How much time do you spend alone?

  _____

- How much time do you spend with others?

  _____

- Who do you spend most your time with at school and at home?

  _____

  _____

- What is a stranger?

  _____

- How long and how well do you need to know someone before that person is not a stranger?

  _____

  _____

- How do you act with strangers and with people you know?

  _____
  _____
  _____
  _____

- How do you feel when you are alone?

  _____

Abused kids can get mixed up about hugging, touching, and kissing other people. Some abused kids don't like to be touched at all while others touch people without asking or let strangers hug and kiss them.

There are red light (Stop) and green light (Go) types of touch and activities. First of all, it is OK to touch yourself (green light) as long as you don't hurt yourself—hurting yourself is red light touch. Touching your own private parts is not OK to do in public but is OK if you do it in a bathroom or in bed when you are alone. Touching someone else's private parts is red light. Letting someone else touch your private parts is red light as well.

How do you know if other kinds of touching are red light or green light? Green light touch makes you feel good. Green light touch is something you can do out in public in front of other people and no one would stop it—like a hug.

Red light touch makes you or someone else feel bad. Picking your nose and eating it in public is red light, because it grosses other people out. Sometimes a person touches you or asks you to touch them but wants you to keep it a secret. That is a red light touch and not OK. Red light touch might also make you feel bad after because you are pretty sure it is wrong.

Activities can also be red light or green light. If a grownup gets naked or has sex in front of you, that is red light. Sex is supposed to be private. And looking at porn is a red light activity; kids should not see sex in adult movies or on TV. Some grownups show kids porn to get them to do red light touch later. Some grownups take pictures of kids without their clothes on. That is also red light activity.

38.4 Touching and Privacy

Here are some very basic rules about touching and privacy. Circle the ones that you agree with.

- It is not a good idea to touch strangers or people you don't know very well.

- Be sure that you ask others before you touch or hug them.

- Don't sit in someone's lap unless it is a person you know very well.

- Don't let anyone in the bathroom with you while you are using the toilet.

- If you are very young, it is OK for a caregiver to help you wipe your bottom.

- Don't let anyone in the bathroom with you (except your caregiver) when you are in the bathtub or shower.

- It is OK if your caregiver helps you wash your hair in the tub or shower when you are really little.

- Even a young child can wash his or her own private parts using a washcloth.

- For dressing, sleeping, undressing, and bathing, as a rule, keep girls with girls and boys with boys.

- Don't sleep in a bed with anyone a lot older or younger than you unless you have a bad dream and can climb in bed with your parent.

- Don't let anyone touch or hug you without asking.

- Strangers or people you don't know very well should not ask to hold you or kiss you.

- No one should touch your private areas, the parts that a bathing suit covers.

- Unless the doctor needs to check you or your mom needs to put medicine on you or wipe your bottom, your private parts are off limits to anyone but you.

- It is OK for you to touch your own private parts in a private place (like your bedroom or the bathtub).

- Persons of all ages have a right to say who touches their bodies. Keep a privacy bubble around your body and don't let anyone pop it.

- If anyone touches you in a way that makes you feel bad, you have a right to say, in a loud voice, "Please stop touching me. I don't like that." If they won't stop, please tell a caregiver or other adult. You need to speak up if this happens.

- Other: _____

38.5 How You Touch Others

- Do you touch or hug others without asking? _____

- Do you let others touch and hold you? _____

- Who can hug or hold you?
  _____
  _____

- Did any adult ever touch you in a way that made you feel bad?
  _____
  _____

- What did you do or say when this happened?
  _____
  _____

- Where and when do you like to have privacy? Does anyone invade your privacy?
  _____
  _____

- What can you do and say about this?
  _____

- Who can you tell?
  _____

After the abuse is over, a grownup might say, "The abuse is over, you are safe now." Well, maybe you are and maybe you aren't. Only time will tell. One kid thinks, "I am safe. My mom stopped the abuse the first time I told her. I know it's not going to happen again." The next kid thinks, "My mom told me *that* the *last* time and she went back to the abuser. I am not safe yet." And even another child thinks, "Yeah, right. My parents hurt me and I got abused in two foster homes. I will *never* be safe."

If you are not sure whether you are safe and who you can trust, you might ask your caregiver, parent, or therapist. Some people can be trusted and others can't—it is important to know the difference.

CHAPTER 39

COPING SKILLS: CONQUER

Thoughts and feelings are related. Negative thoughts can lead to negative feelings, and negative feelings give you negative thoughts. This part of the book is about changing your thoughts and feelings by checking out the facts. You may remember that when you have trauma symptoms, your feelings take over and you go into *freak out, freeze, flight* or *fight*. You can learn to do things to take charge of your feelings. One way is to control, change, and argue with your thoughts.

39.1 Negative Self-Talk

Negative thoughts are ones like . . .

- My life sucks—nothing good ever happens.

- My life is never going to get any better.

- I'm worthless.

- If I try, I will fail.

- Everyone hates me.

- Everyone picks on me.

- Nothing ever goes right.

- If I ignore my problems, they will go away.

- It's in the past—leave it there.

- Talking about it won't help.

- It's all my fault.

- I am never going to be happy.

- I can't win.

- I can't trust anyone.

- All adults are mean.

- No one cares about me.

- I'm never going to feel better.

- I wish I had never been born.

- I can't change.

- Nothing good ever happens to me.

- No one understands me.

- Other: _____

Go back and circle any of the statements that you think apply to you. Read them out loud. How does each statement make you feel? Statements like these usually make kids (and grownups) feel *bad*.

Do you think these statements are facts or beliefs? The answer is that these statements are not facts. They are beliefs or opinions. They are too *absolute*. Words like *always, never, no one*, and *nothing* are absolutes— they are not facts, because they are not always true.

A fact is 100% true. The statements above aren't facts because if you think hard, you can find an exception to the statement. An exception is a time when the statement was not true. For the list of statements above, you can find a fact to prove that the statement is wrong.

Let me tell you what I mean.

If you say, "No one likes me", ask yourself, "Was there ever someone who liked me?" You might answer, "Yes, my Math teacher likes me and the lady next door seems to like me. Even my therapist seems to like me." So it is not true to say, "No one likes me."

You have to really careful about negative beliefs, thoughts and feelings. If you act as though they are true, you will have an unhappy life.

39.2 Changing Self-Talk

You are able to change negative thoughts. Most people have a critical voice inside their head that says bad things about them like, "You're stupid" or "No one likes you." Close your eyes and say one of these two things over and over. It will probably make you feel bad. Now change that little voice in your head. Make it your favorite cartoon character, like Bugs Bunny or one of the Chipmunks or even a Sponge Bob character. Say the same thought over and over in the new cartoon voice. It should feel better. It might even make you smile to hear it. Why is it different when it is the same words? It is different because it is now a silly voice and you don't have to take it seriously. You don't believe the voice any more and you don't have to listen to it.

Another thing you can do is talk back to your *absolute* beliefs and opinions. Imagine two sides of you having a debate or argument. You might call one the Grouch and the other the Helper. The Grouch is the negative side of you that states negative (but untrue) beliefs, opinions, or judgments. The Helper uses facts to prove the Grouch wrong. It is like a debate. When arguing with the Grouch, The Helper voice stays very quiet and calm.

Here are some examples . . .

1   The Grouch voice says, "No one loves you."

The Helper might say, "That's not true. The fact is my Grandma loves me."

2   The Grouch says, "Adults are all mean—you can't trust anyone."

The Helper can say, "Some adults are nice. The fact is my fifth-grade teacher and my coach are nice, and I trust them."

3   The Grouch says, "It was a horrible day."

Then the Helper can say, "The fact is five things went right today and only three things went wrong. It was a so-so day, not a horrible day."

The Helper voice can also argue with the Grouch about being abused. Here are some examples . . .

1   The Grouch says, "The abuser can't help it" or "It's your fault".

The Helper replies, "He can help it—he's a grownup and there is no excuse for abusing a child" and "It's not my fault I got abused."

2   The Grouch says, "You could have stopped it" or "You should have told."

The Helper can say, "I was just a child and it was his job to stop it" or "I was afraid he would hurt me if I told."

3   The Grouch says, "You need to forgive him and see him again."

Then the Helper might say, "I'm not ready to see him again. I can forgive him but I don't have to forget."

Of course, the Grouch voice is not real. The Grouch is your own negative thoughts. And of course, the Helper is not real. The Helper is really your own strong voice (inside your head). It is your voice sticking up for yourself and using the facts. You become your own Helper.

39.3 Practice Changing Self-Talk

- Pick one of the negative statements you circled. It is not a fact. Which one did you pick? ___
  _____

- List one or more facts that prove the statement wrong or false. _____
  _____

- Now write a new statement that is true. _____
  _____

Draw your face in the middle circle of the figure on p. 218. Pick a second negative statement that you circled on the list. Put the negative statement in the Grouch bubble. Come up with facts to prove the Grouch wrong.

- Facts that prove the Grouch wrong: _____
  _____
  _____
  _____

- Put a fact-based, more positive statement in the Helper bubble.

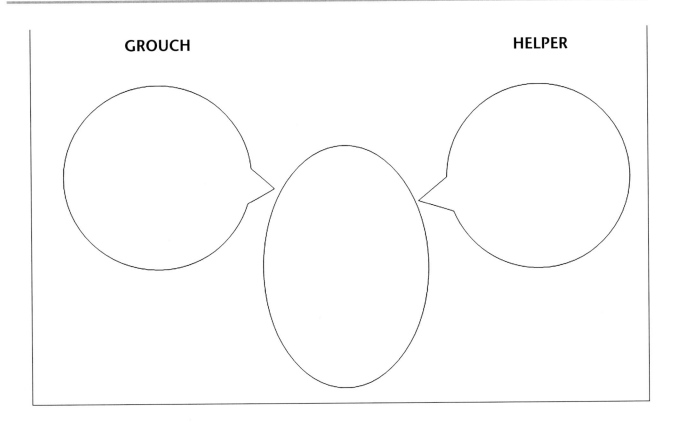

GROUCH   HELPER

39.4 Gratitude

Another thing you can do to conquer negative thoughts and feelings is to *pay attention to* good things that happen each day. Most of us have good and bad days. Or we have good and bad things happen during the day. We just seem to pay more attention to the bad things. Sometimes we even forget about the good things, as if they don't matter.

Dr. Martin Seligman is a scientist who studies *positive psychology* and gratitude. He has found that when people pay attention to the good things in their lives, they start to feel better. Gratitude is saying what you are thankful for. He suggests using a gratitude journal before going to bed. You might try doing this. Right before you go to bed, write down some good things that happened that day and why you are grateful. Your caregiver can help you with this.

39.5 Being Around Your Abuser

As you read this part of the book, remember that the author understands some abusers are men and some are women. When I say "he," it can mean any abuser. At some point after your abuse, someone might tell you that you need to be around your abuser or talk to him. No one should pressure you to spend time with an abuser that has hurt you or someone else in your family. You can say, "I don't feel safe around him" or "I don't want to talk to him." It is not good to make kids do things that feel unsafe. Even when you love and miss your abuser, you need to be safe. You should not be around your abuser unless it is supervised and *you want to* see the abuser or until that person has changed.

Kids and their caregivers ask me, "How can you tell when someone has really changed?"

Here are some clues about how to tell when an abuser has really changed. As you read, circle the things that you think are most important. Which of the things has your abuser done?

- The abuser gets counseling, stops drinking or using drugs, or goes to classes for anger.

- The person should apologize to you and say he was wrong.

- He should ask how you feel and how you think the abuse hurt you.

- He should ask you what he can do to help you trust him again.

- He should ask you before he touches you or asks you to touch him (even a hug).

- He should not make excuses for what happened.

- He should not say the abuse was due to stress or having a hard time.

- He should not blame you or anyone else for what happened.

- He should not blame drugs or alcohol for what happened. Lots of adults use drugs or alcohol and most don't hurt others. That is an excuse.

- He should tell you that it was not your fault.

- He doesn't get mad when you disagree with him about something.

- He doesn't act like everything is your fault.

- Other: _____

Your abuser might say, "I'm sorry. I promise I'll never do it again," and want to come back home, but nothing has really changed. Promises are too *easy*. *Changing behavior* is hard for most abusers and it takes time.

Circle the things below that you would like to try and talk them over with your therapist, because you can't be sure how your abuser will respond. Make sure you are safe and someone will protect you before you do or say these things.

- Tell the abuser how the abuse made you feel. Or write a letter. If the abuser blames you or gets mad at you, it is a sign that he has not changed yet.

- Say, "I'm not sure I believe your words. Show me in your actions."

- You can say, "Tell me some things you are sorry for doing."

- You can say, "What you did to me was wrong. Why did you think it was OK?"

- Ask the person, "Why should I trust you?" and see what he or she says.

- Tell the person, "I love you but I don't trust you. I don't want you to make promises you can't keep."

- Say, "Please don't touch me without asking. I don't trust you yet."

- Say, "I don't want to give you a hug or a kiss. I don't feel safe yet."

- Say, "I don't want to be alone with you or sleep over. I'm not ready."

- Ask, "What are you going to do to change? How will you be different?"

39.6 Questions About Your Abuser

- What would you like your abuser to do to show you he is sorry? _____
  _____

- What can your abuser do to take responsibility for what he did?_____
  _____

- Has your abuser made promises to you or to your caregiver? Do you believe them or not?
  _____ Why?_____

- How does your abuser's behavior match or not match his or her words and promises?
  _____
  _____

PART VI

CAREGIVER'S GUIDE TO TRAUMA

CHAPTER 40

THE IMPACT OF TRAUMA ON DEVELOPMENT

Children and their caregivers need developmentally appropriate, scientifically informed answers to their questions about trauma. The abused children I have worked with ask questions like:

- Why do I feel sort of *crazy* after being abused?
- If the abuse is over, why do I still feel scared?
- Why do adults sometimes think I am being "bad" when I am trying to cope?

Many child treatment resources are simplistic and do not adequately address children's questions and caregivers' concerns. This Caregiver's Guide to Trauma will help caregivers become better informed about the impact of abuse and neglect on child functioning. Teachers, parents, foster parents, and others all help children grow and develop, so the word *caregivers* in this book section refers to all those who contribute to the wellbeing of abused or neglected children. Once a caregiver understands the impact of trauma on a child, he or she will be better able to help that child recover. If you are reading this book, then you are a concerned caregiver that is important in the life of an abused child.

According to Dr. Bruce Perry's training materials, a child's brain remains *in a state of fear* following abuse (2004a, 2004b). So what does that mean? Humans and other primates respond with increased stress to perceived danger or threats to survival. High levels of stress lead to changes in the child's brain—this is a form of brain injury (Cozolino, 2006; Bremner, 2002, 2012; McCollum, 2006; Perry, 2006, 2009; Perry & Hambrick, 2008; Perry & Pollard, 1998; Siegel, 1999). The degree and type of injury depends on the age of the child at the time of the trauma, the child's temperament and coping resources, the duration of the traumatic events, and the caregiver's response following the trauma.

There are many things that trigger stress and fear in children. Non-abused children might be triggered by (and afraid of) things like sleeping in the dark, singing a solo in the chorus, having a bad dream, seeing a spider crawling near them, or being on the school bus during a bad storm. This is considered low-level stress. This type of stress might be compared to a leaky faucet that is easily turned off, and it causes no lasting harm; in fact, it actually leads to improved coping and resilience (McCollum, 2006).

It is very stressful for a child to witness violence or be the victim of abuse or severe neglect, however. *Freak out, freeze, flight* and *fight* (the four "F" words) are words I use to describe how children attempt to cope with stress at a brain level. This is the kind of stress that remains after abuse and severe neglect and it is hard to turn off. It is more like a broken fire hydrant than a leaky faucet; the water gushes out over the pavement and pretty soon it floods the road.

A traumatized child and his or her brain can heal from abuse through relationships with consistent, positive caregivers and therapeutic interventions that match the developmental capacity of the child. Helping a child recover from trauma involves *scaffolding*, where the caregiver response is *one step ahead* of the child. Notice I said *one step ahead*, not five or six steps (which would be stressful and frustrate the child) and not *two steps behind the child* (which would be non-stimulating or neglectful). Through nurturing relationships with caring adults, abused children learn to trust, self-soothe, and learn new emotional and cognitive coping skills. A caregiver can make a tremendous difference in the life of an abused child.

40.1 Impact of Abuse and Neglect

Brain development in the first year of life is dependent on the quality of parent–child interactions. High stress during a mother's pregnancy, abuse and neglect following birth, and witnessing violence can damage a developing child's brain. The earlier the trauma, the more likely it is that a child's brain development will be impacted.

Children abused or severely neglected during infancy and preschool years are at high risk of *neurobiological* deficits; and caregivers might notice developmentally delayed thinking or processing, speech, social skills, and expression or control of emotions. Trauma can lead to any or all of the following in children at different ages:

- Language delay
- Verbal processing
- Obsessive compulsive behavior
- Symptoms of Pervasive Developmental Disorder (PDD)
- Poor attention and concentration
- Impulse control and hyperactivity
- Memory deficits
- Rage or anger outbursts

40.2 Attunement and Attachment

Interpersonal neurobiology is a term for how abuse interferes with the development of attunement and secure attachment. From birth on, there is *brain to brain* interaction between infant and caregiver that sets the stage for later cognitive and interpersonal development. Babies gaze into the caregiver's eyes and *know/sense* when they are loved and safe. They also sense when they are not. It is no accident that breastfeeding allows optimal eye contact and facial proximity for mothers and infants. Neurobiological co-regulation starts to occur early in the first year of life when parents are attentive and responsive to their infants (Badenach 2008, 2011; Cozolino, 2006, 2010; Siegel, 1999). Mirror neurons in the infant brain are activated by parent–child interaction and this sets the stage for later reciprocal interpersonal communication and development of empathy. A child eventually learns to self-regulate through the parent's consistent caregiving, lack of which can result in sleep, mood, and behavioral difficulties.

Drug and alcohol abuse and parental depression are adult problems that interfere with attunement. It is hard for an infant or young child to read a parent's moods (through the face and eyes) when that caregiver is under the influence of a mood- or mind-altering substance. Research by Muir and Lee (2003) has shown that seeing a parent's *still face* distresses an infant, so consider what an infant will see in the eyes and face of a mother who is frequently drunk or high. Perhaps the infant will see glazed eyes and hear slurred speech; certainly that infant will not receive the expected interpersonal stimulation. Also, the *impaired* mother will not be able to consistently recognize or respond to the infant's distress. Impaired mothers keep odd hours, sleep at times their children are awake, do not understand a child's need for regularity, and tend to leave their children alone too much.

It is well known that maternal depression negatively impacts parent–child relationships and child development (Knitzer, Theberge, & Johnson, 2008). Depressed mothers miss signals for caregiving and are less responsive to their children's needs. The depressed mother has difficulty regulating her own mood, and children of depressed mothers may withdraw due to lack of social stimulation. It is hard for an infant to *read* the facial expressions of a depressed parent, and infant–mother co-regulation can be impaired as a result.

Attachment at birth is about survival, but in the second six months of life and thereafter, it includes a strong emotional component (Blaustein & Kinniburgh, 2010; Bowlby, 1958; Cozolino, 2006; Grossmann, Grossmann, & Waters, 2005; Kinniburgh, Blaustein, Spinnazzola, & van der Kolk, 2005; Kozlowska & Hanney, 2002; Lieberman & Van Horn, 2008; Sfroufe, Carlson, Levy, & Egeland, 1999; Solomon & George, 1999; Solomon & Siegel, 2003).

The Attachment Behavioral System (ABS), a biological system to ensure a child's survival, is triggered by situations that threaten safety or security and activate distress. The most congruent attachments develop with caregivers who are reliable sources of comfort. When caregivers are insensitive, unreliable, rejecting, inconsistent, disregarding, or ambivalent about providing care, the child can't trust that his or her needs will be met. It is hard to be securely attached when the person caring for you is hurting you or not meeting some of your needs. When a child's attachment is disrupted, it is hard for that child to have close, trusting relationships later in life. Avoidant, anxious, ambivalent, or disorganized behavior is the child's attempts to adapt and cope.

Intimate partner violence (IPV) symbolically or realistically threatens the survival of the child by endangering the life of the primary attachment figure. It is highly stressful for a child to live in an environment where there is frequent physical or verbal fighting. Regardless of whether the child is ever physically assaulted, witnessing IPV (hearing, seeing, or being told about what happened) arouses the ABS and leads to high interpersonal stress. A longitudinal study of adverse childhood experiences (ACE) has shown that the experience of abuse, neglect, or witnessing IPV in childhood, places one at risk of later physical and mental health problems and increases the likelihood of becoming a victim or perpetrator of IPV (see the website of the Centers for Disease Control, www.cdc.gov/ace).

It is recommended that caregivers read the book *Parenting from the Inside Out* by Siegel and Hartzell (2003) to better understand how their own upbringing impacts parent–child interaction. Some caregivers have difficulty talking at all about childhood, reporting few or only vague memories. Others report *perfect* childhoods in glowing terms and have difficulty sharing a range of feelings about childhood experiences. Still others are bitter about childhood, indicating in their stories that there are many unresolved issues that remain emotionally salient. Caregivers need to be able to discuss their own good and less-good childhood experiences in realistic ways with appropriate affect. This self-understanding will better equip them to nurture the abused children in their care.

An abused or neglected infant or young child develops behavioral strategies to cope with parental inconsistency, abandonment, fear or pain. See Appendix C for ways that abuse and neglect impact children at each stage of development. An abused or neglected infant may cry more than usual and have sleep problems; he or she can't self-soothe or regulate affect. Alternatively, an infant may reduce contact, tune out, or turn away. An abused or neglected toddler will have trouble relating to and communicating with others. Such toddlers might show demonstrate eye contact and seem less connected to others. An abused or neglected child's vocabulary may be limited, and that child might not speak in sentences until age three or four because the trauma may have affected the language areas of his or her brain. In a day care or preschool setting, an abused or neglected child might hit, bite, or avoid playing with other children. An abused (or neglected) child might *regress* (need more help to do things), and toilet training may be delayed. Some abused children seem hyperactive due to hyper-arousal or agitation that often follows abuse.

You as the caregiver might notice or be concerned about any of the following with an abused or neglected infant or young child:

40.2.1 Behavior in Infants

- My baby cries too much.
- My baby is fussy and/or irritable.
- My baby never cries (is a "very good baby").

- My baby does not make eye contact.
- My baby is not responsive.
- My baby doesn't babble.
- My baby has delayed motor development (crawling, fine motor, walking).
- My baby can't stand to be alone.
- My baby rolled off the bed and got hurt.
- My baby is not gaining weight as she should.
- My baby won't sleep.
- My baby is not afraid of strangers (and should be).
- My baby won't eat.
- My baby doesn't want to be held.
- My baby wants to be held all the time.
- My baby is spoiled.

40.2.2 Behavior in Toddlers

- My toddler hits or bites others.
- My toddler has a bad temper.
- My toddler is really hyper.
- My toddler seems off in her own world.
- My toddler is stubborn.
- My toddler won't talk.
- My toddler won't look at me.
- My toddler is accident-prone.
- My toddler won't play with others.
- My toddler won't sleep alone.
- My toddler doesn't talk.
- My toddler is a late bloomer.
- My toddler ignores what I say.
- My toddler is a spoiled brat.
- My toddler "doesn't know a stranger."
- My toddler doesn't know how to play.
- My toddler gets in trouble at day care.
- My toddler has sleep problems (bad dreams, wakes at night, can't get to sleep).

40.2.3 Behavior in Preschool Children

- My child is very grown-up for her age (gets own breakfast, tucks herself in at night, helps feed the baby).
- My child won't listen.
- My child won't sleep alone.
- My child has poor eye contact.
- My child is bad or misbehaves.

- My child defies me.
- My child is clumsy.
- My child still wets his pants.
- My child is scared of everything.
- My child poops his pants.
- My child isn't talking yet.
- My child talks back/curses/calls names.
- My child takes things.
- My child is really hyper.
- My child wakes up during the night.
- My child doesn't pay attention.
- My child can't play with others.
- My child expects me to entertain him.
- My child is "mean" (hits others, has a bad temper).
- My child pees (in trash cans, in closets, on furniture, on the carpet).
- My child sets fires.
- My child has hurt animals.

All of the above behaviors can arise following exposure to a traumatic event, although before coming to that conclusion, a caregiver would want to seek a thorough assessment. The assessment and treatment of infants, toddlers, and young children needs to be trauma-informed, so as to not mistake the behavior for something else.

40.3 Developmental Skills and Interventions

Beginning at birth, trauma can interrupt normal development and lead to delays in functioning due to neurobiological deficits. By observing a child's strengths and limitations, an adult can understand the extent of and remediate the deficits. Developmental skills are like building blocks that reflect the child's brain development. Hands-on, developmentally appropriate interventions allow the child's brain to *catch up* and develop in areas that were hurt by the trauma. Much of this catch-up work takes place in the home, day-care, and school setting, where skills already mastered can be reinforced so that higher order skills can emerge.

40.4 Trauma and Stages of Development

The sensorimotor stage of infant development is the period within which babies interact with the world using their hands (touching and grasping), legs and feet (kicking and bending), ears (listening to sounds and voices), eyes (looking at faces), and mouths (sucking, chewing, and tasting). Babies use eye contact, smiling, cooing, and touching with caregivers. They pass objects to their caregivers and get attention by throwing things on the floor. They learn that others are watching them and interested in what they are doing. Toward the end of the first year, babies use repetition, such as banging things together, stacking, and sorting.

Abuse or neglect during infancy can result in poor sensorimotor integration and language delays. Children abused as infants often continue to put things in their mouths and chew on things. They may become *hyperactive, agitated*, and physically aggressive when anxious, because they don't know how to use words to express their feelings. The play of abused children is often repetitious and mechanical, with delayed emergence of make-believe play behaviors.

A child who displays delays in play behavior and language will respond well to non-verbal sensorimotor play and expressive activities. The therapist and caregiver should remain highly verbal (talk to the child) during these activities and encourage the child's emotional expression and verbalization. Sensorimotor activities require little to no language on the child's part and will help the child calm down, self-soothe, and self-regulate. These activities will also stimulate higher-level brain development. Sensorimotor and visual-motor activities include such things as:

- Rhythmic play using the body and rhythm or percussion instruments (drums, maracas, xylophone, clapping, marching, bells, etc.).
- Simple songs with motions ("Where is Thumbkin?," "The Wheels on the Bus," "Ring Around the Rosy," "London Bridge Is Falling Down").
- Musical DVDs for babies and children.
- Relaxation techniques and simple guided imagery.
- Listening to or making music.
- Yoga or therapeutic massage.
- Dancing or moving to music.
- Nursery rhymes.
- Rocking and swinging.
- Repetitive movement such as crawling or bicycle legs for bilateral brain stimulation.
- Copycat games (to stimulate mirror neurons) such as making faces with emotions and *Simon Says*.
- Any games and music that use good eye contact, active engagement, and face-to-face emotional connecting.

Older babies and toddlers play social games like *Peek-A-Boo, Hide and Find Me*, or *Chase Me, Catch Me, and Tickle Me* with caregivers. Toddlers enjoy activities that use motor skills, like bouncing and throwing balls, putting together large Lego blocks, building towers, jumping, and climbing. Mastery play is seen when children string beads, work on puzzles, and engage in simple art. Singing and rhyming integrates a toddler's brain and helps with language development.

Children abused when they were toddlers might bite, have tantrums, or throw things when they are stressed. They may have trouble using words to communicate their needs and can get easily frustrated. They don't interact well or play with other children, reverting to parallel play. They might bang blocks together without using them to build. If a child or toddler can't make eye contact, has trouble reading social cues, or has poor empathy, the caregiver can engage the child in face-to-face activities that do not place demands on the child for peer interaction until the child is ready.

Preschool children typically engage in make-believe, fantasy, and pretend-play with a narrative component. They use language in their play to communicate about what they are doing. They start to play dress up and imitate adults. They might use a dollhouse to act out a family scene, use blocks to build things and trucks to carry stuff. They play back and forth with other children. Preschool children use play themes of safety and protection, often creating bad guys and good guys. They need reassurance, attention, and praise from adults. Children abused during their preschool years often have very mechanical, rote, repetitive play. They don't use much make-believe and their play might lack emotional expression and mastery.

A child abused after learning to talk is likely to play out themes of abuse (danger and safety) and respond emotionally when using a dollhouse, puppets, or action figures. Expressive play with puppets, dolls, games, and make-believe can help these children express feelings, solve problems, and talk about their abuse. Children having trouble using make-believe play will need help from caregivers in initiating such play. They can learn to use make-believe play through puppets, action figures, dollhouses or sand trays, as well as story-telling. When abused children start to use make-believe play, they often display themes of power–control, victimization, monsters, good–evil, and safety. They may bury "bad guys," fight alligators, or seek help from super-heroes.

Many abused children first enter treatment during their elementary school years. Most school-age children like to play games with rules as well as advanced pretend play. They can tell stories, use cause–effect thinking, and talk about their feelings. At this age, abused kids might become frustrated or aggressive during play. Their power–control issues are easily triggered by competition, and they may become defensive or impulsively angry.

School-age abused children can have trouble managing their impulses and regulating their moods. They might seem immature, hyperactive, or fearful in stressful social situations. These types of children get bullied more than non-abused children and may get into trouble at school. School-age children with prior abuse or neglect can also have peer problems due to being too competitive (vigilance) or passive (flight). Abused or neglected children at this age might need help with language-based expression, both written and oral. It is good to talk with them about problem solving, choices and feelings.

Traumatized pre-adolescents or teens may seem overly withdrawn, angry, sexually- precocious, socially regressed (playing with younger children), or begin using drugs or alcohol to improve sleep and avoid or numb the pain. They become sleep-deprived when they stay up all night to avoid nightmares, since so much abuse typically occurs when children are sleeping. Marijuana and alcohol are often drugs of choice since both are effective in *anesthetizing or* reducing emotional pain, and nightmares. Each child will react differently as puberty approaches. Some young teens realize for the first time the truly sexual nature of what happened to them in the past. Others will show interest in pornography or behave in a sexually explicit manner due to earlier exposure to sexuality. Around puberty, many abused children experience shame, alienation, and depersonalization. If adults do not talk with them about their feelings, they assume that those adults judge them or blame them for what happened. They often blame themselves for what happened to them and in their families. Some adolescents neglect hygiene and stop bathing, as if to avoid touching their bodies or to keep others away from them. Caregivers need to communicate that abuse happened only because adults crossed relational boundaries, and understand that sexually reactive behavior can develop in response to childhood abuse.

With treatment and caregiver involvement, many abused children *catch up* developmentally and eventually meet developmental milestones. As a child's brain heals and develops, he or she becomes more capable of advanced play and communication. Children abused very young may take longer to master tasks that require abstract verbal reasoning, self–other comparison, social reciprocity, emotional control, and complex visual-motor integration; some will require occupational or speech therapy. In any case, by understanding a child's strengths and limitations a caregiver can set realistic expectations, provide appropriate support, and guide the child as he or she moves toward the next set of developmental tasks.

CHAPTER 41

NEUROBIOLOGY AND TRAUMA

In discussing trauma and neurobiology, I draw heavily from researchers such as Bremner, Briere, Cozolino, Perry, and Siegel. Dr. Bruce Perry's Child Trauma Academy in Houston, Texas, is dedicated to research and education on child maltreatment, and its training materials on state-dependent learning (2004a, 2004b) are recommended for clinicians and caregivers. He has been consulted on many high-profile incidents involving traumatized children, including the school shootings in Columbine, Colorado, the Oklahoma City bombing, and the Branch Davidian siege in Waco, Texas. Perry and Szalavitz's book, *The Boy Who Was Raised As a Dog* (2006), is a fairly easy read about how abuse affects the brain.

Perry's training materials (2004a, 2004b) and scientific writings (2006, 2009), including those with Hambrick and Pollard, illustrate how a child's brain moves from higher order functioning (language and reasoning) to lower order (protection and survival) during times of increased stress or when triggered by a trauma reminder. This order is the opposite of the order in which the brain develops (lower to higher). The stress response, often referred to as the *fight or flight response*, is a protective response that frees up survival resources (Cozolino, 2006; Perry, 1998, 2004a, 2004b, 2009; Perry & Hambrick, 2008; Perry & Pollard, 1998; Perry & Szalavitz, 2006). Perry points out that as a child's brain moves to a lower level of functioning to cope and self-protect, he or she is less able to think and reason and the child's behavior becomes less goal-directed. While coping under stress, the child's brain moves from cortex-level brain activity to brainstem-level brain activity. It is important for the caregiver to match his or her response to the child's functioning state when responding to a child under stress. I will discuss later how a sensitive caregiver can observe changes in a child's state or functioning and respond accordingly.

41.1 The Order of Brain Area Development

As mentioned above, and as detailed in Perry's training materials (2004a, 2004b), the brain develops from primitive, lower order to more complex, higher order functioning, and during increased stress, functioning moves in the opposite direction:

1   Brainstem survival (blood pressure, heart rate, body temperature). Abuse or severe neglect soon after birth can result in failure to thrive.
2   Diencephalon/cerebellum (sleep, appetite, arousal, sensation). This brain area develops early in the first year of life, and consistent caregiver interaction helps the child learn to regulate waking and sleeping. When abuse or neglect impairs a child's brain development at this stage, the child may have resultant sensory-integration problems, sleep difficulties, and feeding problems.
3   Limbic (emotional reactivity, attachment, sexual, affiliation). When these brain areas are impacted by early abuse or neglect, the child has difficulty regulating mood and developing stable

attachments. The child may be irritable, difficult to soothe, and highly reactive to change or stress. As a result, the child does not learn to self-soothe and becomes emotionally dysregulated.

4   Neo-cortex and cortex (concrete to abstract thinking, language and verbal memory). Language, which emerges during the second year of life, parallels cortex development, which is delayed following abuse or neglect. The capacity for verbal memory parallels language and cortex development. Thus, abuse or neglect in the first two years of life can lead to slower cortex development and resultant delays in language and conceptual thinking.

41.2 The Difference Between Purposeful and "On Purpose" Behavior

I discussed earlier the need for traumatized children to be given control over as many choices as possible. I have heard some caregivers say, "He wants his own way," as if having control is a bad thing. Everyone likes autonomy and having his or her own way. Children, especially abused children, need to feel in control of their lives and decisions. Remember, when the abuse happened, the child was out of control and had no way to stop what was happening. It makes sense that an abused child needs more control after the abuse is over and to be given reasonable choices.

Children also need structure, discipline, and nurture from caring adults. In using discipline, it is important to know that abused children may interpret *normal discipline* as a threat or risk of abuse. Their brains have become programmed to misinterpret typical parenting behaviors as cues of danger and then over-react with fear.

The behavior of abused children is *purposeful* but not always *on purpose*. Their behavior is an attempt to cope with stress and to protect their bodies and feelings from harm. The goal or purpose of their behavior is to remain safe. Some of their emotions and behaviors are automatic neurobiological responses, triggered by things in their world that *remind them* of past abuse.

We can't expect children to use skills (at home, school, or in therapy) they have not yet mastered; thus we should screen carefully and take developmental strengths and delays into account in setting expectations and when planning interventions (Perry, 2009). To set appropriate expectations for children, we first need to understand the ways in which abuse and neglect interfere with brain development at different ages (see Appendix D).

As noted above, a child's brain remains in a state of fear following trauma (Perry, 2004a, 2004b; Perry and Hambrick, 2008). When something or someone triggers memories of past abuse, that child will experience increased stress and seek to stay safe. Triggers may be non-conscious or conscious and will not always be obvious to the caregiver. As a child's fear increases, the brain goes from higher functioning (thinking and using language) to lower functioning (using senses, feelings, and survival instincts). I refer to this stress response as a *trauma response* or *trauma sequence*.

For example, a toddler abused prior to learning to talk might well experience language and communication delays. The same child now in preschool might use sensorimotor behavior as a coping resource under stress—hitting, banging, throwing, and pounding while screaming loudly. He or she might engage in parallel play and have difficulty paying attention to stories. Treatment for such a child would need to use his sensorimotor strengths and simple concrete verbal communication.

It is possible for a professional to assess and map a child's neurobiological strengths and limitations once trained in Dr. Perry's Neurosequential Model of Therapeutics, but that training is extensive and beyond the scope of this handbook. It is enough to say that one should pay close attention to a child's *typical and most commonly used* coping skills, play behaviors, and means of communication and emotional expression. The tasks of therapy will be more manageable when they utilize a child's developmental competencies.

During my years working with parent–child dyads in a family reunification program, it became clear that certain types of caregiver behaviors reliably increased fear in traumatized children, and that these children could move quickly into survival mode when they perceived risk or stress. It also became clear that certain caregiver interventions could prevent emotional and behavioral "meltdowns." An attentive, attuned caregiver can respond to signs of stress in ways that help the child calm down, decrease fear, and allow the child to think more clearly and make better choices. I refer clinicians and caregivers to the earlier mentioned Perry's training materials on state-dependent functioning, as they succinctly describe the ways in which adults can help abused children lower stress and develop new coping skills that help the brain grow and function better (2004a, 2004b). See Appendix B for this author's example of parent–child interaction and state-dependent functioning in a traumatized child.

41.3 Helping a Child Remain Calm or Return to a Calm State

You probably know that it does not take very long for an abused child to go from a calm state to a state of fear or anger when a child perceives a threat. It does not mean there *is* a threat; it means the child *feels* threatened, *because of* the past, however.

When an abused child perceives a threat, he or she can go through up to four stages (the four "F" words) very quickly: *freak out* (Alert or Arousal), *freeze* (Alarm or High Emotion), *flight* (Fear), and *fight* (Terror). An attuned caregiver notices clues (in the child's behavior) about what the child is experiencing and use those clues to help the child calm down. If an adult misses the clues and does things to increase the child's fear, the child will be unable to calm down or think.

41.4 The Stages of the Trauma–Stress Continuum

41.4.1 Vigilance

Abused kids never feel as calm as non-abused kids; because after abuse, a child (and his or her brain) remains *vigilant*. *Vigilance* is a state of watchfulness, and a *vigilant* child is easily startled by anything that reminds him or her of the abuse. The child may not be aware of his or her startle response—or at least not consciously—but once the child's fear is activated, he or she will start to become *dysregulated* and freak out.

Vigilance Summary
- What Can Trigger Child's Fear
  - Anything that reminds child of past abuse or the abusive person/situation (sights, sounds, smells, persons, tone of voice, locations, reactions of others)
- Child's Response
  - Alert (carefully watches caregiver and others)
  - Less calm than non-abused child
  - "Ready" to react due to past abuse and *on lookout for danger*
  - Easily startled
- How a Caregiver can Help
  - Less focus on punishment
  - Keep stress low in the environment
  - Praise good coping (catch child 'being good')
  - Give choices and teach/use problem-solving skills
  - Build in regular relaxing activities: yoga, Tai Chi, swimming, walking, music, art
  - Pick your battles and say "yes" often
- Caregiver Behaviors to Avoid
  - Poking, grabbling, horseplay, tickling

- ○ Hanging out with past abuser
- ○ Making excuses for past abuser and expecting child to agree
- ○ Blaming child for abuse
- ○ Becoming drunk or high
- ○ Showing porn to child
- ○ Having sex in front of child
- ○ Leaving child to fend for self
- ○ Expecting child to take care of siblings

41.4.2 Freak Out

Freak out takes place in the part of the brain that is sensitive to perceived danger. When danger is sensed, fear is triggered. There are many things that trigger fear in a vigilant abused child: A frustrated facial expression or angry voice can remind the child of danger, for example. A freaking out *child* responds well to eye contact, a quiet voice, simple directions, and *time in* or positive time with the child focused on the child's needs and interests. When a caregiver notices a child becoming agitated or aroused, he or she can do and say things to help the startled child calm down.

If an adult can't tell that the child is freaking out, he might do the *wrong thing,* like raise his voice, move too quickly toward the child, or give an ultimatum. At this point, the freaking out child is likely to *freeze.*

Freak Out Summary
- • Child's Response
  - ○ Child startled by something that triggers fear
  - ○ Child experiences increased heart rate and higher muscle tension
  - ○ Shows stress in one or more ways:
    - ▪ Seems nervous, anxious, or grouchy
    - ▪ Increase in somatic complaints
    - ▪ Clingy or fails to separate
    - ▪ Has bowel or bladder accidents
    - ▪ Whines, complains, or cries more
    - ▪ Acts hyper, silly
    - ▪ Less attentive
    - ▪ Starts to bully or pick on others
    - ▪ Refuses to obey
    - ▪ Curses or argues
    - ▪ Changes eating or sleeping habits
- • How a Caregiver can Help
  - ○ Reassure child (calm, quiet voice and empathy)
  - ○ Make eye contact
  - ○ Calmly re-direct child
  - ○ Distract child
  - ○ Use humor
  - ○ Keep face calm
  - ○ Give simple, clear directions
  - ○ Stay close (proximity)
  - ○ Use time in

- Engage in mindfulness activities, relaxation, or guided imagery. Music, sound machines, and fans can help.
- Examples:
  - Reflect: "You seem upset and stressed."
  - Apologize: "I'm sorry I startled you. I'm not mad."
  - Ask: "Do you need to take a break? Would you like a hug?"
  - Offer relaxing music or activity like a walk, rocking chair, or swinging.
  - Suggest something calm or fun to do elsewhere in the house.
  - Suggest child use coping skills (pretend to be a turtle, count, practice relaxation, use imagery).
- Caregiver Behaviors to Avoid
  - Moving too fast toward child
  - Complaining or lecturing
  - Making loud demands
  - Raising voice
  - Reciting a list of things child was supposed to do
  - Ultimatums
  - Showing frustration or anxiety (in face, voice, eyes)
  - Arguing with partner in front of child
  - Harsh punishment
  - Demeaning child
  - Sarcasm
  - Ignoring child's requests
  - Invading privacy (bathing or dressing)
  - Getting upset about adult matters in front of child
  - Sending child to room for anything more than a regular time-out

41.4.3 Freeze

A child in *freeze* may suddenly become quite emotional (start to cry), disorganized (does random things without a clear goal), or paralyzed (becomes very still). The caregiver who notices this response can distract the child or help the child move to a quieter place. During *freeze*, a child might respond to a slow, sure touch, invited contact ('do you want to sit in my lap?' or 'do you want a hug?'), and quiet, soothing words. These responses can shut off *fear* and help the child calm down. Some adult behaviors further upset a child in *freeze*: a raised or threatening voice, a raised hand, and a shaking finger in the child's face or a strong warning. If this happens, the child might run or hide. This is *flight,* the next stage of the trauma stress sequence.

Summary of Freeze
- Child's Response
  - State of *alarm (high arousal and increased stress)*
  - Becomes very emotional or *freezes*
  - Can't think clearly
  - Acts confused (might not remember what was said or done)
  - Looks *paralyzed,* disorganized, or inattentive
  - Seems distracted and unfocused
  - Does not do what you asked
  - Does not respond to your questions

- How a Caregiver Can Help
  - Use gentle touch
  - Slow down movement toward child
  - Sing or hum to or around child
  - Use quiet, soothing words
  - Maintain closeness
  - Provide comfort object (blanket, toy)
  - Change the setting
  - Tell the child he or she is safe
  - Reassure child that you are not mad
  - Calm face and voice
  - Examples:
    - Reflect and reassure: "You look scared", "Everything's OK", You're safe."
    - Ask: "What are you feeling? What can I do to help?"
    - Touch child gently on shoulder to re-orient to room, in case child has dissociated or tuned out.
    - Lower voice and speak quietly to child. Say, "I want you to be safe."
    - Offer a hug or cuddle. Remind child to keep breathing.
    - Distract by offering a favorite activity or snack.
- Caregiver Behaviors to Avoid
  - Raising hand or shaking finger at child
  - Moving toward child too quickly
  - Grabbing child
  - Raising voice or yelling
  - Making threats or ultimatums
  - Asking a lot of questions and demanding an answer
  - Allowing someone else to tease or bully child

41.4.4 Flight

A child in *flight experiences increased fear and wants to get away;* he or she might leave the room or run outside. The child can't think and does or says things without thinking. There was a little girl in the group home that *flashed back* to the past when staff raised their voices or came too close. Her first response after freezing was to head out the door and run across campus. What helps during this phase is the quiet presence of an attachment figure or attachment object (pet, blanket, stuffed animal, etc.). When the little girl bolted, a staff person was assigned to follow closely and *calmly talk her down.* When a child is in *flight,* it also helps to reduce noise and distractions and to back off a little or give the child some space. *It is a bad time* for a caregiver to talk, lecture, ask the child to *make a good decision* or give warnings (threats or ultimatums). When the child is in *flight,* the caregiver should not yell louder, show increased frustration, show fear, grab the child or make demands. If the adult responds in any of these ways, the child is likely to move into full blown *fight.*

Summary of Flight
- Child's Response
  - State of *fear and panic* (child feels urgent need to hide or escape)
  - Feels confused and can't think
  - Leaves the room
  - Leaves the house

- ○ Runs away
- ○ Hides
- ○ Tunes out, dissociates, or shuts down emotionally (especially with complex trauma or when escape is not possible)
- How a Caregiver Can Help
  - ○ Quietly remain with the child as a calm presence
  - ○ Tell the child you are confident in his or her ability to regain control
  - ○ Remind the child to breathe
  - ○ Pull back a bit
  - ○ Offer safe space and remove any feared person that is in the room
  - ○ Examples:
    - Give space but tell child you are going to stay close (for safety). Say, "I want you to be safe. I'll walk with you. No, I can't go away—I need to be sure you are OK."
    - Follow child (keep a little distance), until child appears to calm down.
    - Don't talk until child is calm. Don't process what happened until later.
- Caregiver Behaviors to Avoid
  - ○ Restraint
  - ○ Cursing or calling names
  - ○ Blocking child's flight
  - ○ Intervening physically
  - ○ Refusing to let child get away from perpetrator
  - ○ Acting afraid of or angry with child

41.4.5 Fight

A child in *fight* is in total *meltdown,* and his or her thinking brain is not working. He or she feels terror and will fight (verbally or physically) without reason. The child's goal at this stage is survival. This type of aggressive behavior is a clear sign of reactive fear, not an indication of defiance.

Verbal fight is a good time to offer a child some space. It is not a good time to lecture or ask questions. Children in *fight* can't think, pick up what they threw, take a time out, wipe up a mess, or make good decisions. When an adult threatens or lectures a child in *fight,* that only makes it worse. The time to talk is *after* the child is calm again. If a child makes a mess or breaks something, he can clean it up or pay for the damage later (because we all know the child is responsible for his behavior).

If a child moves into *physical fight,* the child may hit, bite, throw things, scratch, or kick anyone that comes too close. If an adult grabs, shakes, harshly restrains, or screams at a child in *fight,* that makes it worse. It helps to get the child away from the situation or remove the *audience* when possible. Safety is the goal, and either appropriate physical restraint or calling 911 may be necessary to keep the child and others safe. Restraint should not be used with an abused child except as a last option to maintain or restore safety.

Of course none of this is necessary when adults watch closely for early signs of *distress* in abused children. One last thing should be mentioned. A child getting over trauma needs to have a safe place in his or her classroom or school as well as a safe place at home. A safe place is a quiet, comfortable setting in which the child can calm down.

Some *meltdowns* arise out of fear (self-protection) and others out of defiance (oppositional), and adults need to be able to tell the difference. Both types of tantrums look very much the same, and when people don't know the difference, children get blamed for *acting out on purpose* when the child is really having a flashback or trying to stay safe.

A child in a state of *fight* can't think. It is recommended that a caregiver gives consequences/assigns restitution for damages only after the child calms down. At that point the child will be able to think more clearly and talk about what has happened. Even then, the caregiver needs to be kind and give a consequence without yelling, blaming or labeling the child's behavior as *bad*.

Summary of Fight
- Child's Response
    - Instinctive state of *terror* (Focused on Survival)
    - Meltdown
    - Out of control behavior
    - Screams, curses, threatens others
    - Reactive anger: child hits, bites, shouts, curses, throws, kicks to *protect and survive*
    - May have a flashback and try to defend him or herself
- How a Caregiver Can Help
    - Stay focused on safety
    - Remove harmful objects
    - For self-injury or hurting others, ask child to stop (without raising voice) and restrain appropriately if child does not stop
    - Use safe physical management (restraint) per policy and only if needed for safety
    - Get child to safe place like time-out room and quietly sit with child.
    - Have weighted blanket/vest available if child typically responds to this
    - Use mindfulness techniques, music or sound machine (white noise or other) once the child can respond
    - Remove audience
    - Call 911 if dangerous situation develops—let child know it is for safety ("I want/need you to be safe")
    - After the meltdown is over, many children feel remorse and guilt. They want and need to re-establish their attachment and trust with the caregiver. Allow and encourage child to make restitution and apologize when ready. Collaborate on this.
    - Examples of What to do with Child in Time-Out
        - Calmly tell child he/she is safe. "I need to be sure you are safe. No one is going to hurt you."
        - Say, "I love you. I'm here if you need me."
        - Say, "When you calm down, I can let you . . .
        - Remind child to breathe; breathe together.
        - Offer non-dangerous object such as squishy ball, stress ball, or a stuffed animal the child likes.
- Caregiver Behaviors to Avoid
    - Locking child alone in time-out room (traumatized child may feel trapped)
    - Threatening a long grounding or loss of privilege
    - Hitting or shaking child
    - Screaming or cursing at child
    - Showing cruelty toward child
    - Manhandling child to force compliance
    - Labeling child's behavior as *bad*
    - Comparing child to abuser
    - Taking away *all coping and calming opportunities* afterward (recess, music, walks, etc.)
    - Taking away all privileges for a long period of time (child needs to be able to *wipe slate clean* and start fresh after a meltdown)
    - Holding grudges (silent treatment, teaching the child a lesson). The goal of discipline is to teach appropriate behavior, not further frustrate the child.

41.5 Professional Help for Traumatized Children

With regard to professional help, wise therapists use therapy activities within the child's developmental repertoire (abilities). Many therapists use the elements of Trauma-focused Cognitive Behavior Therapy (TF-CBT), an evidence-based model, with abused children (Cohen, Mannarino, & Deblinger, 2012).

P stands for *Psycho-education about IPV and trauma* as well as *Parenting Intervention*: Your child's therapist can offer you some books and handouts about abuse, neglect, and the effects of IPV. You will want to know what is *normal* after abuse and *signs* that your child needs medication or other professional help. You also need to know how to notice risks and to keep your child safe in the future. Parenting intervention helps you learn new skills in order to be a more consistent, nurturing, and effective parent.

R stands for *Relaxation (and stress reduction)*: As mentioned earlier, before a child can think and plan, he or she must be able to calm down. Techniques for relaxation range from guided imagery to physical relaxation techniques, mindfulness, music therapy, yoga, and massage.

A stands for *Affective expression and regulation*: Abused children have trouble managing their moods. They need help labeling, expressing, and controlling feelings so that they don't flood, rage, or panic.

C stands for *Cognitive coping (and sets the stage for later Cognitive restructuring work)*: This allows children to understand the connections among thoughts, feelings, and behaviors. Children need to eventually make sense of what happened to them, understand it in a new way, and know that they were not to blame.

T stands for *Trauma narrative development and processing*: Creating a story about the child's abuse can be done in words, art, or play. The child shares the memory of the abuse and the therapist assists the child to tell it, step by step. This helps the child stop avoiding the thoughts and feelings related to the abuse.

I stands for *in vivo exposure to avoided situations*: The child sometimes avoids people and places where the abuse happened or that remind the child of the abuse. He may not want to sleep in his bed or go to school. *In vivo* exposure allows the child to safely think about and deal with what has been avoided.

C stands for *Conjoint sessions with children*: Caregivers and children need to have some therapy together. It is important for the child to share his or her trauma narrative with the caregiver so the adult can offer support. Parents and other caregivers sometimes avoid doing this because it is painful, but it is important to proceed with it for the sake of the child.

E stands for *Enhancing future safety and healthy relationship/self development*: Parents need to work with the therapist to set up safety plans with their child so that he or she feels safe and secure. Adults must think about the persons they socialize with and how they supervise the child. They need to set up a very consistent schedule, since abused children respond well to predictable routines. Adults must also consider the child's level of development when they set rules and privileges.

Some therapists who work with abused children also use Eye Movement Desensitization and Reprocessing (EMDR), Mindfulness-Based Stress Reduction, Trauma Play Therapy, and parent–child interaction-type therapies. Therapy with preschool and some school-age children often includes play therapy, expressive activities with little verbal demand, and games. These are *good fit interventions* because of the delays in an abused child's verbal expression and abstract thinking. Cognitive behavioral therapy (CBT) can be used with children that have at least average verbal abilities. Cognitive behavioral therapies such as social skills or self-control training require higher level brain development. To respond to CBT, a child must have adequate executive functioning (be able to think and plan ahead, use self-direction and self-control), be able to use cause–effect thinking, be able to sequence (think about things step by step), be able to use pretend play, and be able to connect thoughts and feelings. Yet as you know from reading this book, the verbal part of the brain develops more slowly in abused and neglected children. For a child to benefit from behavior modification, he or she must be able to connect behavior with consequences. To do that, a child must understand cause and effect.

Components of TF-CBT may be implemented using play techniques, games, puppets, stories and art until a child is capable of higher level cognitive functioning. For example, a trauma narrative (telling a story about the abuse) is done using art or play until a child has the capacity for executive functioning, conceptual understanding, and expressive language, at which point the narrative may be done verbally (in an autobiography, dictated story, or dramatic enactment).

Traumatized children often respond well to activities with sensory integration components that help them self-regulate, calm down, and focus. They benefit from deep muscle massage and mindfulness-based activities, interventions that promote relaxation. One technique for relaxation involves a caregiver or therapist blowing bubbles over the child's head. The adult encourages the child to watch the bubbles until they are about 12 inches from the child's face. The child can then pop the bubbles, one at a time. As children watch the bubbles, their breathing slows and their muscles relax. Abused children also benefit from daily routines, such as a bedtime ritual that uses a calming activity and attachment-based story. They may enjoy doing yoga with their caregivers, listening to and dancing to music, and engaging in daily exercise. During make-believe play, they can pretend to be babies again and let the caregiver feed them, playing out earlier attachment strategies. The caregiver can follow the child's lead in these types of activities and promptly stop activities that lead to increased agitation or arousal.

Trauma-informed care should be individualized to the child. If you question whether your child should be receiving trauma-informed care, talk to the child's therapist. You have a right to seek care that is a good fit for the child and a responsive therapist will be open to your questions. A child's view of the abuse changes over time as he or she gains competency and feels empowered. With good care, children heal from traumatic experiences.

CHAPTER 42

CAREGIVER STRESS AND SELF-CARE

It is good to consider the ways in which family members respond to stress and the impact of this on each person's functioning. Coping with stress is a matter of risk and resilience. Risk factors are those things that make stress worse, while resilience factors are those things that make it easier to cope with stress. You might ask yourself the following questions when seeking treatment for your child and share the answers with your child's therapist:

- Was your pregnancy planned? If no, what was your and your partner's reaction to the pregnancy?
- How did the birth of this child change your life?
- What do you most enjoy about your child?
- What about your child's behavior do you find most stressful?
- What activity is most stressful for you with your child?
- Every family has stress. How would someone be able to tell when you are under stress?
- Everyone has ways of disagreeing or expressing anger. What do people in your family do when they are angry with one another?
- Has your child ever seen or heard you and your partner argue or fight? What has the child seen or heard? During a fight, has there ever, even once, been throwing, pushing or hitting?
- On a scale from one to ten, how patient are you with your child?
- When you *lose it with your child,* what types of things do you do or say?
- Do your children have the same sleep schedule as you or different? How do you handle that?
- Write down your family schedule of waking up to bedtime—a typical day in your family life. What time of day is most stressful for you as a parent?
- What do you do to relax and cope with stress?
- Do you or your partner have trouble with chronic pain or illness? What do you do to cope with that? Do you take any medication?
- How do your mood and behavior affect your child?
- What worries you the most about your child?
- If you could change one thing about your child, what would that be?
- Is there anyone your child reminds you of?
- What would your child say if asked how you (parent) act when you are drunk or high?
- Pretend it is ten years from now. What would your child say if asked for his or her three best and three worst memories from childhood?
- What would your child say if asked, "How do you want to grow up and be just like your (mom, dad)?" and "How do you *want to be different than* your mom/dad when you grow up?"
- What do you most enjoy doing with your child? What does your child most enjoy doing with you?
- What has been the adult use of alcohol or drugs over the past five years?

- Did you or your partner grow up with abuse or neglect?
- Did you or your partner witness intimate partner violence (IPV) as a child?

Your answers to these questions will give you and your child's therapist some insight into the ways your moods and behavior impact your child and how you deal with stress.

As a caregiver, you need to remember to take care of yourself also, since is very stressful to care for a traumatized child. You may find it difficult to listen to the child's story and wish you could avoid the feelings it brings up. It will be especially hard if you were abused or neglected as a child. You may find the child's therapy process troubling if you believe you are in any way responsible for what happened or that you missed signs of what was going on. You may want to believe that the abuse is in the past and does not need to be brought up. You may even think that the withdrawn, quiet child has *gotten over it* and not recognize signs of tuning out or dissociation.

As you help the child process his or her abuse, you will see positive changes in the child's adaptive functioning and behavior. I want to remind you that a child does not just *get over* abuse. Ignoring it and not talking about it does not make the pain go away. It is like choosing not to treat a bad wound, hoping it will get better on its own. When the wound gets infected, you realize that it needs to be cleaned out and treated in order to heal and develop a clean scar.

When you make the decision to help a child get over past abuse, you will need extra support (someone to talk to), patience, and good energy reserves. An abused child will test your patience. He or she will say and do things to see if you will *give up on* him or her, and an angry child will expect you to send him or her somewhere else to live. Before the child can trust you, he or she needs to know that you can love unconditionally and tolerate the child's pain and other feelings. The child needs to tell you his or her trauma story during the course of treatment and you need to be able to listen and provide empathy. If the child starts to remind you of someone that hurt you, you need to remember that you are dealing with a child, not an angry, abusive adult.

This is all very difficult for even the strongest, most loving caregiver. And it does not matter whether you are related to the child or not. A traumatized child will tax the resources of any caregiver, and you need to remain nurturing and consistent in the face of stress.

You may wish to seek professional help of your own if you find yourself struggling with these tasks. That is especially important if you went through abuse or neglect yourself, since you might get *triggered by* things the child talks about or by the child's behavior. The child's trauma work could bring back painful memories or remind you of things you have not thought about in a very long time. It is never too late to do trauma work; even as an adult, you can process the trauma and find ways to cope with the left-over feelings.

Take care of yourself—fill your cup. Don't let it get too empty, for your sake and for that of the child you are caring for. Find respite as needed and rely on the child's therapist to guide you. No one needs to deal with trauma alone.

RESOURCES FOR ABUSED CHILDREN AND THEIR CAREGIVERS

Appropriate Touch

Freeman, L. (1984). *It's My Body*. Parenting Press.

Hansen, D. (2003). *Those Are MY Private Parts*. Empowerment Productions.

Kleven, S. and Bergsma, J. (1997). *The Right Touch: A Read-Aloud Story to Help Prevent Child Sexual Abuse*. Illumination Arts.

Attachment and Bedtime Stories

Boynton, S. (1982). *The Going to Bed Book*. Little Simon Publisher.

Brown, M. and Hurd, C. (2006). *Over the Moon*. HarperCollins.

Brown, M. and Hurd, C. (2005). *The Runaway Bunny*. HarperCollins.

Brown, M. and Hurd, C. (2005). *Goodnight Moon*. HarperCollins.

Brown, M. and Hurd, C. (2001). *My World: A Companion to Goodnight Moon*. HarperCollins.

Carle, E. (2009). *The Very Hungry Caterpillar*. Philomel Publishers.

DiCamillo, K. (2009). *The Miraculous Journey of Edward Tulane*. Candlewick Press.

Kunhardt, D. (2001). *Pat the Bunny*. Golden Books.

McBratney, S. and Jeram, A. (2011). *Guess How Much I Love You?* Candlewick Press.

Munsch, R. and McGraw, S. (1995). *Love You Forever*. Firefly Books.

Child Development

Zero to Three, see www.zerotothree.org/

Collaborative Problem Solving

Greene, R. (2009). *Lost at School: Why Our Kids with Behavioral Challenges are Falling Through the Cracks and How We Can Help Them*. HarperCollins.

Greene, R. (2005). *Treating Explosive Kids: The Collaborative Problem-Solving Approach*. HarperCollins.

Ross Greene Websites, see www.livesinthebalance.org or www.ccps.info

Dealing with Angry (Explosive) Behavior

Greene, Ross (2010). *The Explosive Child: A New Approach for Understanding and Parenting Easily Frustrated, Chronically Inflexible Children*. HarperCollins

Ross Greene websites, see www.livesinthebalance.org or www.ccps.info

Emotional Abuse

Loftis, C. and Gallagher, C. (1997). *The Words Hurt: Helping Children Cope with Verbal Abuse.* New Horizon Press.

Feelings and Feeling Expression

Cain, J. (2000). *The Way I Feel.* Parenting Press.
Cook, J. and Hartman, C. (2006). *My Mouth Is a Volcano!* National Center for Youth Issues.
Curtis, J. (1998). *Today I Feel Silly: And Other Moods That Make My Day.* HarperCollins.
Lamia, M. (2010). *Understanding Myself: A Kid's Guide to Intense Emotions and Strong Feelings.* Magination Press.
Metzger, S. (2010). *The Way I Act.* Parenting Press.
Parr, T. (2005). *The Feelings Book.* Little, Brown and Company

Metaphorical Stories for Change

Burns, G. (2004). *101 Healing Stories for Kids and Teens: Using Metaphors in Therapy.* Wiley.
Markell, K. and Markell, M. (2008). *The Children Who Lived: Using Harry Potter and other Fictional Characters to Help Grieving Children and Adolescents.* Routledge.
Pernicano, P. (2011). *Outsmarting the Riptide of Domestic Violence.* Jason Aronson Press.
Pernicano, P. (2010). *Family-Focused Trauma Intervention.* Jason Aronson Press.
Pernicano, P. (2010). *Metaphorical Stories for Child Therapy.* Jason Aronson Press.

Mindfulness

Greenland, S. (2010). *The Mindful Child: How to Help Your Kid Manage Stress and Become Happier, Kinder, and More Compassionate.* Free Press.
Hanh, T. (2011). *Planting Seeds: Practicing Mindfulness with Children.* Parallax Press.
Hanh, T. (2008). *Mindful Movements: Ten Exercises for Well-being.* Parallax Press.
MacLean, K. (2009). *Moody Cow Meditates.* Wisdom Publications.
Silver, G. and Kromer, C. (2009). *Anh's Anger.* Plum Blossom Books.

Parent–Child Attachment

Siegel, D. J. and Hartzell, M. (2003). *Parenting from the Inside Out: How a Deeper Self Understanding Can Help You Raise Children Who Thrive.* Penguin.

Sexual Abuse

Foltz, L. (2003). *Kids Helping Kids Break the Silence of Sexual Abuse.* Lighthouse Point Press.
Jessie (1991). *Please Tell: A Child's Story About Sexual Abuse.* Hazeldon Foundation.

Talking About Abuse

Holmes, M. (2000). *A Terrible Thing Happened: A Story for Children Who Have Witnessed Violence or Trauma.* Magination Press.

Trauma

Child Trauma Academy Website, see www.childtrauma.org

Perry, B. and Szalavitz, M. (2006). *The Boy Who Was Raised As a Dog—And Other Stories from a Child Psychiatrist's Notebook: What Traumatized Children Can Teach Us About Loss, Love, and Healing.* Basic Books.

EXAMPLE OF TRAUMA STRESS CHAIN REACTION AND STATE-DEPENDENT FUNCTIONING[1]

Situation: Traumatized child at home, three months following the trauma

From across the room, a caregiver tells a child (who is absorbed in watching TV or playing a video game) to pick up his toys. Fifteen minutes later, the child has not done so. Remember, an abused child is never as calm as a non-abused child. The child is vigilant, alert, and easily startled.

Table B.1 Freak Out

Child's State	What Adult Is Thinking	What Adult Does That Makes It Worse (Gets Child More Upset)	What Child Feels, Thinks, and Does	What Is Likely to Happen Next
Vigilant and Watchful Due to prior abuse, child is *on guard*. Any sudden change or noise will startle him and set off a stress response. Rarely as calm as non-abused child.	Adult thinks, "I told him to pick up his toys. He's not listening to me. I need to do something to get his attention." *Parent makes an assumption instead of checking things out with the child.	Adult looks annoyed/frustrated, moves closer to the child and raises voice. Puts hands on hips and says, "Look at me when I'm talking to you! I told you to pick up those toys 15 minutes ago. Do it right now!"	Child did not hear the first request to pick up toys. Child is startled by the raised voice. Child thinks, "That's the *Mean Mom* voice—I'm in trouble! What did I do?" Child feels high stress level. Child's heart starts to pound. Child puts his head down and does not move. Has hard time listening.	Child will become alarmed and more stressed. Might get very emotional (cry harder, over-react) or freeze.

Table B.2 Freeze

Child's State	What Adult Is Thinking	What Adult Does That Makes It Worse	What Child Feels, Thinks, and Does	What Is Likely to Happen Next
Increased Arousal Child is startled and does not move. Child is anxious and has trouble listening. Might stare blankly and hold breath. Acts like a deer in the headlights.	Adult thinks, "That child has not moved to pick up those toys—he is ignoring and disrespecting me! He never does what I ask." *The parent goes into black-and-white, all-or-nothing thinking. This increases the parent's negative emotion. It is time for the adult to take a deep breath and calm down.	Adult moves closer, raises a finger and shakes it at the child. Adult raises voice and threatens. "You heard me! Pick up those toys right now. Do you want to go to time-out?" Adult moves quickly—turns off TV that child was watching.	Child feels scared. He thinks, "Of course I don't want to go to time-out. I want to know why Mom is so mad. She's coming closer. I'm not safe. She might hurt me. I need to get away." Child feels threatened. Muscles get tight. Child is not able to think clearly. Does not respond to the adult. Child looks for an escape route.	Child will go into a full state of fear. At that point, child will go into Flight. Child will run away, leave the room, or tune out and look even more disengaged.

Table B.3 Flight

Child's State	What Adult Is Thinking	What Adult Does That Makes It Worse	What Child Feels, Thinks, and Does	What Is Likely to Happen Next
Panic Child senses impending danger and takes off. Child hides, tunes out (dissociates), or runs.	Adult sees child leaving and thinks, "I need to show that child who is boss. If it's the last thing I do, I'm going to teach that child to listen to me. I'm the parent. I need to move fast and catch him before he leaves. I need to teach him some respect."	Adult quickly follows the child. Raises voice and gives orders while following child. Adult's face looks angry and stressed. Adult grabs the child's arm or blocks the door to keep the child from leaving the room.	Fear state: "Oh no, here it comes, just like before. She's grabbing me. That hurts! Something bad is going to happen. I'm not safe. I can't escape. I'm trapped. I need to protect myself." Child is not really thinking. Heart is pounding, face red. Child pulls away and runs. Child tries to escape. If child can't get away, child will fight.	If adult does not let go or back away, child moves into Fight (total meltdown).

Table B.4 Fight

Child's State	What Adult Is Thinking	What Adult Does That Makes It Worse	What Child Feels, Thinks, and Does	What Is Likely to Happen Next
Meltdown Child is in *primitive survival* mode. Not rational. Child will not be able to think. Child has a meltdown. Child shouts, curses, bites, lashes out, screams, kicks, throws, or hits. Seeks safety.	Adult becomes scared seeing child's intense aggression. Adult thinks, "I can't handle him/her. This child is dangerous. I need to restrain this child. I need to get help." If adult is an abuse victim, adult might be quite afraid of child and think, "He is just like [my dad, his father]!"	Adult panics and shows fear to the child. Lectures the child. In a loud voice, warns the child about what will happen if the child doesn't stop. Orders child to go to his room. Might put the child in a hold *for his own good* or drag the child to a time-out room.	Child drops to the floor, kicking, hitting, biting, and screaming. Might curse or call names. Might shout, "I hate you!" or "I'm going to kill you!" Feels raw *terror*: "I need to get away right now!" Might have a flashback. Might not recognize the caregiver. Heart is pounding, brain in a *fog*, face red.	Child will hurt self or others unless adult allows child some space to calm down. Adult needs to keep everyone away—clear the room and no audience. If danger, call 911. Need to use safety plan.

Note

1 *Living and Working with Traumatized Children. Video Series I.* (2004), by B. D. Perry, 2004, Houston, TX: The Child Trauma Academy.

APPENDIX C

SIGNS OF TRAUMA AT DIFFERENT AGES AND STAGES

Table C.1

Age Group	Trauma-Related Symptoms (Attachment, Behavior, Mood Regulation, Social/Interpersonal)	
Infancy	Very little, or too much, crying Slow developmental milestones (and parents might not "remember" milestones) Lack of babbling and slow language development Failure to thrive—eating problems Sleep problems Doesn't like to be cuddled Irritability Might shut down and fail to engage (poor eye contact, less baby talk, less smiling) Poor mood regulation (can't self-soothe)	
Preschool	Clingy or distant with strangers—poor eye contact Fearful to separate from mother Hyperactivity with an anxious feel to it Parallel play lasts a long time—social delay Poor self-care Long temper tantrums (over 20 minutes each) Hitting and aggressive behavior Has trouble doing make-believe Delayed potty training or accidents after being potty-trained Hoarding food	Not well bonded—angry, clingy, or avoidant Compulsive or PDD behaviors Language delays and slow milestones Too independent or dependent (clingy) for age Sexual reactivity Too quiet—hardly ever gets upset Play very repetitious or lacks imagination Excessive crying Sleep problems
School Age	Expressive language delays (talking or writing) Temper tantrums or mood problems Accidents (wetting or soiling) Hoarding food Might look ADHD or compulsive Sexual reactivity Oppositional behavior Immature or pseudo-mature for age	Receptive language delays (listening) Trouble making or keeping friends Stealing Tunes out or stares into space Imaginary playmates last a long time Play not age appropriate Aggressive with others or overly withdrawn Avoids bathing or going to bed
Teens	Suicidal ideation and dramatic emotional reactions Self-harm (Cutting, burning) Intense Anger Onset of drug/alcohol use following trauma (including "huffing," or inhalant abuse) Drop in grades, increase in suspensions or truancy Increased withdrawal	Poor hygiene Immaturity, playing with younger children Precocious sexuality Seems paranoid and protective Intense dreams and sleeping problems

OVERLAP OF TRAUMA SYMPTOMS WITH OTHER DISORDERS

Table D.1

Diagnosis	Symptoms that Co-Occur with Trauma	Differences with Trauma	Source of the Symptom in Trauma
Attention Deficit Hyperactivity Disorder (ADHD)	• Hyperactivity • Distractibility • Tuned out • Poor concentration	• Trauma symptoms—onset during or after period of high stress (witnessed or experienced) • ADHD onset ongoing and non-dramatic, no identifiable causal factors, symptoms can be exacerbated by stress • Trauma-related frantic hyperactivity—child reactive to anger, abandonment, criticism (ADHD child not as watchful of parent response) • Trauma-related agitation gets worse when a parent gets upset around the child (yells or threatens) or is inconsistent in response	• Attachment disorganized or ambivalent • Heightened stress response when triggered by fear • Hyperarousal from overactive limbic system (amygdala) • Slow or impaired development of left hemisphere pre-frontal cortex—results in poor executive functioning and self-regulation
Autism Spectrum	• Speech delay • Poor eye contact • Poor social reciprocity • Poor emotion recognition • Ritualized play with objects	• Social-emotional development of child declines following trauma and improves once child has "normal" nurturing relationships (preschool, therapist, day care) • Autistic spectrum child has delayed social-emotional development regardless of parental response	• Cognitive development impaired—delays in language centers • Poor reciprocal social skills due to poor mirroring and attunement • Avoidant attachment strategies
Oppositional Defiant Disorder (ODD)	• Defies adults • Does not comply with adult directives	• With trauma, defiance often "worse" at home or around perpetrator than at school. • "Disobedience" occurs when child is tuned out or not listening • Oppositional child enjoys the "game"—watches adult, smiles when adult gets mad, displays a stubborn or playful quality • Traumatized child shows fear or anxiety when parent gets upset	Self-Protection: • Hyper-vigilance • Needs control • Vulnerability means being hurt • Traumatized child disobeys out of fear and in order to stay safe • May re-enact prior trauma by disobeying or defying

Table D.2

Diagnosis	Symptoms That Co-Occur with Trauma	Differences with Trauma	Source of the Symptom in Trauma
Psychosis	• Apparent hallucinations • Not grounded in reality	• "Voices" more likely to be child's own voice/thoughts or memory of punitive adult voice • Social delays in traumatized kids can lead to imaginary playmates later into the elementary years • Psychotic children have more odd behaviors and mannerisms, odd reasoning • With child dissociative identity disorder (DID), child hears different age voices inside head and they are like "characters"	• Trauma-related flashbacks, intrusive thoughts, dissociation
OCD (Obsessive Compulsive Disorder)	• Rituals and compulsive habits • Very regulated play • Emotions overly regulated • OCD symptoms	• Play of traumatized kids very controlled and non-social • Play will have themes of danger and protection • Compulsive behaviors are protective—they compartmentalize emotions and distract the child from the trauma	• Delays in cognitive development lead to repetitive, non-make-believe play, social delays result in parallel play at older ages and inability to make-believe • Anxiety-driven • Basal ganglia development delayed
Conduct Disorder	• Stealing • Bullying • Hurting other people or animals	• Strong fear and angry affect underlie trauma-related conduct problems. Strong ambivalence in traumatized kids. Might see need for approval, guilt, or remorse. Projective testing will show underlying anxiety, anger, and fear. • Truly conduct disordered child shows less vulnerability and little affect or emotion in testing—more sealed over and less ambivalence about the behavior.	Self-Protection: • Fear turns into anger • Does not want to feel vulnerable—hurting others feels better than being victimized • Hurting others is sometimes due to internalizing the abuser. It can be a form of repetition compulsion (replaying the trauma).

APPENDIX E

TUNING IN TO YOUR CHILD

A sensitive caregiver needs to understand the ways in which an abused child *changes the self* to be what he or she thinks a caregiver wants. The child behaves like a Transformer toy. When you twist and turn a Transformer, it becomes something else that looks nothing like the original toy. Sometimes what the child shows on the outside is not what the child feels inside. When a child *hides his/her real thoughts or feelings* and acts in ways intended to please the caregiver, this results in a "false self." The child puts on a false self to get positive attention or to avoid punishment, ridicule, rejection, and abandonment.

Please complete the following worksheet. Your answers will help you and your child's therapist understand the ways in which your child *changes* his / her behavior around you to put on a "false self."

How My Behavior and Mood Affect My Child

- When I am in a good mood my child_____

- How does my child act after I lose my temper with him/her?_____
_____

- When I ignore my child while I watch TV or talk on the phone, my child _____
_____

- When my child wants to show me something or wants me to play with him or her and I say, "maybe later", my child_____
_____

- How does my child act after I lose my temper with someone else?_____
_____

- When I wake up in a bad mood, my child_____

- When I am feeling sad, my child_____

- When I am tired or in a bad mood, I expect my child to_____
_____

- When I am busy doing something, I expect my child to_____
_____

- When I am in pain, I expect my child to_____

- When I am sleeping, my child should_____

- When I am drunk or high, my child_____

- When I leave and don't tell my child where I'm going, my child_____
- What do I do and say to my child to show love?_____
  _____
- When my child is afraid of something, I_____
- When my child makes a mistake, I am likely to_____
- When I raise my voice at my child for acting up, he or she_____

My Child's Coping Strategies

- When my child is scared, he or she_____
  _____
- Does your child ever show anger when he / she is afraid?_____
  _____
- Does your child ever act silly when upset?_____
  _____
- Does your child ever try to take care of you or cheer you up? _____
  _____
- How can you tell when your child is feeling left out or lonely?_____
  _____
- How can you tell when your child is ashamed?_____
  _____
- How can you tell when your child feels guilty or sorry?_____
  _____
- How can you tell when your child wants your approval? _____
  _____
- How can you tell when your child wants your attention? What happens if you are too busy to respond?
  _____
- What does your child do when he/she needs your help with something? _____
  _____
- How can you tell when your child is sad or disappointed? _____
  _____
- How can you tell when your child wants affection or nurture?_____
  _____
- Does your child ever get coy, cute, or flirtatious so that you will change your mind or to get something he / she wants? _____
- How does your child act when he/she does not get his or her way?_____
  _____
- How does your child act when he/she is disappointed? _____
  _____

REFERENCES

Adverse Childhood Experiences (ACE) Study. Atlanta, GA: Centers for Disease Control. See www.cdc.gov/ace.

Badenach, B. (2008). *Being a brain-wise therapist: A practical guide to interpersonal neurobiology.* New York: W. W. Norton & Company, Inc.

Badenach, B. (2011). *The brain-savvy therapist's workbook: A companion to being a brain-wise therapist.* New York: W.W. Norton & Company, Inc.

Blaustein, M. & Kinniburgh, K. (2010). *Treating traumatic stress in children and adolescents: How to foster resilience through attachment, self-regulation and competency.* New York: The Guilford Press.

Bowlby, J. (1958). The nature of the child's tie to his mother. *International Journal of Psycho-Analysis, 39,* 350–373.

Bremner, J. D. (2002). Neuroimaging of childhood trauma. *Semin. Clin. Neuropsychiatry, 7*(2), 104–112.

Bremner, J. D. (2003). Long term effects of childhood abuse on brain and neurobiology. *Child and Adolescent Clinics of North America, 12,* 271–292.

Bremner, J. D. (2006). The relationship between cognitive and brain changes in posttraumatic stress disorder. *Annals of the New York Academy of Sciences, 1071,* 80–86.

Bremner, J. D. (2012). *Does stress damage the brain?* New York: W. W. Norton & Company, Inc.

Briere, J. (November, 2012). *An integrated approach to complex trauma.* Louisville, KY: Kentucky Psychological Association Conference Presentation.

Briere, J. & Jordan, C. E. (2009). The relationship between childhood maltreatment, moderating variables, and adult psychological difficulties in women: An overview. *Trauma, Violence, and Abuse: A Review Journal, 10,* 375–388.

Briere, J. & Langtree, C.B. (2008). *Integrative treatment for complex trauma in adolescents (ITCT-A): A guide for the treatment of multiply-traumatized youth.* Long Beach, CA: MCAVIC-USC Child and Adolescent Trauma Program, National Child Traumatic Stress Network, Substance Abuse and Mental Health Services Administration, U.S. Department of Health and Human Services.

Briere, J. & Scott, C. (2006). *Principles of trauma therapy: A guide to symptoms, evaluation, and treatment.* Thousand Oaks, CA: SAGE Publications, Inc.

Burns, G. (2005). *101 Healing stories for kids and teens: using metaphor in therapy.* New York: John Wiley & Sons, Inc.

Burns, G. (2007). *Healing with Stories: Your Casebook Collection for Using Therapeutic Metaphors.* New York: John Wiley & Sons, Inc.

Centers for Disease Control (www.cdc.gov/ace).

Child Trauma Academy website: http://wwwchildtrauma.org.

Cohen, J., Mannarino, A. & Deblinger, E. (2006). *Treating trauma and traumatic grief in children and adolescents.* New York: The Guilford Press.

Cohen, J., Mannarino, A. & Deblinger, E. (2012). *Trauma-focused CBT for children and adolescents: Treatment applications.* New York: The Guilford Press.

Cozolino, L. (2006). *The Neuroscience of human relationships: Attachment and the developing social brain* (Norton Series on Interpersonal Neurobiology). New York: W.W. Norton & Company, Inc.

Cozolino, L. (2010). *The neuroscience of psychotherapy: Healing the social brain.* 2nd edition. New York: W.W. Norton & Company, Inc.

Crittenden, P. (2008). *Raising parents: Attachment, parenting and child safety.* Abingdon: Taylor & Francis.

Crittenden, P. (February, 2013). *The Dynamic-Maturational Model of Attachment, Parts One and Two: Introduction and Application.* Louisville, KY: KPA Workshop.

Crittenden, P. & Landini, A. (2011). *Assessing adult attachment: A dynamic-maturational approach to discourse analysis.* New York: W.W. Norton & Company, Inc.

Crowell, J. A. & Treboux, D. (1995). A review of adult attachment measures: Implications for theory and research. *Social Development, 4,* 294–327.

Drewes, A. (Ed.). (2009). *Blending play therapy with cognitive behavioral therapy: evidence-based and other effective treatments and techniques.* New York: John Wiley & Sons, Inc.

Gardner, R. (1971). *Therapeutic communication with children: the mutual storytelling technique.* New York: Science House.

Gil, E. & Briere, J. (2006). *Helping abused and traumatized children: integrating directive and nondirective approaches.* New York: The Guilford Press.

Gomez, A. (2013). *EMDR therapy and adjunct approaches with children: Complex trauma, attachment, and dissociation.* New York: Springer Publishing Company.

Greene, R. (2001). *The explosive child: A new approach for understanding and parenting easily frustrated, chronically inflexible children.* New York: HarperCollins Books.

Greene, R. Websites: http://www.ccps.info & http://www.livesinthebalance.org.

Greene, R. & Ablon, J. (2006) *Treating explosive kids: The collaborative problem-solving approach.* New York: The Guilford Press.

Grossmann, K., Grossmann, K. & Waters, E. (2005). *Attachment from infancy to adulthood: The major longitudinal studies.* New York: The Guilford Press.

Kaduson, H. G. & Schaffer, C. E. (Eds.). (2003). *101 favorite play therapy techniques, vol. III.* North Vale, NJ: Jason Aronson.

Kinniburgh, K., Blaustein, M., Spinnazzola, J. & van der Kolk, B. (2005). Attachment, self-regulation and competency. *Psychiatric Annals, 35*(5), 424–430.

Knitzer, J., Theberge, S. & Johnson, K. (2008). *Reducing maternal depression and its impact on young children: Toward a responsive early childhood policy framework (project thrive issue brief number two).* New York: Columbia University National Center for Children in Poverty.

Kopp, R. (1995). *Metaphor therapy: using client generated metaphors in psychotherapy.* Bristol, PA: Brunner-Mazel.

Kozlowska, K. & Hanney, L. (2002). The network perspective: An integration of attachment and family systems theories. In Wood. B. (Ed.), *Family Process, 41,* 285–312.

Landreth, G. & Bratton, S. (2006). *Child parent relationship therapy (CPRT): A 10-session filial therapy model.* New York: Routledge.

Le Guin, U. (1968). *A wizard of earthsea.* New York: Random House.

Lieberman, A. & Van Horn, P. (2005). *Don't hit my mommy!: A manual for child–parent psychotherapy with young witnesses of family violence.* Washington, D.C.: Zero to Three.

Lieberman, A. & Van Horn, P. (2008). *Psychotherapy with infants and young children: Repairing the effects of stress and trauma on early attachment.* New York: The Guilford Press.

Lovett, J. (2007). *Small wonders: Healing childhood trauma with EMDR.* New York: Free Press.

Malchiodi, C. (Ed.). (2008). *Creative interventions with traumatized children.* New York: The Guilford Press.

Markell, K. & Markell, M. (2008). *The children who lived: Using Harry Potter and other fictional characters to help grieving children and adolescents.* New York: Routledge.

McCollum, D. (2006). Child maltreatment and brain development. *Minnesota Medicine, 89*(3), 48–50.

McGee, S. & Holmes, C. (2008). *Finding the sunshine after the storm: A workbook for children healing from sexual abuse.* Oakland, CA: New Harbinger Publications.

McKay, M., Wood, J. & Brantley, J. (2007). *The dialectical behavior therapy skills workbook: Practical DBT exercises for learning mindfulness, interpersonal effectiveness, emotion regulation, and distress tolerance.* Oakland, CA: New Harbinger Publications.

Muir, D. & Lee, K. (2003). The still-face effect: Methodological issues and new applications. *Infancy, 4*(4), 483–491

Murray, H. Thematic Apperception Test. Pearson Education, Inc. (http://www.pearsonassessments.com)

Pernicano, P. (2010a). *Metaphorical stories for child therapy: Of magic and miracles.* Lanham, MD: Jason Aronson.

Pernicano, P. (2010b). *Family-focused trauma intervention: Using metaphor and play with victim of abuse and neglect.* Lanham, MD: Jason Aronson.

Pernicano, P. (2011). *Outsmarting the riptide of domestic violence: Metaphor and mindfulness for change.* Lanham, MD: Jason Aronson.

Perry, B. (2004a). *Living and working with traumatized children.* In Video Series I. Houston, TX: The Child Trauma Academy.

Perry, B. (2004b). *Violence and childhood.* In Video Series I. Houston, TX: The Child Trauma Academy.

Perry, B. (2006). Applying principles of neurodevelopment to clinical work with maltreated and traumatized children: The Neurosequential model of therapeutics. In Boyd Webb (Ed.) *Working with traumatized youth in child welfare* (pp. 27–52). New York: The Guilford Press.

Perry, B. (2009). Examining child maltreatment through a neurodevelopmental lens: Clinical applications of the neurosequential model of therapeutics. *Journal of Loss and Trauma, 14,* 240–255.

Perry, B. & Hambrick, E. (2008). The neurosequential model of therapeutics. *Reclaiming Children and Youth, 17*(3), 40.

Perry, B. & Pollard, R. (1998). Homeostasis, stress, trauma, and adaptation: A neurodevelopmental view of childhood trauma. *Child and Adolescent Psychiatric Clinics of North America, 7,* 33–51.

Perry, B. & Szalavitz, M. (2006). *The boy who was raised as a dog: and other stories from a child psychiatrist's notebook: What traumatized children can teach us about loss, love, and healing.* New York: Basic Books.

Prochaska, J. O. & DiClemente, C. C. (1982). Transtheoretical therapy: Toward a more integrative model of change. *Psychotherapy: Theory, Research and Practice, 19*(3), 276–288.

Saltzman, A. (2007). *Still quiet place: Mindfulness for young children.* CD Baby.

Saltzman, A. (2010). *Still quiet place: Mindfulness for teens.* CD Baby.

Saltzman, A. & Goldin, P. (2008). Mindfulness based stress reduction for school-age children. In S. C. Hayes & L. A. Greco (Eds.), *Acceptance and mindfulness interventions for children, adolescents and families* (pp. 139–161). Oakland, CA: Context Press/New Harbinger.

Schore, A. (2001). The effects of a secure attachment relationship on right-brain development, affect regulation, and infant mental health. *Infant Mental Health Journal, 22,* 7–66.

Seligman, M. (2003). *Authentic happiness: Using the new positive psychology to realize your potential for lasting fulfillment.* New York: Free Press.

Sfroufe, L., Carlson, A., Levy, K. & Egeland, B. (1999). Implications of attachment theory for developmental psychopathology. *Development and Psychopathology, 11,* 1–13.

Siegel, D. J. (1999). *The developing mind: How relationships and the brain interact to shape who we are.* New York: The Guilford Press.

Siegel, D. J. (2010). *The mindful therapist: A clinician's guide to mindsight and neural integration.* New York: W.W. Norton & Company, Inc.

Siegel, D. J. & Hartzell, M. (2003). *Parenting from the inside out: How a deeper self-understanding can help you raise children who thrive.* New York: Penguin.

Solomon, J. & George, C. (1999). *Attachment disorganization.* New York: The Guilford Press

Solomon, M. & Siegel, D. (Eds.). (2003) *Healing trauma: attachment, mind, body, and brain.* New York: W.W. Norton & Company, Inc.

Tinker, R. & Wilson, S. (1999). *Through the eyes of a child.* New York: W.W. Norton & Company, Inc.

Van der Kolk, B. (2005). Developmental trauma disorder. *Psychiatric Annals,* May 2005, *35*(5), 1–18

VanFleet, R. (2005). *Filial therapy: strengthening parent–child relationships through play* (2nd ed.). Sarasota, FL: Professional Resource Press.

Winnicott, D. W. (1953). *Symptom tolerance in paediatrics. Proc R Soc Med., 46*(8): 675–684.

Zero to Three: Early experiences matter (www.zerotothree.org). Washington, D.C.: National Center for Infants, Toddlers and Families.

Zisser, A. & Eyberg, S. M. (2010). Treating oppositional behavior in children using parent–child interaction therapy. In A.E. Kazdin & J.R. Weisz (Eds.), *Evidence-based psychotherapies for children and adolescents* (2nd ed., pp. 179–193). New York: The Guilford Press.

INDEX